Secrets to the Law of Attraction:
from the
Go Thunk Yourself Reference Library

A collection of essays derived from
the Law of Attraction Classics Series

Dr. Robert C. Worstell

Beta release 0.1

"Go Thunk Yourself!" and the Go Thunk Yourself logo are trademarks owned by Robert C. Worstell

Publisher: Midwest Journal Press - ISBN: 978-0-6151-4810-6

Secrets to the Law of Attraction:
from the
Go Thunk Yourself Reference Library

**A collection of essays derived from
the Law of Attraction Classics Series**

Table of Contents

Introduction

There is nothing more fascinating than the Law of Attraction. Like a multi-faceted jewel, you turn it one way and then another, seeking to find the most beautiful side – but they all sparkle and bedazzle.

The secret to the Law of Attraction is no secret – but people have been holding it as such all through the centuries. Earl Nightingale was surprised to find his simple recording of what he found ("The Strangest Secret") to go Gold due to its sales and popularity – as a 78 RPM LP.

But Nightingale was doing nothing except telling others what he had found – that people were "discovering" this "secret" for themselves all through the centuries.

For the oddest thing is that the Law of Attraction is both a self-fulfilling prophecy and the universal solvent. Nothing can contain it, but once you find it, everything is explained – and predicted.

My trail in this lead through "The Secret" DVD. And of course I told everyone important to me about it. Even explaining it in a single sentence ("You are what you think.") was the easiest philosophical discussion I have ever had.

One day, I was looking for a reference and typed in the phrase "Law of Attraction" - and found that there were dozens upon dozens of references stashed on my computer from the various researches I had been doing – of course, figuring that I'd "get around to them" at some point.

And it was then I knew I had my work cut out for me. These were books in all sorts of formats and stylings – from authors who had written in the earlier century, if not earlier.

I knew that my job was to present these authors to the world again – so people don't have to reinvent the wheel in this century. People who were searching for information deserved to find it, simply. But most of it was unavailable for easy search – since many of these didn't show up on any fast Google search, or on Amazon or eBay.

Our modern Internet Age is the way these books came my way – and so I had to give back. I had to dig out these authors, format their works for easy reading, and provide marketing so that people could find that they again existed.

For any student of the Law of Attraction, you deserve to be able to find the data you need – that data you want to attract into your life. I hope I've helped contribute to your success in some way.

While I'll be back to tell you a bit about each of our contributing authors, let me leave you here with my best wishes:

Good Luck and Good Hunting!

Dr. Robert C. Worstell

22 May, 2007

How to Read This Book

Simply put: skip around.

Don't try to read it at one sitting.

Some of these chapters are way too long and too heavy to digest at a single sitting – so snack lightly and frequently. Flip through the pages and see which ones appeal to you.

Start randomly and see what you find. See if you are reading the same sections over and over – and then discover what lesson or message you are attracting into your life...

You have attracted this book into your life. I wrote it for you, but am not the real author of it – all these brilliant people quoted here have done all the heavy lifting. If you like what you read, get their full books. (They are all listed in the back of this book.)

And test out everything you read. See if what they say works for you. Stick to what works.

And above all, have fun – feel good.

RCW

Thomas Troward

Judge Thomas Troward was one of the founding influences of New Thought, having studied all the major religions in their own language while he practiced Law in India.

Troward is no easy read. His was a very logical and analytical mind, one which was able to deduce the very basic principles upon which all Life operates.

You will see, as you read, why Troward's name constantly surfaces when you study the classics.

Two of his many works are excerpted here. The Hidden Power was a collection of unpublished essays, while The Edinburgh Lectures was his first surprising bestseller.

The Hidden Power

VIII - DESIRE AS THE MOTIVE POWER

THERE are certain Oriental schools of thought, together with various Western offshoots from them, which are entirely founded on the principle of annihilating all desire. Reach that point at which you have no wish for anything and you will find yourself free, is the sum and substance of their teaching; and in support of this they put forward a great deal of very specious argument, which is all the more likely to entangle the unwary, because it contains a recognition of many of the profoundest truths of Nature. But we must bear in mind that it is possible to have a very deep knowledge of psychological facts, and at the same time vitiate the results of our knowledge by an entirely wrong assumption in regard to the law which binds these facts together in the universal system; and the injurious results of misapprehension upon such a vital question are so radical and far-reaching that we cannot too forcibly urge the necessity of clearly understanding the true nature of the point at issue. Stripped of all accessories and embellishments, the question resolves itself into this: Which shall we choose for our portion, Life or Death? There can be no accommodation between the two; and whichever we select as our guiding principle must produce results of a kind proper to itself.

The whole of this momentous question turns on the place that we assign to desire in our system of thought. Is it the Tree of Life in the midst of the Garden of the Soul? or is it the Upas Tree creating a wilderness of death all around? This is the issue on which we have to form a judgment, and this judgment must color all our conception of life and determine the entire range of our possibilities. Let us, then, try to picture to ourselves the ideal proposed by the systems to which I have alluded--a man who has succeeded in entirely annihilating all desire. To him all things must be alike. The good and the evil must be as one, for nothing has any longer the power to raise any desire in him; he has no longer any feeling which shall prompt him to say, "This is good, therefore I choose it; that is evil, therefore I reject it"; for all choice implies the perception of something more desirable in what is chosen than in what is rejected, and consequently the existence of that feeling of desire which has been entirely eliminated from the ideal we are contemplating.

Then, if the perception of all that makes one thing preferable to another has been obliterated, there can be no motive for any sort of action whatever. Endue a being who has thus extinguished his faculty of desire with the power to create a universe, and he has no motive for employing it. Endue him with all knowledge, and it will be useless to him; for, since desire has no place in him, he is without any purpose for which to turn his knowledge to account. And with Love we cannot endue him, for that is desire in its supreme degree. But if all this be excluded, what is left of the man? Nothing, except the mere outward form. If he has actually obtained this ideal, he has practically ceased to be. Nothing can by any means interest him, for there is nothing to attract or repel in one thing more than in another. He must be dead alike to all feeling and to all motive of action, for both feeling and action imply the preference for one condition rather than another; and where desire is utterly extinguished, no such preference can exist.

No doubt some one may object that it is only evil desires which are thus to be suppressed; but a perusal of the writings of the schools of thought in question will show that this is not the case. The foundation of the whole system is that all desire must be obliterated, the desire for the good just as much as the desire for the evil. The good is as much "illusion" as the evil, and until we have reached absolute indifference to both we have not attained freedom. When we have utterly crushed out all desire we are free. And the practical results of such a philosophy are shown in the case of Indian devotees, who, in pursuance of their resolve to crush out all desire, both for good and evil alike, become nothing more than outward images of men, from which all power of perception and of action have long since fled.

The mergence in the universal, at which they thus aim, becomes nothing more than a self-induced hypnotism, which, if maintained for a sufficient length of time, saps away every power of mental and bodily activity, leaving nothing but the outside husk of an attenuated human form--the hopeless wreck of what was once a living man. This is the logical result of a system which assumes for its starting-point that desire is evil in itself, that every desire is per se a form of bondage, independently of the nature of its object. The majority of the followers of this philosophy may lack sufficient resolution to carry it out rigorously to its practical conclusions; but whether their ideal is to be realized in this world or in some other, the utter extinction of desire means nothing else than absolute apathy, without feeling and without action.

How entirely false such an idea is--not only from the standpoint of our daily life, but also from that of the most transcendental conception of the Universal Principle--is evidenced by the mere fact that anything exists at all. If the highest ideal is that of utter apathy, then the Creative Power of the universe must be extremely low-minded; and all that we have hitherto been accustomed to look upon as the marvelous order and beauty of creation, is nothing but a display of vulgarity and ignorance of sound philosophy.

But the fact that creation exists proves that the Universal Mind thinks differently, and we have only to look around to see that the true ideal is the exercise of creative power. Hence, so far from desire being a thing to be annihilated, it is the very root of every conceivable mode of Life. Without it Life could not be. Every form of expression implies the selection of all that goes to make up that form, and the passing-by of whatever is not required for that purpose; hence a desire for that which is selected in preference to what is laid aside. And this selective desire is none other than the universal **Law of Attraction**.

Whether this law acts as the chemical affinity of apparently unconscious atoms, or in the instinctive, if unreasoned, attractions of the vegetable and animal worlds, it is still the principle of selective affinity; and it continues to be the same when it passes on into the higher kingdoms which are ruled by reason and conscious purpose. The modes of activity in each of these kingdoms are dictated by the nature of the kingdom; but the activity itself always results from the preference of a certain subject for a certain object, to the exclusion of all others; and all action consists in the reciprocal movement of the two towards each other in obedience to the law of their affinity.

When this takes place in the kingdom of conscious individuality, the affinities exhibit themselves as mental action; but the principle of selection prevails without exception throughout the universe. In the conscious mind this attraction towards its affinity becomes desire; the desire to create some condition of things better than that now existing. Our want of knowledge may cause us to make mistakes as to what this better thing really is, and so in seeking to carry out our desire we may give it a wrong direction; but the fault is not in the desire itself, but in our mistaken notion of what it that it requires for its satisfaction. Hence unrest and dissatisfaction until its true affinity is found; but, as soon as this is discovered, the **law of attraction** at once asserts itself and produces that better condition, the dream of which first gave direction to our thoughts.

Thus it is eternally true that desire is the cause of all feeling and all action; in other words, of all Life. The whole livingness of Life consists in receiving or in radiating forth the vibrations produced by the **law of attraction**; and in the kingdom of mind these vibrations necessarily become conscious out-reachings of the mind in the direction in which it feels attraction; that is to say, they become desires. Desire is therefore the mind seeking to manifest itself in some form which as yet exists only in its thought. It is the principle of creation, whether the thing created be a world or a wooden spoon; both have their origin in the desire to bring something into existence which does not yet exist.

Whatever may be the scale on which we exercise our creative ability, the motive power must always be desire.

Desire is the force behind all things; it is the moving principle of the universe and the innermost center of all Life. Hence, to take the negation of desire for our primal principle is to endeavor to stamp out Life itself; but what we have to do is to acquire the requisite knowledge by which to guide our desires to their true objects of satisfaction. To do this is the whole end of knowledge; and any knowledge applied otherwise is only a partial knowledge, which, having failed in its purpose, is nothing but ignorance. Desire is thus the sum-total of the livingness of Life, for it is that in which all movement originates, whether on the physical level or the spiritual. In a word, desire is the creative power, and must be carefully guarded, trained, and directed accordingly; but thus to seek to develop it to the highest perfection is the very opposite of trying to kill it outright.

And desire has fulfillment for its correlative. The desire and its fulfillment are bound together as cause and effect; and when we realize the law of their sequence, we shall be more than ever impressed with the supreme importance of Desire as the great center of Life

XIV - THE SPIRIT OF OPULENCE

IT is quite a mistake to suppose that we must restrict and stint ourselves in order to develop greater power or usefulness. This is to form the conception of the Divine Power as so limited that the best use we can make of it is by a policy of self-starvation, whether material or mental. Of course, if we believe that some form of self-starvation is necessary to our producing good work, then so long as we entertain this belief the fact actually is so for us. "Whatsoever is not of faith"--that is, not in accordance with our honest belief--"is sin"; and by acting contrary to what we really believe we bring in a suggestion of opposition to the

Divine Spirit, which must necessarily paralyze our efforts, and surround us with a murky atmosphere of distrust and want of joy.

But all this exists in, and is produced by, our belief; and when we come to examine the grounds of this belief we shall find that it rests upon an entire misapprehension of the nature of our own power. If we clearly realize that the creative power in ourselves is unlimited, then there is no reason for limiting the extent to which we may enjoy what we can create by means of it. Where we are drawing from the infinite we need never be afraid of taking more than our share. That is not where the danger lies. The danger is in not sufficiently realizing our own richness, and in looking upon the externalized products of our creative power as being the true riches instead of the creative power of spirit itself.

If we avoid this error, there is no need to limit ourselves in taking what we will from the infinite storehouse: "All things are yours." And the way to avoid this error is by realizing that the true wealth is in identifying ourselves with the spirit of opulence. We must be opulent in our thought. Do not "think money," as such, for it is only one means of opulence; but think opulence, that is, largely, generously, liberally, and you will find that the means of realizing this thought will flow to you from all quarters, whether as money or as a hundred other things not to be reckoned in cash.

We must not make ourselves dependent on any particular form of wealth, or insist on its coming to us through some particular channel--that is at once to impose a limitation, and to shut out other forms of wealth and to close other channels; but we must enter into the spirit of it. Now the spirit is Life, and throughout the universe Life ultimately consists in circulation, whether within the physical body of the individual or on the scale of the entire solar system; and circulation means a continual flowing around, and the spirit of opulence is no exception to this universal law of all life.

When once this principle becomes clear to us we shall see that our attention should be directed rather to the giving than the receiving. We must look upon ourselves, not as misers' chests to be kept locked for our own benefit, but as centers of distribution; and the better we fulfill our function as such centers the greater will be the corresponding inflow. If we choke the outlet the current must slacken, and a full and free flow can be obtained only by keeping it open. The spirit of opulence--the opulent mode of thought, that is--consists in cultivating the feeling that we possess all sorts of riches which we can bestow upon others, and which we can bestow liberally because by this very action we open the way for still greater supplies to flow in. But you say, "I am short of money, I hardly know how to pay for necessaries. What have I to give?"

The answer is that we must always start from the point where we are; and if your wealth at the present moment is not abundant on the material plane, you need not trouble to start on that plane. There are other sorts of wealth, still more valuable, on the spiritual and intellectual planes, which you can give; and you can start from this point and practice the spirit of opulence, even though your balance at the bank may be nil. And then the universal **law of attraction** will begin to assert itself. You will riot only begin to experience an inflow on the spiritual and intellectual planes, but it will extend itself to the material plane also.

If you have realized the spirit of opulence you cannot help drawing to yourself material good, as well as that higher wealth which is not to be measured by a money standard; and because you truly understand the spirit of opulence you will neither affect to despise this form of good, nor will you attribute to it a value that does not belong to it; but you will co-ordinate it with your other more interior forms of wealth so as to make it the material instrument in smoothing the way for their more perfect expression. Used thus, with understanding of the relation which it bears to spiritual and intellectual wealth, material wealth becomes one with them, and is no more to be shunned and feared than it is to be sought for its own sake.

It is not money, but the love of money, that is the root of evil; and the spirit of opulence is precisely the attitude of mind which is furthest removed from the love of money for its own sake. It does not believe in money. What it does believe in is the generous feeling which is the intuitive recognition of the great law of circulation, which does not in any undertaking make its first question, How much am I going to get by it? but, How much am I going to do by it? And making this the first question, the getting will flow in with a generous profusion, and with a spontaneousness and rightness of direction that are absent when our first thought is of receiving only.

We are not called upon to give what we have not yet got and to run into debt; but we are to give liberally of what we have, with the knowledge that by so doing we are setting the law of circulation to work, and as this law brings us greater and greater inflows of every kind of good, so our out-giving will increase, not by depriving ourselves of any expansion of our own life that we may desire, but by finding that every expansion makes us the more powerful instruments for expanding the life of others. "Live and let live" is the motto of the true opulence.

Edinburgh Lectures

V. FURTHER CONSIDERATIONS REGARDING SUBJECTIVE AND OBJECTIVE MIND.

AN intelligent consideration of the phenomena of hypnotism will show us that what we call the hypnotic state is the normal state of the subjective mind. It always conceives of itself in accordance with some suggestion conveyed to it, either consciously or unconsciously to the mode of objective mind which governs it, and it gives rise to corresponding external results. The abnormal nature of the conditions induced by experimental hypnotism is in the removal of the normal control held by the individual's own objective mind over his subjective mind and the substitution of some other control for it, and thus we may say that the normal characteristic of the subjective mind is its perpetual action in accordance with some sort of suggestion. It becomes therefore a question of the highest importance to determine in every case what the nature of the suggestion shall be and from what source it shall proceed; but before considering the sources of suggestion we must realize more fully the place taken by subjective mind in the order of Nature.

If the student has followed what has been said regarding the presence of intelligent spirit pervading all space and permeating all matter, he will now have little difficulty in recognizing this all-pervading spirit as universal subjective mind. That it cannot as universal mind have the qualities of objective mind is very obvious. The universal mind is the creative power throughout Nature; and as the originating power it must first give rise to the various forms in which objective mind recognizes its own individuality, before these individual minds can re-act upon it; and hence, as pure spirit or first cause, it cannot possibly be anything else than subjective mind; and the fact which has been abundantly proved by experiment that the subjective mind is the builder of the body shows us that the power of creating by growth from within is the essential characteristic of the subjective mind. Hence, both from experiment and from a priori reasoning, we may say that where-ever we find creative power at work there we are in the presence of subjective mind, whether it be working on the grand scale of the cosmos, or on the miniature scale of the individual. We may therefore lay it down as a principle that the universal all-permeating intelligence, which has been considered in the second and third sections, is purely subjective mind, and therefore follows the law of subjective mind, namely that it is amenable to any suggestion, and will carry out any suggestion that is impressed upon it to its most rigorously logical consequences. The incalculable importance of this truth may not perhaps strike the student at first sight, but a little consideration will show him the enormous possibilities that are stored up in it, and in the concluding section I shall briefly touch upon the very serious conclusions resulting from it. For the present it will be sufficient to realize that the subjective mind in ourselves is the same subjective mind which is at work throughout the universe giving rise to the infinitude of natural forms with which we are surrounded, and in like manner giving rise to ourselves also. It may be called the supporter of our individuality; and we may loosely speak of our individual subjective mind as our personal share in the universal mind. This, of course, does not imply the splitting up of the universal mind into fractions, and it is to avoid this error that I have discussed the essential unity of spirit in the third section, but in order to avoid too highly abstract conceptions in the present stage of the student's progress we may conveniently employ the idea of a personal share in the universal subjective mind.

To realize our individual subjective mind in this manner will help us to get over the great metaphysical difficulty which meets us in our endeavor to make conscious use of first cause, in other words to create external results by the power of our own thought. Ultimately there can be only one first cause, which is the universal mind, but because it is universal it cannot, as universal, act on the plane of the individual and particular. For it to do so would be for it to cease to be universal and therefore cease to be the creative power which we wish to employ. On the other hand, the fact that we are working for a specific definite object implies our intention to use this universal power in application to a particular purpose, and thus we find ourselves involved in the paradox of seeking to make the universal act on the plane of the particular. We want to effect a junction between the two extremes of the scale of Nature, the innermost creative spirit and a particular external form. Between these two is a great gulf, and the question is how is it to be bridged over. It is here, then, that the conception of our individual subjective mind as our personal share in the universal subjective mind affords the means of meeting the difficulty, for on the one hand it is in immediate connection with the universal mind, and on the other it is immediate connection with the individual objective, or intellectual mind; and this in its turn is in immediate connection with the world of externalization, which is conditioned in time and space; and thus the relation between the subjective and objective minds in the individual forms the bridge which is needed to connect the two extremities of the scale.

The individual subjective mind may therefore be regarded as the organ of the Absolute in precisely the same way that the objective mind is the organ of the Relative, and it is in order to regulate our use of these two organs that it is necessary to understand what the terms "absolute" and "relative" actually mean. The absolute is that idea of a thing which contemplates it as existing in itself and not in relation to something else, that is to say, which contemplates the essence of it; and the relative is that idea of a thing which contemplates it as related to other things, that is to say as circumscribed by a certain environment. The absolute is the region of causes, and the relative is the region of conditions; and hence, if we wish to control conditions, this can only be done by our thought-power operating on the plane of the absolute, which it can do only through the medium of the subjective mind. The conscious use of the creative power of thought consists in the attainment of the power of Thinking in the Absolute, and this can only be attained by a clear conception of the interaction between our different mental functions. For this purpose the student cannot too strongly impress upon himself that subjective mind, on whatever scale, is intensely sensitive to suggestion, and as creative power works accurately to the externalization of that suggestion which is most deeply impressed upon it. If then, we would take any idea out of the realm of the relative, where it is limited and restricted by conditions imposed upon it through surrounding circumstances, and transfer it to the realm of the absolute where it is not thus limited, a right recognition of our mental constitution will enable us to do this by a clearly defined method.

The object of our desire is necessarily first conceived by us as bearing some relation to existing circumstances, which may, or may not, appear favorable to it; and what we want to do is to eliminate the element of contingency and attain something which is certain in itself. To do this is to work upon the plane of the absolute, and for this purpose we must endeavor to impress upon our subjective mind the idea of that which we desire quite apart from any conditions. This separation from the elements of condition implies the elimination of the idea of time, and consequently we must think of the thing as already in actual existence. Unless we do this we are not consciously operating upon the plane of the absolute, and are therefore not employing the creative power of our thought. The simplest practical method of gaining the habit of thinking in this manner is to conceive the existence in the spiritual world of a spiritual prototype of every existing thing, which becomes the root of the corresponding external existence. If we thus habituate ourselves to look on the spiritual prototype as the essential being of the thing, and the material form as the growth of this prototype into outward expression, then we shall see that the initial step to the production of any external fact must be the creation of its spiritual prototype. This prototype, being purely spiritual, can only be formed by the operation of thought, and in order to have substance on the spiritual plane it must be thought of as actually existing there. This conception has been elaborated by Plato in his doctrine of archetypal ideas, and by Swedenborg in his doctrine of correspondences; and a still greater teacher has said, "All things whatsoever ye pray and ask for, believe that ye have received them, and ye shall receive them." (Mark XI. 24, R.V.) The difference of the tenses in this passage is remarkable. The speaker bids us first to believe that our desire has already been fulfilled, that it is a thing already accomplished, and then its accomplishment will follow as a thing in the future. This is nothing else than a concise direction for making use of the creative power of thought by impressing upon the universal subjective mind the particular thing, which we desire as an already existing fact. In following this direction we are thinking on the plane of the absolute and eliminating from our minds all consideration of conditions, which imply limitation and the possibility of adverse contingencies; and we are thus planting a seed which, if left undisturbed, will infallibly germinate into external fruition.

By thus making intelligent use of our subjective mind, we, so to speak, create a nucleus, which is no sooner created than it begins to exercise an attractive force, drawing to itself material of a like character with its own, and if this process is allowed to go on undisturbed, it will continue until an external form corresponding to the nature of the nucleus comes out into manifestation on the plane of the objective and relative. This is the universal method of Nature on every plane. Some of the most advanced thinkers in modern physical science, in the endeavor to probe the great mystery of the first origin of the world, have postulated the formation of what they call "vortex rings" formed from an infinitely fine primordial substance. They tell us that if such a ring be once formed on the minutest scale and set rotating, then, since it would be moving in pure ether and subject to no friction, it must according to all known laws of physics be indestructible and its motion perpetual. Let two such rings approach each other, and by the **law of attraction**, they would coalesce into a whole, and so on until manifested matter as we apprehend it with our external senses, is at last formed. Of course no one has ever seen these rings with the physical eye. They are one of those abstractions, which result if we follow out the observed law of physics and the unavoidable sequences of mathematics to their necessary consequences. We cannot account for the things that we can see unless we assume the existence of other things, which we cannot; and the "vortex theory" is one of these assumptions. This theory has not been put forward by mental scientists but by purely physical scientists as the ultimate conclusion to which their researches have led them, and this conclusion is that all the innumerable forms of Nature have their origin in the infinitely minute nucleus of the vortex ring, by whatever means the vortex ring may have received its initial impulse, a question with which physical science, as such, is not concerned.

As the vortex theory accounts for the formation of the inorganic world, so does biology account for the formation of the living organism. That also has its origin in a primary nucleus which, as soon as it is established, operates as a center of attraction for the formation of all those physical organs of which the perfect individual is composed. The science of embryology shows that this rule holds good without exception throughout the whole range of the animal world, including man; and botany shows the same principle at work throughout the vegetable world. All branches of physical science demonstrate the fact that every completed manifestation, of whatever kind and on whatever scale, is started by the establishment of a nucleus, infinitely small but endowed with an unquenchable energy of attraction, causing it to steadily increase in power and definiteness of purpose, until the process of growth is completed and the matured form stands out as an accomplished fact. Now if this were the universal method of Nature, there is nothing unnatural in supposing that it must begin its operation at a stage further back than the formation of the material nucleus. As soon as that is called into being it begins to operate by the **law of attraction** on the material plane; but what is the force which originates the material nucleus? Let a recent work on physical science give us the answer; "In its ultimate essence, energy may be incomprehensible by us except as an exhibition of the direct operation of that which we call Mind or Will." The quotation is from a course of lectures on " Waves in Water, Air and Ether," delivered in 1902, at the Royal Institution, by J. A. Fleming. Here, then, is the testimony of physical science that the originating energy is Mind or Will; and we are, therefore, not only making a logical deduction from certain unavoidable intuitions of the human mind, but are also following on the lines of the most advanced physical science, when we say that the action of Mind plants that nucleus which, if allowed to grow undisturbed, will eventually attract to itself all the conditions necessary for its manifestation in outward visible form. Now the only action of Mind is Thought; and it is for this reason that by our thoughts we create corresponding external conditions, because we thereby create the nucleus which attracts to itself its own correspondences in due order until the finished work is manifested on the external plane. This is according to the strictly scientific conception of the universal law of growth; and we may therefore briefly sum up the whole argument by saying that our thought of anything forms a spiritual prototype of it, thus constituting a nucleus or center of attraction for all conditions necessary to its eventual externalization by a law of growth inherent in the prototype itself.

The complete text of the books behind these excerpts may be found in -

The Complete Thomas Troward Collection

(Please see Bibliography for details.)

Charles M. Bristol

I first ran into Bristol through a single reference in Earl Nightingale's "Strangest Secret" recording. As I continued to listen to that MP3, I started checking into the recommended authors.

They were each gems – and each nearly impossible to find, as they had dropped off the apparent face of the earth. But not off the Internet.

Once I acquired the reference and started my studies, I was entranced by his direct style and practical advice. Here was someone who was a professional reporter and also a success in his own life well before writing this book.

And now you can find if his truths are true for you...

Magic of Believing

Chapter 4 - Suggestion is Power

How many times have you heard it said, "Just believe you can do it and you can"? Whatever the task, if begun with the belief that you can do it, it will be done perfectly. Often belief empowers a person to do what others consider impossible. The act of believing is the starting force, the generating power that leads to accomplishment.

"Come on, fellows, we can beat them," shouts someone in command, whether in a football game, on the battlefield, or in the strife of the business world. That sudden voicing of belief, challenging and electrifying, reverses the tide and---Success! From defeat to victory---and all because some mighty believer knew that it could be done.

You may be shipwrecked and tossed into the water near a rocky shore. Momentarily, you may fear that there isn't a chance for you. Suddenly a feeling comes that you will be saved---or that you can save yourself. The moment you have that feeling, it begins to take the form of belief. And along with the belief comes the power to assist you.

You may be in a fire, surrounded by flames and enveloped in smoke, and frantic with fear. This same power asserts itself---and you may be saved. Emerson explains it by saying that in a difficult situation or a sudden emergency, our spontaneous action is always the best. Many stories have been told of the great reserves of the subconscious mind, how under its direction (and by imparting its superhuman strength), frail men and women have been able to perform feats far beyond their normal powers. Speakers, stand-up comedians, and writers are often amazed at the subconscious mind's power to furnish them with a steady flow of thoughts that their audiences enjoy.

After studying the various mystical religions and different teachings and systems of mind-stuff, I'm impressed that they all have the same basic modus operandi. That is, they achieve success through repetition---the repeating of certain mantras, words, or formulas. William Seabrook declared that witch doctors, Voodoo high priests, "hexers," and many other followers of strange cults use just plain mumbo-jumbo to invoke the spirits or work black magic. One finds the same principle at work in the chants, incantations, litanies, daily lessons (to be repeated at frequently as possible during the week), and the frequent praying of the Buddhists and Moslems alike. Or consider the affirmations of the Theosophists and the followers of Unity, the Absolute, Truth, New Thought, Divine Science. In fact, it is basic in all religions, although here it is white magic instead of black.

When you seek further, you find the same principle at work in the beating of tom-toms or kettledrums by primitive peoples in all parts of the globe. The sound vibrations arouse similar vibrations in the psychic nature of these so-called "primitives," so that they become stimulated, excited, and emotionalized to the point where they can defy death. The war dances of the American Indians, with their repeated rhythmic physical movements; the tribal ceremonies to bring rain; the dancing of the whirling dervishes---even the playing of martial music at critical times, and the soothing background music played for the workers in industrial plants---all embody the same principle.

In his book, Penthouse of the Gods, published in 1939, Theos Bernard recounts some interesting facts as to the repetition of certain mystical chants and prayers. When he wrote it, he claimed to be the first white person to enter the mysterious Tibetan city of Lhasa, high in the Himalayas, where the monasteries contained thousands of lamas---

followers of Buddha. On reading the book, you get the impression that when the lamas, and monks are not eating or attending to the material wants of their bodies, they are constantly and continuously engaged in their mystical chants, using their prayer wheels. Bernard declared that in one temple, the monks started at daybreak and spent the entire day repeating prayers. The exact number of their repetitions was 108,000. He told also of how lamas accompanying him repeated certain fixed chants in order to give him additional strength.

In all religions, cults, and orders, there is an obvious, prescribed ritual in which the repetition of words (mystical or otherwise) plays an important part. And this brings us to the law of suggestion.

Forces operating within its limits are capable of producing phenomenal results. That is, the power of suggestion---either autosuggestion (your own to yourself) or heterosuggestion (coming to you from outside sources)---starts the machinery into operation, causing the subconscious mind to begin its creative work---and right here is where the affirmations and repetitions play their part.

Repetition of the same chant, the same incantations, the same affirmations leads to belief, and once that belief becomes a deep conviction, things begin to happen. A builder or contractor looks over a set of plans and specifications for a bridge or a building, and, urged by a desire to get the contract for the work, declares to himself, "I can do that. Yes, I can do that." He may repeat it silently to himself a thousand times without being conscious of doing it. Nevertheless, the suggestion finds a place in which to take root, he gets the contract, and the structure is eventually built. Conversely, he may say that he can't do it---and he never does.

Hitler used the identical force and the same mechanics in inciting the German people to attack the world. A reading of his Mein Kampf will verify that. Dr. René Fauvel, a famous French psychologist, explained it by saying that Hitler had a remarkable understanding of the law of suggestion and its different forms of application, and that he mobilized every instrument of propaganda in his mighty campaign of suggestion with uncanny skill and masterly showmanship.

Hitler openly stated that the psychology of suggestion was a terrible weapon in the hands of anyone who knew how to use it.

Let's see how he worked it to make the Germans believe what he wanted them to. Slogans, posters, huge signs, massed flags appeared throughout Germany. Hitler's picture was everywhere. "One Reich, one People, one Leader" became the chant. It was heard everywhere that a group gathered.

"Today we own Germany, tomorrow the entire world," the marching song of the German youths, came from thousands of throats daily. Such slogans as "Germany has waited long enough," "Stand up, you are the aristocrats of the Third Reich," "Germany is behind Hitler to a man," and hundreds of others, bombarded them twenty-four hours a day from billboards, sides of buildings, the radio, and the press. Every time they moved, turned around, or spoke to one another, they got the idea that they were a superior race, and once that belief took hold, they started their campaign of terror.

Under the hypnotic influence of this belief, strengthened by repeated suggestion, they started out to prove it. Unfortunately for them, other nations also had strong national beliefs that eventually became the means of bringing defeat to the Germans.

Mussolini, too, used the same law of suggestion in an attempt to give Italy a place in the sun. Signs and slogans such as "Believe, Obey, Fight," "Italy must have its great place in the world," "We have some old scores and new scores to settle," covered the walls of thousands of buildings, and similar ideas were dinned into the people via the radio and every other means of direct communication.

Joseph Stalin, too, used the same science to build Russia into what she is today. In November, 1946, the Institute of Modern Hypnotism, recognizing that Stalin had been using the great power of the repeated suggestion in order to make the Russian people believe in their strength, named him as one of the ten persons with the "most hypnotic eyes in the world," and rated him as a "mass hypnotist." The Japanese warlords used it to make fanatical fighters out of their people. From the very day of their birth, Japanese children were fed the suggestion that they were direct descendants of Heaven and destined to rule the world. They prayed it, chanted it, and believed it; but here again, it was used wrongly.

For forty-four years, ever since the Russo-Japanese war, the Japanese immortalized Naval Warrant Officer Magoshichi Sugino, one of Japan's early suicide fighters and greatest heroes. Thousands of statues were erected to his memory. In repeated song and story, young Nipponese were taught to believe that they could die in no more heroic manner than by following his example. Millions of them believed it, and during the war thousands of them did die as Kamikaze pilots. Yet Sugino, who was supposed to have gone to his death while scuttling a ship to bottle up the Russian fleet at Port Arthur, didn't die in battle! He was picked up by a Chinese boat. Upon learning that he was being lauded by his people as a great martyr, he decided to remain obscure and became an exile in Manchuria. Although he was alive and well, it continued to be dinned into the ears of young Nipponese that there was no greater heroic act than to die as Sugino had. This terrible, persistent and deeply founded belief, though based entirely on a fable, caused thousands of Japanese to throw away their lives during the war. Finally, Associated Press dispatches from Tokyo in November, 1946, told how he was discovered after many years and was being returned home.

Americans, too, were subjected to the power of suggestion long before World War I, and got it again in a big way under the direction of General Hugh Johnson with his N.R.A. plan. In World War II, we were constantly told that Germany and Japan had to be defeated unconditionally. Under the constant repetition of the same thought, all individual thinking was paralyzed and the mass mind became grooved to a certain pattern---win the war unconditionally. As one writer so ably said, "In war, the voice of dissension becomes the voice of treason." Again we see the terrific force of thought repetition---it is our master, and we do as we are ordered.

This subtle force of the repeated suggestion overcomes our reason, acting directly on our emotions and our feelings, finally penetrating to the very depths of our subconscious minds. This is the basic principle of all successful advertising---the continued and repeated suggestion that first makes you believe, after which you are eager to buy.

For centuries tomatoes were looked upon as poisonous. People dared not eat them until some fearless person tried them and lived. Today millions of people eat tomatoes, not knowing that they were considered unfit for human consumption. Conversely, the lowly spinach nearly went into the garbage pail after the United States Government declared that it did not contain the food values attributed to it for decades. Millions believed this and refused to honor Popeye's favorite dish any longer.

Clearly, the founders of all great religious movements knew much about the power of the repeated suggestion and gained far-reaching results with it. Religious teachings have been hammered into us from birth, into our mothers and fathers before us and into their parents and their parents before them. There's certainly white magic in that kind of believing.

Such statements as "What we don't know won't hurt us" and 'Ignorance is bliss" take on greater significance when you realize that only the things you become conscious of can harm or bother you. We have all heard the story of the man who didn't know it couldn't be done and went ahead and did it. Psychologists tell us that as babies we have only two fears: the fear of loud noises and the fear of falling. All of our other fears are passed on to us or develop as a result of our experiences; they come from what we are taught or what we hear and see. I like to think of men and women as staunch oak trees that can stand firm amid the many crosscurrents of thought that whirl around them. But far too many people are like saplings that, swayed by every little breeze, ultimately grow in the direction of some strong wind of thought that blows against them.

The Bible is filled with examples of the power of thought and suggestion. Read Genesis, Chapter 30, verses 36 to 43, and you'll learn that even Jacob knew their power. The Bible tells how he developed spotted and speckled cattle, sheep, and goats by placing rods from trees, partially stripping them of their bark so they would appear spotted and marked, in the watering troughs where the animals came to drink. As you may have guessed, the flocks conceived before the spotted rods and brought forth cattle, "ring-straked, speckled, and spotted." (And incidentally, Jacob waxed exceedingly rich.) Moses, too, was a master at suggestion. For forty years he used it on the Israelites, and it took them to the promised land of milk and honey. David, following the suggestive forces operating on him, slew the mighty, heavily armed Goliath with a pebble from a slingshot.

Joan of Arc, the frail little Maid of Orleans, heard voices and under their suggestive influences became imbued with the idea that she had a mission to save France. She was able to transmit her indomitable spirit to the hearts of her soldiers and she defeated the superior forces of the English at Orleans.

William James, father of modern psychology in America, declared that often our faith in advance of a doubtful undertaking is the only thing that can assure its successful conclusion. Man's faith, according to James, acts on the powers above him as a claim and creates its own verification. In other words, the thought becomes literally father to the fact. For further illumination of faith and its power, I suggest that you read the General Epistle of James in the New Testament.

Actually everyone who has ever witnessed a football or baseball game has seen this power of suggestion at work. Knute Rockne, the famous coach at Notre Dame, knew the value of suggestion and used it repeatedly, but always suited his method of applying it to the temperament of the individual team. On one Saturday afternoon, Notre Dame was playing in a particularly grueling game, and at the end of the first half was trailing badly. The players were in their dressing room nervously awaiting Rockne's arrival. Finally the door opened, and Rockne came in slowly. His eyes swept inquiringly over the squad---"Oh, excuse me, I made a mistake. I thought these were the quarters of the Notre Dame team." The door closed, and Rockne was gone.

Puzzled and then stung with fury, the team went out for the second half---and won the game.

Other writers, too, have explained the psychological methods Rockne used and have told how Fielding Yost of Michigan, Dan McGuin of Vanderbilt, Herbert Crisler of Princeton, and dozens of others used the "magic" of suggestion to arouse their teams to great emotional heights. Before the Rose Bowl game of 1934, the "wise" tipsters rated the Columbia team as underdogs. They hadn't counted on Coach Lou Little and his stirring talks to his players day after day. When the whistle blew for the end of the game, the Columbia men were the top dogs over the "superior" Stanford team.

In 1935, Gonzaga University beat powerful Washington State 13 to 6 in one of the biggest upset games ever seen in the West. Gonzaga was a nonconference team, while the Washington State team, because of its great record, was thought to be unbeatable. Newspapers at the time reported assistant coach Sam Dagley as having declared that Gonzaga played inspired football. He revealed that for half an hour before the game, Coach Mike Pecarovich played "over and over" a phonograph record of one of Rockne's most rousing pep talks.

Years ago, Mickey Cochrane of the Detroit Tigers literally drove a second-division-minded group of baseball players to the top of the American League by using the power of the repeated suggestion. I quote from a newspaper dispatch: "Day after day, through the hot, hard grind, [Cochrane] preached the gospel of victory, impressing on the Tigers the 'continued thought' that the team which wins must go forward." You see the same force actively at work in the fluctuations of the stock market. Unfavorable news immediately depresses prices, while favorable news raises them. The intrinsic values of stocks are not changed, but there is an immediate change in the thinking of the market operators, which is reflected at once in the minds of the holders. Not what will actually happen, but what security holders believe will happen causes them to buy or sell.

In the Depression years---and there may be years like them in the future---we saw this same suggestive force working overtime. Day after day we heard expressions such as, "Times are hard," "Business is poor," "The banks are failing," "Prosperity hasn't a chance," and wild stories about business failures on every hand, until they became the national chant. Millions believed that prosperous days would never return. Hundreds, yes thousands, of strong-willed men go down under the constant hammering, the continuous tap-tapping of the same fearful thoughts. Money, always sensitive, runs to cover when fear suggestions begin to circulate, and business failures and unemployment quickly follow. We hear thousands of stories of bank failures, huge concerns going to the wall, etc., and people readily believe them and act accordingly.

There will never be another business depression if people generally realize that their own fearful thoughts literally create hard times. They think hard times, and hard times follow. So it is with wars. When peoples of the world stop thinking of depressions and wars, they will become non-existent, for nothing comes into our economic sphere unless we first create it with our emotional thinking.

Dr. Walter Dill Scott, eminent psychologist and long president of Northwestern University, told the whole story when he said, "Success or failure in business is caused more by mental attitudes even than by mental capacities."

You may have read of the night of October 20, 1938, when Orson Welles and his Mercury Theater players broadcast a dramatization of H. G. Wells' novel, The War of the Worlds. It was a story of an invasion by some strange warriors from the planet Mars, but it caused fright among thousands of people. Some rushed out-of-doors, police stations were besieged, eastern telephone exchanges were blocked, New Jersey highways were dogged. In fact, for a few hours following the broadcast, there was genuine panic among millions of listeners who believed our earth was being attacked by invaders from Mars. Yes, indeed, belief does cause some strange and unusual happenings!

Human beings are human beings the world over, all subject to the same emotions, the same influences, and the same vibrations. And what is a big business, a village, a city, a nation but merely a collection of individual humans controlling and operating it with their thinking and believing? As individuals think and believe, so they are. As a whole city of them thinks, so it is; and as a nation of them think, so it is. This is an inescapable conclusion. Every person is the creation of themselves, the image of their own thinking and believing. As King Solomon put it, 'For as he thinketh in his heart, so is he."

Rallies held in schools and colleges just before important athletic contests are based on the same principles---speeches, songs, and yells become the means of creating suggestion and arousing the will to win. Many sales managers employ the same principle in their morning sales meetings when frequently music is used to emotionalize the salesmen and to get the idea over to them that they can beat all their previous sales records. The same principle with varying technique is basic in the Army---in fact, all armies. The commands and formations constantly repeated in close-order drill develop in the men instant obedience, which ultimately becomes instinctive. The commands and formations become so fixed in their minds and bodies that their movements are almost automatic---all of which in turn creates that self-confidence which is absolutely necessary in active conflict.

It is very important to remember that the subconscious will go into action at once under the impetus of the commands or suggestions it receives from the conscious mind (or which come from outside sources and are transmitted to it via the conscious mind). But it gets results quicker if the conscious mind accompanies its message with a mental picture of the desired goal. It may be faint, sketchy, or even unfinished, but even if only an outline, it will be enough for the subconscious to act upon.

And this brings us to the rituals and ceremonies performed amid dramatic settings in churches and secret orders, all designed to appeal to the emotions and to create a mystical picture in the beholders' minds. These rituals, no matter what the setting, are there to hold your attention and link these symbols' hidden meanings with the particular ideas to be implanted in your mind. Various lighting arrangements, different paraphernalia, often a special garb for those directing the operations, all to the accompaniment of soft, often religious, music, all help to put you in the proper emotional (and incidentally, receptive) state. The idea is as old as history. Not only the most civilized peoples but also the most primitive tribes have their characteristic ceremonials. Similar methods for impressing the individual are employed at mediumistic stances and crystal-gazing performances; even the gypsy phrenologist considers it a part of her "props." Without this atmosphere, which tends to make our conscious mind drowsy and even puts it temporarily to sleep, we would not be so easily convinced, for by itself, the desire to satisfy completely our longings for the mystical and miraculous is often not strong enough to permit conviction.

This is not said with any idea of being sacrilegious, but to present a picture of the historic method of appealing to the masses. Appeal by drama is the first step in arousing people's emotions, no matter for what purpose. Awakening and stirring their emotional interest prepares the way to approach their reasoning minds.

Could Aimee Semple McPherson, she with the long flowing white robe and picturesque auburn hair-do, have put over her great act of saving souls as well as achieving healings, without her superb understanding of the power of the dramatic? It's something to wonder about, because Billy Sunday in his best table-sliding act was a novice compared to Aimee when it came to showmanship and plain impressiveness. She with her many artifices and stage settings put on a most solemn performance, and her followers---on the Pacific Coast at least---declare that the results she got were real and lasting. This is no reflection on Mrs. McPherson, for her followers were very sincere and believed in her work, her teachings, and the results---and that's all that matters.

However, men and women with strong personal magnetism and great orators can get the same emotional effect without props or stage settings to aid them. They are masters of tone effects, emotional appeal, gesticulations, bodily movements, eye magnetism, etc., by which your attention is held and you yourself are thrown wide open to their driving appeal.

Let's consider charms, talismans, amulets, good-luck pieces, four-leaf clovers, old horseshoes, rabbits' feet, and countless other trinkets which thousands of people believe in. By themselves, they are harmless inanimate objects with no power. But when people breathe life into them by their thinking, they do have power, even though the power isn't in them per se. The power comes only with the believing---which alone makes them effective.

An outstanding illustration of this is found in the story of Alexander the Great and Napoleon. In Alexander's day, an oracle proclaimed that whoever unloosened the Gordian knot would become ruler of all Asia. Alexander cut the knot with one stroke of his sword--- and rose to tremendous heights and power. Napoleon was given a star sapphire when a child, with the prophecy that it would bring him luck and some day make him Emperor. Could anything but the supreme belief in the prophecy have carried this great man to become Emperor of France? He and Alexander became supermen because they had supernormal beliefs.

A cracked or broken mirror isn't going to bring you bad luck unless you believe in it. But as long as the belief is fertilized, nurtured, and made a part of your inner self, believe it or not, it is going to bring you bad luck---because the subconscious mind always brings to reality what it is led to believe.

Bird claimed there are people with certain mind powers which, when directed at plant life such as grain, vegetables, flowers, and trees, can make them grow more abundantly. A number of years ago we had an old Swiss gardener who insisted that we replace a number of small trees and shrubs in our yard. At first I couldn't see the reason for digging up the old ones and replanting others, but the old man's insistence prevailed. I observed that while planting them, just after he got the small trees in the soil and covered the roots, he engaged in some sort of audible Mumbo Jumbo. He did the same with the shrubs. One day, my curiosity piqued, I asked him what he was mumbling about as he placed the trees and shrubs in the ground. He looked at me searchingly for a moment, then said, "You may not understand, but I'm talking to them, telling them they must live and bloom. It's something I learned as a boy from my teacher in the old country. Anything that grows should have encouragement, and I'm giving it to them." Certain humans appear to have a kind of affinity for plants, which the plants seem to feel. Thousands of professional gardeners will plant seeds only at certain times of the moon. Superstition, you say? Perhaps it is practical mysticism. The Yale investigators concluded that electrical fields play a major part in plant life, and certainly that is a scientific observation.

It is a long way from Switzerland to British Columbia, but in that Canadian province is a tribe of Indians, the members of which always talk to their lines and hooks before actually starting to fish, claiming that if they didn't, the halibut and salmon wouldn't bite. Many are the tales of South Sea Islanders who offer food to their tools and implements, talking to them as though they were alive and beseeching them to get results. It isn't a great jump from those customs to the blessings offered at ship launchings or at sailing times of large fishing fleets in civilized countries, where prayers are offered even today, for successful voyages or ventures.

I recall a thrifty neighbor of mine who, although a man of intelligence and mature years, had his hair cut at only certain times of the moon. I don't remember whether it was when the moon was waxing or waning, but he maintained that whatever phase he selected caused his hair to grow less abundantly than if he had visited the barber at other times. I asked him once where he got such an idea. He glared at me as though I were belittling his intelligence, and I never did get an answer to my question.

What I have said about plant and animal life may cause a lot of materialistic people to take violent issue, but it must be remembered that at work in the world are many forces of which we know little or nothing. Consider how many new principles were developed in World War II. In the late 1940s, the American Rocket Society made application to the United States Government for land on the moon.

Without question, human imagination, visualization, and concentration are the chief factors in developing the subconscious mind's magnetic forces. You have often heard the statement, "Hold that pose!" That, of course, means holding the mental picture or vision. Here again, suggestion---repeated suggestion---plays its part.

For example, you would like a new home. Your imagination goes to work. At first, you have only a hazy idea of the kind of house you would like. Then, as you discuss it with other members of your family---or ask questions of builders or look at illustrations of new houses---the mental picture becomes clearer and clearer, until you can visualize your ideal house in all its particulars.

After that, the subconscious goes to work to provide you with that house. It may come into manifestation in any number of ways. But do you really care whether you build it with your own hands, or whether it comes to you through purchase, or from the actions of outsiders? How it comes to you is of no great consequence! When you are after a better job or planning a vacation trip, the process is the same. You've got to see it in your mind's eye, see yourself as holding that job or actually taking the trip. Some of our fears become realities through our imaginations, just as Job's did. Fortunately, many of them do not---as long as we hold the mental picture only temporarily, or at least not long enough to focus it fully upon the screen of our subconscious. The Biblical warning, "Where there is no vision, the people perish," is a fundamental truth, whether considered individually or collectively. For without the mental picture of accomplishment, little is done. You want a better job? You'll get it when you give your subconscious mind a mental picture of yourself holding that job.

As I write this, I think of the many experiences confided to me by those who have used this science during the years. I want to give you some of their stories, for in them you may perhaps find clues to an even more effective use of the principles and the mechanics which I am setting forth.

A friend got the idea of building a boat. He knew nothing about boat construction, but believed that with some simple instructions, he could build one. So he went ahead. In the course of the work, he found that he needed an electric drill, but he didn't want to spend $75 or $80 for the kind he wanted, especially when he would be using it for only a few months. First, he tried renting a drill, but inasmuch as he could use it only at night and had to return it early the next morning, he found such an arrangement very inconvenient.

He told me, "I got to thinking one night that somewhere there was a drill for me and I would have it placed in my hands. The more I thought about it, the more I thought it possible. However, nothing happened for several days; then one evening a friend who owned a sizable garage---a man I hadn't seen for a couple of years---came to see me. He, too, was interested in boats, and hearing that I was building one, said he'd like to look it over. He saw me floundering around with the heavy half-inch drill I was using and asked me where I got it. I told him I had rented it and he laughed, saying, 'Come over to the shop tomorrow and I'll lend you a smaller one which you can handle much easier.' Needless to say, I got it and kept it during all the period I was constructing the boat.

"A somewhat similar experience happened when I was cutting the ribs. I found that a small jig saw wouldn't cut through three-quarter-inch lumber. Then I caught myself wishing for a band saw---that thought led me to a woodworking shop a few blocks away from my house. I could use the band saw if I paid the owner fifty cents an hour for its use. However, I found that I was running to and from my home, first to fit the ribs and then to shape them, and losing much time in the process.

I frequently said to myself during those days that there must be some easier way to get the use of a band saw, and there was.

"The following Sunday another friend came to see how the boat was getting along. When I told him that I had been slowed down without the use of a band saw, he too laughed, saying, 'I bought one Thursday and won't be using it for some time. Got to get my shop fixed up, and in the meantime, you're welcome to use it.' As a matter of fact, he delivered it to me that same day and I kept it a number of months. I finished the boat!" Another man told me how he got the use of a thirty-foot extension ladder with which to paint his house. "I thought I would undertake the painting in my spare time," he told me, "and began looking around to find where I could get the use of a ladder. I found places where I could rent one, but their fixed time requirements didn't fit into my plans. I don't know how many times I said to myself, You're going to find a ladder. And I did. It was Memorial Day, and while in my back yard, I happened to notice that a neighbor across the street was using a long ladder to wash off the walls of his house. I called to him, asking where he got the ladder. He told me he had bought it when he purchased the house. That afternoon it was in my back yard, and I had the loan of it for several weeks!" Another man told me that shortly after Pearl Harbor, he had been looking for a garbage can of a certain size, but because of wartime priorities, he was unable to locate what he wanted. He visited second-hand stores, junk shops, bakeries, and garages to find the kind of container he wanted, but without success. He was about to give up hope when one morning he noticed workmen making repairs on a concrete building across from his home. They were using some waterproofing material from exactly the kind of can he had pictured for his own use. He asked the man in charge of the work what would be done with the container when the work was finished, and was told it would be left on the ground to be hauled away. He then explained his wants, and a couple of days later the container was in his garage---the workmen had not only emptied it but had washed and scrubbed it before delivery!

I had taken my car to a shop owner for repairs to the ignition system, after several mechanics had failed to locate the trouble. I told him how the car had been acting, and after listening he said, "I believe I can fix it."

I casually remarked, "Belief is a great thing, isn't it?" "You bet it is. Thought is the greatest force in the world, and the dumb ducks laugh when you talk about it," he answered rather caustically.

"I don't, I'm interested," I replied. 'Tell me of some instances where you have demonstrated the power of thought."

"I could keep you here all day telling you of its power---at least in my own life."

'Tell me a few. When did you first become aware of it?"

"Oh, I guess about twelve years ago, when I fell and broke my back. I was in a cast for a long time, and the doctors told me that even if I recovered, I would be crippled the rest of my life. As I lay on my back in the hospital worrying about my future, I frequently thought of the words used by my mother to the effect that 'One just has to believe.' One day it dawned on me that if I could hold on to the mental picture I was going to be all right, and if I believed in it sufficiently, I could get well. To make a long story short, here I am crawling over and underneath cars, and far from being a cripple, as you can see for yourself."

"Very interesting," I urged. 'Tell me more."

"Well, I've used it frequently to get more business. As a matter of fact, this present location is a result of it. As you know, I was burned out at my old place a few weeks ago and space like this in the city is well-nigh impossible to find. For two or three days, I worried about not being able to find another location and deliberated whether I should attempt to go to work for someone else. Then one night I made up my mind I would continue in business for myself. That was the turning point. Just before I went to sleep I said to myself, 'Oh, you'll find a place within the next few days. This thought power hasn't failed you yet.' I went to sleep with full confidence that the place would be forthcoming. The very next day I went over to see the painter where I had taken the car I saved from the fire and mentioned I was looking for another place. 'That's funny,' he commented, 'You can rent this space. I've just bought the building in the next block from an owner who wanted to retire.' And so now here I am, on a main thoroughfare and with more business than I can possibly handle!"

I know that some readers will say that these are merely coincidences, but my files are filled with similar "coincidences." To some of you they may be just that, but those acquainted with this science know that these things come about as the result of intensified thought or mental picture- making. However, we come again to a matter of opinion---the difference in conclusions between those who think this is all nonsense and those who know that the things we think materialize after their kind. Again we are reminded of what Paracelsus said: "Men devoid of the power of spiritual perception are unable to recognize anything that cannot be seen externally." It is pretty well agreed that the subconscious mind works as a result of images thrown upon its screen, but if there is something wrong with your projection apparatus or the original slide, then the projected image is blurred, inverted, or a total blank. Doubts, fears, counter-thoughts, all manage to blur the pictures you consciously desire to project.

Those who have well-developed imaginations, such as great artists, writers, and inventors, possess the ability to visualize or to make mental pictures almost at will. However, with the mechanics which I will enlarge upon later and the explanations already given, anyone following them should have no difficulty in being able to see in their mind's eye the things, objects, or situations that they desire in reality.

One of the greatest fishermen I ever knew used this visualizing method. He could sit in a boat with one or two others and pull trout after trout out of the water, while his companions--using the same kind of bait and with apparently the same mechanical technique--- dropped their hooks in the same places repeatedly, without results.

I asked him about it one time, and he laughingly replied: "I put the old 'squeeza-ma-jintum' [his word for magic] on them. I figuratively or mentally get down there where they are, and tell them to hook the bait or fly. In other words, I see them snapping at the hook and believe that it will work. That's all I can give you in the way of explanation."

This story was told to another fisherman not blessed with the first fisherman's luck, and he scoffed at it. "Ridiculous," he declared. "Any good fisherman must know the stream, the holes, the habits of fish, the type of bait or flies to use, and he'll catch them if they are there." However, he couldn't explain how others skilled in fishing technique could fish in an identical spot and still not catch them like the man who used the old "squeeza-ma-jintum."

Ben Hur Lampman was associate editor of The Oregonian, author of many articles and books on fishing and kindred subjects and a recognized naturalist. Upon reading this story, he said: "The man who says that it is ridiculous to consider there's some sort of magic or attraction at work makes himself ridiculous by displaying his ignorance. I can't explain how your friend is always so fortunate in making his catches beyond saying that there is decidedly something psychic about successful fishing. Anyone who has studied the habits of fish and tried to catch them, sooner or later realizes that there is more to successful fishing than merely throwing a lure or bait into a place where the fish are supposed to be. Just what the relationship is between mind and fish - if any - I cannot explain. But having been a student of fish, their ways and habits practically all my life, I do know that in successful fishing there is an unexplainable element or factor at work - call it what you please. Undoubtedly in the realm of psychic phenomena lies the explanation of the so-called fisherman's "luck" or the "squeeza-ma-jintum" of your successful fisherman friend."

I am not a fisherman, but surely if this **law of attraction** works in other ways, there is no reason why it could not be used advantageously in fishing.

For many years I was interested in the game of golf and was a member of several clubs. I frequently played with a man who had been one of the world's tennis champions in his younger days. He was one of the most amazing short-shot players on the Pacific Coast. With his mashie or mashie niblick, he could place the ball on any desired spot on the green with a dead stop, as close to or as far from the pin as he desired, and he was usually down in one putt. His putting, too, was an art to marvel at.

One day he amazed everyone in our foursome with what could be called phenomenal shots. "How did you do it, George?" I asked.

"Well," he replied, "you've played handball and squash, and you know what it means to place your shots on the front wall. You intuitively place it high or low or so it will rebound to a side wall or result in a kill or an extremely low ball. I learned placement years ago in tennis. You have sort of a mental picture where you want the ball to go or land before you hit it with your racket. I use the same principle with my short shots and putting. In other words, when I face the green and before I swing my club, I have an instant mental picture of where I want the ball to land, and when I putt, I actually see the ball dropping into the hole. Of course, a proper stance and knowledge of handling the clubs are vital. But most golfers have that and still don't get results. It is true that I spend many hours in practice. So do others; but the main thing is that I just seem to know where the ball is going to land before the club hits it. There's a confidence or a belief existing that I can do it, and with a mashie or mashie niblick I cause a backspin that will bring the ball to a dead stop when it lands."

For you who may raise your eyebrows at this, let's examine the facts given in a newspaper story written in the middle thirties by the famous sports writer, Grantland Rice. Rice declared that the phenomenal amateur golf player, John Montagu, could run rings around anyone. The ball always landed where he wanted to place it, whether 300 yards down the fairway or a chip shot to within two or three feet of the cup, and then when he putted, it was like the crack of doom. Rice said that the ball went where Montagu wanted it to go. Now let's read Montagu's own explanation as given in the same newspaper story. "Golf to me is played with the head, mind or brain or whatever you wish to call it. Of course, there are fundamentals of stance, grip, swing; but I must have a clear, clean mental picture of what I am doing before I play the shot. That mental picture takes charge of the muscular reaction. If there is no mental picture---what happens is a mere guess. This means almost endless concentration of thought if you are under pressure, and there is no thrill in any game unless you are under pressure."

Gene Sarazen, one of the greatest golf professionals of all times, used similar methods in his matches. His little book. Golf Tips, has much to say about mental pictures, objectives, concentration, and confidence. All golfers have heard of "mental hazards." In reality, they are bunkers, traps, water hazards, etc. But in the imaginations of many, they are formidable handicaps that put fear into the hearts of the players.

On one course where I often played there was a water hole. The distance from the tee to the hole was about one hundred and twenty yards spanning a small pond approximately fifty feet wide---an easy shot with a mashie or a mashie niblick for the average player. For a long time one member of the club, who had been a great baseball and football player in his younger days, could never get over this water hazard. Invariably he would put ball after ball into the water with his irons, to the accompaniment of profanity on his part and laughter on ours. Finally, as the months went by he took to using his spoon and hitting the ball far beyond the green.

One day I said to him, "I know the water fools you, but the next time, just blot out of your mind the picture of water between the tee and the green and see instead, mentally, an easy short fairway before you." The first time he followed the suggestion, his ball fell a few inches from the pin. And from that time, on, he later told me, as long as he followed the blotting-out technique, he never had any trouble. But when he was unable to concentrate on his own mental picture, due to the joshing from other members of his foursome, he landed in difficulties.

In observing many pool and billiard games, I am convinced that certain skilled players influence the direction and fall of the balls by mind control, although they may be in complete ignorance of the power they are using. If it can work on a golf ball, it certainly can work on a billiard ball.

The naturalist Roy Chapman Andrews told the story of a man from San Antonio, Texas, who with a .22 caliber rifle fired more than 14,500 shots at small blocks of wood tossed into the air without a single miss. Mr. Andrews emphasized his perfect timing and remarkable accuracy. Nothing was said of the mind-pictures; but if you have ever done any prolonged trap or target shooting, you know the part visualizing plays.

One finds the same sort of "magic" at work in all fields of sports. Great baseball batters, expert forward-passers in football, accurate drop-kickers---all consciously or unconsciously picture connecting with the ball and placing it where they want it to go. Certainly, practice and timing all have their primary importance, but the mental side must never be overlooked.

In this connection, I was impressed by several statements made by Dr. Marcus Bach in one of his first books, They Have Found a Faith. Dr. Bach tells of bowling with Father Divine, and of observing---from the way Father Divine selected a ball, and from his stance and delivery---

that he was no bowler. Yet Father Divine made a strike on his first try and it was one of the prettiest strikes Dr. Bach ever saw. "Father's nonchalance was characteristic. He rubbed the soft palms of his hands together as if to say, 'Well, what do you expect when the Lord rolls one!'"

Dr. Bach also wrote of an interview with Rickert Fillmore, manager of Unity City and son of one of the founders of the Unity movement. Dr. Bach asked if the works of Unity could be applied to a real estate venture. Mr. Fillmore replied, "If it works at all, it works everywhere."

Many readers of this book may not be golfers or billiard players, but a simple experiment will demonstrate to you this strange power of attraction through visualizing---or making the mental picture actually work. Find a few small stones or pebbles which you can easily throw and locate a tree or post between 6 and 10 inches in diameter. Stand away from it twenty-five or thirty feet and start throwing the pebbles in an attempt to hit it. If you have average aim, most of the stones will go wide of their mark. Now stop and tell yourself that you can hit the objective. Get a mental picture of the tree figuratively stepping forward to meet the stone or of the pebble actually colliding with the tree in the spot where you want it to strike, and you'll soon find yourself making a perfect score. Don't say it's impossible. Try it, and you'll prove it can be done---if only you will believe it.

In the early days of wartime gasoline rationing, most people didn't consider getting additional coupons a criminal offense. A friend found he didn't have enough gas to take him to his duck lake.

One Sunday he told me how he had secured enough coupons to make several trips to the shooting grounds. "I had just about given up the idea of duck shooting this fall when the thought occurred to me that I could put this Mind Stuff to work and get some more gas. Of course, everyone around the office knew that I wanted to go duck shooting and most of them knew of my problem. Whether they passed out word to their friends I do not know, but I got more coupons than you could shake a stick at. I had a constant picture of going hunting and using my automobile and of someone giving me gasoline coupons. It may be hooey, but I got the coupons. Even a farmer friend gave me gas out of his allotment."

Now let's take this same science into the kitchen. Did it ever occur to you that the so-called good cooks use this same science, some consciously and others unconsciously? Two people can attempt to make the same kind of pie, use identical ingredients and follow instructions to the letter. One will be a failure while the other will be the last word in culinary achievement.

Why? In the first case, the one cook approaches pie-making with trepidation. She knows she has had pie failures in the past and worries how this one is going to come out. She doesn't have a perfect mental picture of an appetite-satisfying golden brown crust with a wonderful zestful filling.

She's upset and nervous, and without her knowing it, her uneasiness is communicated to her pie-making. The second one is aware, she knows that her pie is going to be tops---and it is. That primary mental picture---her belief---makes it so.

If you are a mediocre chef but you like to cook---that's a very necessary requisite too---sell yourself on the idea that you can prepare superior dishes. You can do it, for you have the forces inside of you, and they will come to your aid if only you will believe in them and call upon them. So put your heart and soul into the next pie you make. Envision it as perfect, and you will be surprised when you see the realization of your mental picture.

The same law will work no matter where it is applied, and that goes for everything from fishing to money-making or success in business. Let's take an example out of the war. When he left the Philippines, General Douglas MacArthur declared "I shall return." With our Pacific Fleet in ruins at Pearl Harbor and with the Japanese in control of most of the South Pacific, MacArthur had no physical evidence that he would ever return. However, it was a statement of confidence or belief.

He must have had a mental picture of his returning, and history relates how he kept his promise.

Thousands of similar cases happened during the war and are happening today.

The complete text of the book containing this excerpt may be found in -

Law of Attraction: Magic of Believing

(Please see Bibliography for details.)

Charles F. Haanel

One of the most downloaded and popular books was featured on "The Secret" DVD and on their website. But I had found his works long before I found that DVD.

Haanel has more urban legends repeated about his books than any other in this genre. What we do know as fact is that he originally wrote this as a mail-subscription course which was such a hit that he turned it into a book. And that book became a bestseller in its time.

Since the advent of the Internet, it has been uploaded onto innumerable websites and become republished by various editors.

His understanding of how the universe works is unparalleled except by those who have studied his works, and those of his mentor, Troward.

These excerpts are not all he has to say about the Law of Attraction – so feel free to get your complete copy of his books.

Master Key System

INTRODUCTION - PART FIVE

Enclosed herewith you will find Part Five. After studying this part carefully, you will see that every conceivable force or object or fact is the result of mind in action.

Mind in action is thought, and thought is creative. Men are thinking now as they never thought before. Therefore, this is a creative age, and the world is awarding its richest prizes to the thinkers.

Matter is powerless, passive, inert. Mind is force, energy, power. Mind shapes and controls matter. Every form which matter takes is but the expression of some pre-existing thought.

But thought works no magic transformations; it obeys natural laws; it sets in motion natural forces; it releases natural energies; it manifests in your conduct and actions, and these in turn react upon your friends and acquaintances, and eventually upon the whole of your environment.

You can originate thought, and, since thoughts are creative, you can create for yourself the things you desire.

PART FIVE

1. At least ninety per cent of our mental life is subconscious, so that those who fail to make use of this mental power live within very narrow limits.

2. The subconscious can and will solve any problem for us if we know how to direct it. The subconscious processes are always at work; the only question is, are we to be simply passive recipients of this activity, or are we to consciously direct the work? Shall we have a vision of the destination to be reached, the dangers to be avoided, or shall we simply drift?

3. We have found that mind pervades every part of the physical body and is always capable of being directed or impressed by authority coming from the objective or the more dominant portion of the mind.

4. The mind, which pervades the body, is largely the result of heredity, which, in turn, is simply the result of all the environments of all past generations on the responsive and ever-moving life forces. An understanding of this fact will enable us to use our authority when we find some undesirable trait of character manifesting.

5. We can consciously use all the desirable characteristics with which we have been provided and we can repress and refuse to allow the undesirable ones to manifest.

6. Again, this mind which pervades our physical body is not only the result of hereditary tendencies, but is the result of home, business and social environment, where countless thousands of impressions, ideas, prejudices and similar thoughts have been received. Much of this has been received from others, the result of opinions, suggestions or

statements; much of it is the result of our own thinking, but nearly all of it has been accepted with little or no examination or consideration.

7. The idea seemed plausible, the conscious received it, passed it on to the subconscious, where it was taken up by the Sympathetic System and passed on to be built into our physical body. "The word has become flesh."

8. This, then, is the way we are consistently creating and recreating ourselves; we are today the result of our past thinking, and we shall be what we are thinking today, the **Law of Attraction** is bringing to us, not the things we should like, or the things we wish for, or the things some one else has, but it brings us "our own," the things which we have created by our thought processes, whether consciously or unconsciously. Unfortunately, many of us are creating these things unconsciously.

9. If either of us were building a home for ourselves, how careful we would be in regard to the plans; how we should study every detail; how we should watch the material and select only the best of everything; and yet how careless we are when it comes to building our Mental Home, which is infinitely more important than any physical home, as everything which can possibly enter into our lives depends upon the character of the material which enters into the construction of our Mental Home.

10. What is the character of this material? We have seen that it is the result of the impressions which we have accumulated in the past and stored away in our subconscious Mentality. If these impressions have been of fear, of worry, of care, of anxiety; if they have been despondent, negative, doubtful, then the texture of the material which we are weaving today will be of the same negative material. Instead of being of any value, it will be mildewed and rotten and will bring us only more toil and care and anxiety. We shall be forever busy trying to patch it up and make it appear at least genteel.

11. But if we have stored away nothing but courageous thought, if we have been optimistic, positive, and have immediately thrown any kind of negative thought on the scrap pile, have refused to have anything to do with it, have refused to associate with it or become identified with it in any way, what then is the result? Our mental material is now of the best kind; we can weave any kind of material we want; we can use any color we wish; we know that the texture is firm, that the material is solid, that it will not fade, and we have no fear, no anxiety concerning the future; there is nothing to cover, there are no patches to hide.

12. These are psychological facts; there is no theory or guess work about these thinking processes; there is nothing secret about them; in fact, they are so plain that every one can understand them. The thing to do is to have a mental house-cleaning, and to have this house-cleaning every day, and keep the house clean. Mental, moral and physical cleanliness are absolutely indispensable if we are to make progress of any kind.

13. When this mental house-cleaning process has been completed, the material which is left will be suitable for the making of the kind of ideals or mental images which we desire to realize.

14. There is a fine estate awaiting a claimant. Its broad acres, with abundant crops, running water and fine timber, stretch away as far as the eye can see. There is a mansion, spacious and cheerful, with rare pictures, a well-stocked library, rich hangings, and every comfort and luxury. All the heir has to do is to assert his heirship, take possession, and use the property. He must use it; he must not let it decay; for use is the condition on which he holds it. To neglect it is to lose possession.

15. In the domain of mind and spirit, in the domain of practical power, such an estate is yours. You are the heir! You can assert your heirship and possess, and use this rich inheritance. Power over circumstances is one of its fruits, health, harmony and prosperity are

assets upon its balance sheet. It offers you poise and peace. It costs you only the labor of studying and harvesting its great resources. It demands no sacrifice, except the loss of your limitations, your servitudes, your weakness. It clothes you with self-honor, and puts a scepter in your hands.

16. To gain this estate, three processes are necessary: You must earnestly desire it. You must assert your claim. You must take possession.

17. You admit that those are not burdensome conditions.

18. You are familiar with the subject of heredity. Darwin, Huxley, Haeckel, and other physical scientists have piled evidence mountain high that heredity is a law attending progressive creation. It is progressive heredity which gives man his erect attitude, his power of motion, the organs of digestions, blood circulation, nerve force, muscular force, bone structure and a host of other faculties on the physical side. There are even more impressive facts concerning heredity of mind force. All these constitute what may be called your human heredity.

19. But there is a heredity which the physical scientists have not compassed. It lies beneath and antecedent to all their researches. At a point where they throw up their hands in despair, saying they cannot account for what they see, this divine heredity is found in full sway.

20. It is the benignant force which decrees primal creation. It thrills down from the Divine, direct into every created being. It originates life, which the physical scientist has not done, nor ever can do. It stands out among all forces supreme, unapproachable. No human heredity can approach it. No human heredity measures up to it.

21. This Infinite Life flows through you; is you. Its doorways are but the faculties which comprise your consciousness. To keep open these doors is the Secret of Power. Is it not worth while to make the effort?

22. The great fact is, that the source of all life and all power is from within. Persons, circumstances and events may suggest need and opportunities, but the insight, strength and power to answer these needs will be found within.

23. Avoid counterfeits. Build firm foundations for your consciousness upon forces which flow direct from the Infinite source, the Universal Mind of which you are the image and likeness.

24. Those we have come into possession of this inheritance are never quite the same again. They have come into possession of a sense of power hitherto undreamed of. They can never again be timid, weak, vacillating, or fearful. They are indissolubly connected with Omnipotence. Something in them has been aroused; they have suddenly discovered that they possess a tremendous latent ability of which they were heretofore entirely unconscious.

25. This power is from within, but we cannot receive it unless we give it. Use is the condition upon which we hold this inheritance. We are each of us but the channel through which the Omnipotent power is being differentiated into form; unless we give, the channel is obstructed and we can receive no more. This is true on every plane of existence and in every field of endeavor and all walks of life. The more we give, the more we get. The athlete who wishes to get strong must make use of the strength he has, and the more he gives the more he will get. The financier who wishes to make money must make use of the money he has, for only by using it can he get more.

26. The merchant who does not keep his goods going out will soon have none coming in; the corporation which fails to give efficient service will soon lack customers; the attorney who fails to get results will soon lack clients, and so it goes everywhere; power is contingent upon a proper use of the power already in our possession; what is true in every field of endeavor, every experience in life, is true of the power from which every other power known among men is begotten -- spiritual power. Take away the spirit and what is left? Nothing.

27. If then the spirit is all there is, upon the recognition of this fact must depend the ability to demonstrate all power, whether physical, mental or spiritual.

28. All possession is the result of the accumulative attitude of mind, or the money consciousness; this is the magic wand which will enable you to receive the idea, and it will formulate plans for you to execute, and you will find as much pleasure in the execution as in the satisfaction of attainment and achievement.

29. Now, go to your room, take the same seat, the same position as heretofore, and mentally select a place which has pleasant associations. Make a complete mental picture of it, see the buildings, the grounds, the trees, friends, associations, everything complete. At first, you will find yourself thinking of everything under the sun, except the ideal upon which you desire to concentrate. But do not let that discourage you. Persistence will win, but persistence requires that you practice these exercises every day without fail.

PART FIVE - Study Questions with Answers

41. What proportion of our mental life is subconscious? At least ninety per cent.

42. Is this vast mental storehouse generally utilized? No.

43. Why not? Few understand or appreciate the fact that it is an activity which they may consciously direct.

44. Where has the conscious mind received its governing tendencies? From heredity -- which means that it is the result of all the environments of all past generations.

45. What is the **law of attraction** bringing to us? Our "Own."

46. What is our "Own"? What we inherently are, and is the result of our past thinking, both conscious and subconscious.

47. Of what is the material with which we construct our mental home composed? The thoughts which we entertain.

48. What is the Secret of Power? A recognition of the omnipresence of omnipotence.

49. Where does it originate? All life and all power is from within.

50. Upon what is the possession of power contingent? Upon a proper use of the power already in our possession.

INTRODUCTION - PART TWELVE

Part Twelve is enclosed herewith. In the fourth paragraph you will find the following statement: "You must first have the knowledge of your power; second, the courage to dare; third, the faith to do."

If you concentrate upon the thoughts given, if you give them your entire attention, you will find a world of meaning in each sentence, and will attract to yourself other thoughts in harmony with them, and you will soon grasp the full significance of the vital knowledge upon which you are concentrating.

Knowledge does not apply itself; we as individuals must make the application, and the application consists in fertilizing the thought with a living purpose.

The time and thought which most persons waste in aimless effort would accomplish wonders if properly directed with some special object in view. In order to do this, it is necessary to center your mental force upon a specific thought and hold it there, to the exclusion of all other thoughts. If you have ever looked through the viewfinder on a camera, you found that when the object was not in focus, the impression was indistinct and possibly blurred, but when the proper focus was obtained the picture was clear and distinct. This illustrates the power of concentration. Unless you can concentrate upon the object which you have in view, you will have but a hazy, indifferent, vague, indistinct and blurred outline of your ideal and the results will be in accordance with your mental picture.

PART TWELVE

1. There is no purpose in life that cannot be best accomplished through a scientific understanding of the creative power of thought.

2. This power to think is common to all. Man is, because he thinks. Man's power to think is infinite, consequently his creative power is unlimited.

3. We know that thought is building for us the thing we think of and actually bringing it nearer, yet we find it difficult to banish fear, anxiety or discouragement, all of which are powerful thought forces, and which continually send the things we desire further away, so that it is often one step forward and two steps backward.

4. The only way to keep from going backward is to keep going forward. Eternal vigilance is the price of success. There are three steps, and each one is absolutely essential. You must first have the knowledge of your power; second, the courage to dare; third, the faith to do.

5. With this as a basis you can construct an ideal business, an ideal home, ideal friends, and an ideal environment. You are not restricted as to material or cost. Thought is omnipotent and has the power to draw on the Infinite bank of primary substance for all that it requires. Infinite resources are therefore at your command.

6. But your ideal must be sharp, clear-cut, definite; to have one ideal today, another tomorrow, and a third next week, means to scatter your forces and accomplish nothing; your result will be a meaningless and chaotic combination of wasted material.

7. Unfortunately this is the result which many are securing, and the cause is self evident. If a sculptor started out with a piece of marble and a chisel and changed his ideal every fifteen minutes, what result could he expect? And why should you expect any different result in molding the greatest and most plastic of all substances, the only real substance?

8. The result of this indecision and negative thought is often found in the loss of material wealth. Supposed independence which required many years of toil and effort suddenly disappears. It is often found then that money and property are not independence at all. On the contrary, the only independence is found to be a practical working knowledge of the creative power of thought.

9. This practical working method cannot come to you until you learn that the only real power which you can have is the power to adjust yourself to Divine and unchangeable principles. You cannot change the Infinite, but you can come into an understanding of Natural laws. The reward of this understanding is a conscious realization of your ability to adjust your thought faculties with the Universal Thought which is Omnipresent. Your ability to cooperate with this Omnipotence will indicate the degree of success with which you meet.

10. The power of thought has many counterfeits which are more or less fascinating, but the results are harmful instead of helpful.

11. Of course, worry, fear, and all negative thoughts produce a crop after their kind; those who harbor thoughts of this kind must inevitably reap what they have sown.

12. Again, there are the Phenomena seekers who gormandize on the so-called proofs and demonstration obtained at materializing seances. They throw open their mental doors and soak themselves in the most

poisonous currents which can be found in the psychic world. They do not seem to understand that it is the ability to become negative, receptive and passive, and thus drain themselves of all their vital force, which enables them to bring about these vibratory thought forms.

13. There are also the Hindu worshipers, who see in the materializing phenomena which are performed by the so-called adepts, a source of power, forgetting, or never seeming to realize that as soon as the will is withdrawn the forms wither, and the vibratory forces of which they are composed vanish.

14. Telepathy, or thought transference, has received considerable attention, but as it requires a negative mental state on the part of the receiver, the practice is harmful. A thought may be sent with the intention of hearing or seeing, but it will bring the penalty attached to the inversion of the principle involved.

15. In many instances, hypnotism is positively dangerous to the subject as well as the operator. No one familiar with the laws governing in the mental world would think of attempting to dominate the will of another, for by so doing, he will gradually (but surely) divest himself of his own power.

16. All of these perversions have their temporary satisfaction and for some a keen fascination, but there is an infinitely greater fascination in a true understanding of the world of power within, a power which increases with use; is permanent instead of fleeing; which not only is potent as a remedial agency to bring about the remedy for past error or results of wrong thinking, but is a prophylactic agency protecting us from all manner and form of danger, and finally is an actual creative force with which we can build new conditions and new environment.

17. The law is that thought will correlate with its object and bring forth in the material world the correspondence of the thing thought or produced in the mental world. We then discern the absolute necessity of seeing that every thought has the inherent germ of truth in order that the law of growth will bring into manifestation good, for good alone can confer any permanent power.

18. The principle which gives the thought the dynamic power to correlate with its object, and therefore to master every adverse human experience, is the **law of attraction**, which is another name for love. This is an eternal and fundamental principle, inherent in all things, in every system of Philosophy, in every Religion, and in every Science. There is no getting away from the law of love. It is feeling that imparts vitality to thought. Feeling is desire, and desire is love. Thought impregnated with love becomes invincible.

19. We find this truth emphasized wherever the power of thought is understood, The Universal Mind is not only Intelligence, but it is substance, and this substance is the attractive force which brings electrons together by the **law of attraction** so that they form atoms; the atoms in turn are brought together by the same law and form molecules; molecules take objective forms; and so we find that the law of love is the creative force behind every manifestation, not only of atoms, but of worlds, of the Universe, of everything of which the imagination can form any conception.

20. It is the operation of this marvelous **law of attraction** which has caused men in all ages and all times to believe that there must be some personal being who responded to their petitions and desires, and manipulated events in order to comply with their requirements.

21. It is the combination of Thought and Love which forms the irresistible force, called the **law of attraction**. All natural laws are irresistible, the law of Gravitation, or Electricity, or any other law

operates with mathematical exactitude. There is no variation, it is only the channel of distribution which may be imperfect. If a bridge falls, we do not attribute the collapse to any variation of the law of gravitation. If a light fails us, we do not conclude that the laws governing electricity cannot be depended upon, and if the **law of attraction** seems to be imperfectly demonstrated by an inexperienced or uninformed person, we are not to conclude that the greatest and most infallible law upon which the entire system of creation depends has been suspended. We should rather conclude that a little more understanding of the law is required, for the same reason that a correct solution of a difficult problem in Mathematics is not always readily and easily obtained.

22. Things are created in the mental or spiritual world be fore they appear in the outward act or event. by the simple process of governing our thought forces today, we help create the events which will come into our lives in the future, perhaps even tomorrow. Educated desire is the most potent means of bringing into action the **law of attraction**.

23. Man is so constituted that he must first create the tools, or implements by which he gains the power to think. The mind cannot comprehend an entirely new idea until a corresponding vibratory brain cell has been prepared to receive it. This explains why it is so difficult for us to receive or appreciate an entirely new idea; we have no brain cell capable of receiving it; we are therefore incredulous; we do not believe it.

24. If, therefore, you have not been familiar with the Omnipotence of the **law of attraction**, and the scientific method by which it can be put into operation, or if you have not been familiar with the unlimited possibilities which it opens to those who are enabled to take advantage of the resources it offers, begin now and create the necessary brain cells which will enable you to comprehend the unlimited powers which may be yours by cooperating with Natural Law. This is done by concentration or attention.

25. The intention governs the attention. Power comes through repose. It is by concentration that deep thoughts, wise speech, and all forces of high potentiality are accomplished.

26. It is in the Silence that you get into touch with the Omnipotent power of the subconscious mind from which all power is evolved.

27. He who desires wisdom, power, or permanent success of any kind will find it only within; it is an unfoldment. The unthinking may conclude that the silence is very simple and easily attained, but it should be remembered that only in absolute silence may one come into contact with Divinity itself; may learn of the unchangeable law and open for himself the channels by which persistent practice and concentration lead to perfection.

28. This week go to the same room, take the same chair, the same position as previously; be sure to relax, let go, both mentally and physically; always do this; never try to do any mental work under pressure; see that there are no tense muscles or nerves, that you are entirely comfortable. Now realize your unity with omnipotence; get into touch with this power, come into a deep and vital understanding, appreciation, and realization of the fact that your ability to think is your ability to act upon the Universal Mind, and bring it into manifestation, realize that it will meet any and every requirement; that you have exactly the same potential ability which any individual ever did have or ever will have, because each is but an expression or manifestation of the One, all are parts of the whole, there is no difference in kind or quality, the only difference being one of degree.

"Thought cannot conceive of anything that may not be brought to expression. He who first uttered it may be only the suggester, but the doer will appear." - Wilson.

PART TWELVE - Study Questions with Answers

111. How may any purpose in life be best accomplished? Through a scientific understanding of the spiritual nature of thought.

112. What three steps are absolutely essential? The knowledge of our power, the courage to dare, the faith to do.

113. How is the practical working knowledge secured? By an understanding of Natural laws.

114. What is the reward of an understanding of these laws? A conscious realization of our ability to adjust ourselves to Divine and unchanging principle.

115. What will indicate the degree of success with which we meet? The degree in which we realize that we cannot change the Infinite but must cooperate with it.

116. What is the principle which gives thought its dynamic power? The **Law of Attraction** which rests on vibration, which in turn rests upon the law of love. Thought impregnated with love becomes invincible.

117. Why is this law irresistible? Because it is a Natural law. All Natural laws are irresistible and unchangeable and act with mathematical exactitude. There is no deviation or variation.

118. Why then does it sometimes seem to be difficult to find the solution to our problems in life? For the same reason that it is sometimes

difficult to find the correct solution to a difficult mathematical problem. The operator is uninformed or inexperienced.

119. Why is it impossible for the mind to grasp an entirely new idea? We have no corresponding vibratory brain cell capable of receiving the idea.

120. How is wisdom secured? By concentration; it is an unfoldment; it comes from within.

Mental Chemistry

6. Transmutation

Abundance is a natural law of the universe. The evidence of this law is conclusive; we see it on every hand. Everywhere Nature is lavish, wasteful, extravagant. Nowhere is economy observed in any created thing. The millions and millions of trees and flowers and plants and animals and the vast scheme of reproduction where the process of creating and re-creating is forever going on, all indicate the lavishness with which nature has made provision for man. That there is an abundance for everyone is evident; but that many seem to have been separated from this supply is also evident; they have not yet come into realization of the universality of all substance and that mind is the active principle which starts causes in motion whereby we are related to the things we desire.

To control circumstances, a knowledge of certain scientific principles of mind-action is required. Such knowledge is a most valuable asset. It may be gained by degrees and put into practice as fast as learned. Power over circumstances is one of its fruits; health, harmony and prosperity are assets upon its balance sheet. It costs only the labor of harvesting its great resources.

All wealth is the offspring of power; possessions are of value only as they confer power. Events are significant only as they affect power; all things represent certain forms and degrees of power.

The discovery of a reign of law by which this power could be made available for all human efforts marked an important epoch in human progress. It is the dividing line between superstition and intelligence; it eliminated the element of caprice in men's lives and substituted absolute, immutable universal law.

A knowledge of cause and effect as shown by the laws governing steam, electricity, chemical affinity and gravitation enables men to plan courageously and to execute fearlessly. These laws are called Natural Laws, because they govern the physical world, but all power is not physical power; there is also mental power, and there is moral and spiritual power.

Thought is the vital force or energy which is being developed and which has produced such startling results in the last half century, as to bring about a world which would be absolutely inconceivable to a man existing only 50 or even 25 years ago. If such results have been secured by organizing these mental powerhouses in 50 years, what may not be expected in another 50 years?

Some will say, if these principles are true, why are we not demonstrating them; as the fundamental principle is obviously correct, why do we not get proper results? We do; we get results in exact accordance with our understanding of the law and our ability to make the proper application. We did not secure results from the laws governing electricity until someone formulated the law and showed us how to apply it. Mental action inaugurates a series of vibrations in the ether, which is the substance from which all things proceed, which in their turn induce a corresponding grosser vibration in the molecular substance until finally mechanical action is produced.

This puts us in an entirely new relation to our environment, opening out possibilities hitherto undreamt of, and this by an orderly sequence of law which is naturally involved in our new mental attitude.

It is clear, therefore, that thoughts of abundance will respond only to similar thoughts; the wealth of the individual is seen to be what he inherently is. Affluence within is found to be the secret of attraction for affluence without. The ability to produce is found to be the real source of wealth of the individual. It is for this reason that he who has his heart in his work is certain to meet with unbounded success. He will give and continually give, and the more he gives the more he will receive.

Thought is the energy by which the **law of attraction** is brought into operation, which eventually manifests in abundance in the lives of men.

The source of all power, as of all weakness, is from within; the secret of all success as well as all failure is likewise from within. All growth is an unfoldment from within. This is evident from all Nature; every plant, every animal, every human is a living testimony to this great law, and the error of the ages is in looking for strength or power from without.

A thorough understanding of this great law which permeates the Universe leads to the acquirement of that state of mind which develops and unfolds a creative thought which will produce magical changes in life. Golden opportunities will be strewn across your path, and the power and perception to properly utilize them will spring up within you, friends will come unbidden, circumstances will ad just themselves to changed conditions; you will have found the "Pearl of greatest price."

Wisdom, strength, courage and harmonious conditions are the result of power, and we have seen that all power is from within; likewise every lack, limitation or adverse circumstance is the result of weakness, and weakness is simply absence of power; it comes from nowhere; it is nothing--the remedy, then is simply to develop power.

This is the key with which many are converting loss into gain, fear into courage, despair into joy, hope into fruition.

This may seem to be too good to be true, but remember that within a few years, by the touch of a button or the turn of a lever, science has placed almost infinite resources at the disposal of man. Is it not possible that there are other laws containing still great possibilities?

Let us see what are the most powerful forces in Nature. In the mineral world everything is sold and fixed. In the animal and vegetable kingdom it is in a state of flux, forever changing, always being created and recreated. In the atmosphere we find heat, light and energy. Each realm becomes finer and more spiritual as we pass from the visible to the invisible, from the coarse to the fine, from the low potentiality to the high potentiality. When we reach the invisible we find energy in its purest and most volatile state.

And as the most powerful forces of Nature are the invisible forces, so we find that the most powerful forces of man are his invisible forces, his spiritual force, and the only way in which the spiritual force can manifest is through the process of thinking. Thinking is the only activity which the spirit possesses, and thought is the only product of thinking.

Addition and subtraction are therefore spiritual transactions; reasoning is a spiritual process; ideas are spiritual conceptions; questions are spiritual searchlights and logic, argument and philosophy are parts of the spiritual machinery.

Every thought brings into action certain physical tissue, parts of the brain, nerve or muscle. This produces an actual physical change in the construction of the tissue. Therefore it is only necessary to have a certain number of thoughts on a given subject in order to bring about a complete change in the physical organization of a man.

This is the process by which failure is changed to success. Thoughts of courage, power, inspiration, harmony, are substituted for thoughts of failure, despair, lack, limitation and discord, and as these thoughts take root, the physical tissue is changed and the individual sees life in a new light, old things have actually passed away; all things have become new; he is born again, this time born of the spirit; life has anew meaning for him; he is reconstructed and is filled with joy, confidence, hope, energy. He sees opportunities for success to which he was heretofore blind. He recognizes possibilities which before had no meaning for him. The thoughts of success with which he has been impregnated are radiated to those around him, and they in turn help him onward and upward; he attracts to him new and successful associates, and this in turn changes his environment; so that by this simple exercise of thought, a man changes not only himself, but his environment, circumstances and conditions.

You will see, you must see, that we are at the dawn of a new day; that the possibilities are so wonderful, so fascinating, so limitless as to be almost bewildering. A century ago any man with an aeroplane or even a Gatling gun could have annihilated a whole army equipped with the implements of warfare then in use. So it is at preset. Any man with a knowledge of the possibilities of modern metaphysics has an inconceivable advantage over the multitude.

Mind is creative and operates through the **law of attraction**. We are not to try to influence anyone to do what we think they should do. Each individual has a right to choose for himself, but aside from this we would be operating under the laws of force, which is destructive in its nature and just the opposite of the **law of attraction**. A little reflection will convince you that all the great laws of nature operate in silence and that the underlying principle is the **law of attraction**. It is only destructive processes, such as earthquakes and catastrophes, that employ force. Nothing good is ever accomplished in that way.

To be successful, attention must invariably be directed to the creative plane; it must never be competitive. You do not wish to take anything away from any one else; you want to create something for yourself, and what you want for yourself you are perfectly willing that every one else should have.

You know that it is not necessary to take from one to give to another, but that the supply for all is abundant. Nature's storehouse of wealth is inexhaustible and if there seems to be a lack of supply anywhere it is only because the channels of distribution are as yet imperfect.

Abundance depends upon a recognition of the laws of Abundance. Mind is not only the creator, but the only creator of all there is. Certainly nothing can be created before we know that it can be created and then make the proper effort. There is no more Electricity in the world today than there was fifty years ago, but until someone recognized the law by which it could be made of service, we received no benefit; now that the law is understood, practically the whole world is illuminated by it. So with the law of Abundance; it is only those who recognize the law and place themselves in harmony with it, who share in its benefits.

A recognition of the law of abundance develops certain mental and moral qualities, among which are Courage, Loyalty, Tact, Sagacity, Individuality and Constructiveness. These are all moods of thought, and as all thought is creative, they manifest in objective conditions corresponding with the mental condition. This is necessarily true because the ability of the individual to think is his ability to act upon the Universal Mind and bring it into manifestation; it is the process whereby the individual becomes a channel for the differentiation of the Universal. Every thought is a cause and every condition an effect.

This principle endows the individual with seemingly transcendental possibilities, among which is the mastery of conditions through the creation and recognition of opportunities. This creation of opportunity implies the existence or creation of the necessary qualities or talents which are thought forces and which result in a consciousness of power which future events cannot disturb. It is this organization of victory or success within the mind, this consciousness of power within, which constitutes the responsive harmonious action whereby we are related to the objects and purposes which we seek. This is the **law of attraction** in action; this law, being the common property of all, can be exercised by any one having sufficient knowledge of its operation.

Courage is the power of the mind which manifests in the love of mental conflict; it is a noble and lofty sentiment; it is equally fitted to command or obey; both require courage. It often has a tendency to conceal itself. There are men and women, too, who apparently exist only to do what is pleasing to others, but when the time comes and the latent will is revealed, we find under the velvet glove an iron hand, and no mistake about it.

True courage is cool, calm, and collected, and is never foolhardy, quarrelsome, ill-natured or contentious.

Accumulation is the power to reserve and preserve a part of the supply which we are constantly receiving, so as to be in a position to take advantage of the larger opportunities which will come as soon as we are ready for them. Has it not been said, "To him that hath shall be given"? All successful business men have this quality, well developed. James J. Hill, who recently died, leaving an estate of over fifty-two million dollars said: "If you want to know whether you are destined to be a success or failure in life, you can easily find out. The test is simple and it is infallible: Are you able to save money? If not, drop out. You will lose. You may think not, but you will lose as sure as you live. The seed of success is not in you."

This is very good so far as it goes, but any one who knows the biography of James J. Hill knows that he acquired his fifty million dollars by following the exact methods we have given. In the first place, he started with nothing; he had to use his imagination to idealize the vast railroad which he projected across the western prairies. He then had to come into a recognition of the law of abundance in order to provide the ways and means for materializing it; unless he had followed out this program he would never had anything to save.

Accumulativeness acquires momentum; the more you accumulate the more you desire, and the more you desire the more you accumulate, so that it is but a short time until the action and reaction acquire a momentum that cannot be stopped. It must, however, never be confounded with selfishness, miserliness or penuriousness; they are perversions and will make any true progress impossible.

Constructiveness is the creative instinct of the mind. It will be readily seen that every successful business man must be able to plan, develop or construct. In the business world it is usually referred to as initiative. It is not enough to go along in the beaten path. New ideas must be developed, new ways of doing things. It manifests in building, designing, planning, inventing, discovering, improving. It is a most valuable quality and must be constantly encouraged and developed. Every individual possesses it in some degree, because he is a center of consciousness in that infinite and Eternal Energy from which all things proceed.

Water manifests on three planes, as ice, as water and as steam; it is all the same compound; the only difference is the temperature, but no one would try to drive an engine with ice; convert it into steam and it easily takes up the load. So with your energy; if you want it to act on the creative plane, you will have to begin by melting the ice with the fire of imagination, and you will find the stronger the fire, and the more ice you melt, the more powerful your thought will become, and the easier it will be for you to materialize your desire.

Sagacity is the ability to perceive and co-operate with Natural Law. True Sagacity avoids trickery and deceit as it would the leprosy; it is the product of that deep insight which enables on to penetrate into the heart of things and understand how to set causes in motion which will inevitably create successful conditions.

Tact is a very subtle and at the same time a very important factor in business success. It is very similar to intuition. To possess tact one must have a fine feeling, must instinctively know what to say or what to do. In order to be tactful one must possess Sympathy and Understanding, the understanding which is so rare, for all men see and hear and feel, but how desperately few "understand." Tact enables one to foresee what is about to happen and calculate the result of actions. Tact enables us to feel when we are in the presence of physical, mental and moral cleanliness, for these are today invariably demanded as the price of success.

Loyalty is one of the strongest links which bind men of strength and character. It is one which can never be broken with impunity. The man who would lose his right hand rather than betray a friend will never lack friends. The man who will stand in silent guard, until death, if need be, besides the shrine of confidence or friendship of those who have allowed him to enter will find himself linked with a current of cosmic power which will attract desirable conditions only. It is conceivable that such a person should ever meet with lack of any kind.

Individuality is the power to unfold our own latent possibilities, to be a law unto ourselves, to be interested in the race rather than the goal. Strong men care nothing for the flock of imitators who trot complacently behind them. They derive no satisfaction in the mere leading of large numbers, or the plaudits of the mob. This pleases only petty natures and inferior minds. Individuality glories more in the unfolding of the power within than in the servility of the weakling.

Individuality is a real power inherent in all and the development and consequent expression of this power enables one to assume the responsibility of directing his own footsteps rather than stampeding after some self-assertive bell-wether.

Inspiration is the art of imbibing, the art of self realization, the art of adjusting the individual mind to that of the Universal Mind, the art of attaching the proper mechanism to the source of all power, the art of differentiating the formless into form, the art of becoming a channel for the flow of Infinite Wisdom, the art of visualizing perfection, the art of realizing the Omnipresence of Omnipotence.

Truth is the imperative condition of all well being. To be sure, to know the truth and to stand confidently on it, is a satisfaction beside which no other is comparable. Truth is the underlying verity, the condition precedent to every successful business or social relation.

Every act not in harmony with Truth, whether through ignorance or design, cuts the ground from under our feet, leads to discord, inevitable loss, and confusion, for while the humblest mind can accurately foretell the result of every correct action, the greatest, most profound and penetrating mind loses its way hopelessly and can form no conception of the result due to a departure from correct principles.

Those who establish within themselves the requisite elements of true success have established confidence, organized victory, and it only remains for them to take such steps from time to time as the newly-awakened thought force will direct, and herein rests the magical secret of all power.

Less than 10 per cent of our mental processes are conscious; the other 90 per cent are subconscious and unconscious, so that he who would depend upon his conscious thought alone for results is less than 10 per cent efficient. Those who are accomplishing anything worth while are those who are enabled to take advantage of this greater storehouse of mental wealth. It is in the vast domain of the subconscious mind that great truths are hidden, and it is here that thought finds its creative power, its power to correlate with its object, to bring out of the unseen the seen.

Those familiar with the laws of Electricity understand the principle that electricity must always pass from a higher to a lower potentiality and can therefore make whatever application of the power they desire. Those not familiar with this law can effect nothing; and so with the law governing in the Mental World; those who understand that Mind penetrates all things, is Omnipresent and is responsive to every demand, can make use of the law and can control conditions, circumstances and environment; the uninformed cannot use it because they do not know it.

The fruit of this knowledge is as it were, a gift of the Gods; it is the "truth" that makes men free, not only free from every lack and limitation, but free from sorrow, worry and care, and, is it not wonderful to realize that this law is no respecter of persons, that it makes no difference what your habit of thought may be, the way has been prepared?

With the realization that this mental power controls and directs every other power which exists, that it can be cultivated and developed, that no limitation can be placed upon its activity, it will be come apparent that it is the greatest fact in the world, the remedy for every ill, the solution for every difficulty, the gratification of every desire; in fact, that it is the Creator's magnificent provision for the emancipation of mankind.

Thoughts Are Things - Henry Van Dyke

I hold it true that thoughts are things;
They're endowed with bodies and breath and wings;
And that we send them forth to fill
The world with good results, or ill.
That which we call our secret thought
Speeds forth to earth's remotest spot,
Leavings its blessings or its woes
Like tracks behind it as it goes.
We build our future, thought by thought,
For good or ill, yet know it not.
Yet, so the universe was wrought.
Thought is another name for fate;
Choose, then they destiny and wait,
For love brings love and hate brings hate.

The complete text of the books behind these excerpts may be found in -

Haanel's Master Key System ,

Law of Attraction: Mental Chemistry, and

THINK, THANK, THUNK!

(Please see Bibliography for details.)

Genevieve Behrend

Genevieve Behrend used the Law of Attraction to become Thomas Troward's only pupil. She set her goal and attracted the funds to make the trip to England and support herself while there (the story of her funds is included here).

Troward was at first reticent to take on a pupil, but Behrend's persistence – and her use of the Law to achieve her goal – ultimately won him over.

While we have room for only a few chapters from one of her books, you will probably want to get her entire book – or collect them all. They are available in different spots on the Internet, as well have been recently republished in hardback.

Her writing style is light and modern, a perfect introduction to the much heavier Troward. Her style actually earned her living after she completed her tutelage under Troward – the rest of her life was spent in writing and lecturing.

Your Invisible Power

Chapter 1 - Order Of Visualization

The exercise of the visualizing faculty keeps your mind in order, and attracts to you the things you need to make life more enjoyable in an orderly way. If you train yourself in practice of deliberately picturing your desire and carefully examining it, you will soon find your thought and desires come and proceed in more orderly procession than ever before. Having reached a state of ordered mentality you are no longer in a constant state of mental hurry. Hurry is Fear and consequently destructive.

In other words, when your understanding grasps the power to visualize your heart's desire and hold it with your will, it attracts to you all things requisite to the fulfillment of that picture by the harmonious vibrations of the **law of attraction**. You realize that since Order is Heaven's first law, and visualization places things in their natural element, then it must be a heavenly thing to visualize.

Everyone visualizes, whether they know it or not. Visualizing is the great secret of Success. The conscious use of this great power attracts to you greatly multiplied resources, intensifies your wisdom, and enables you to make use of advantages which you formerly failed to recognize.

We now fly through the air, not because anyone has been able to change the laws of Nature, but because the inventor of the flying machine learned how to apply Nature's laws and, by making orderly use of them, produced the desired result. So far as natural forces are concerned, nothing has changed since the beginning. There were no airplanes in "the Year One," because those of that generation could not conceive the idea as a practical working possibility. "It has not yet been done" was the argument, "and it cannot be done." Yet the laws and materials for practical flying machines existed then as now.

Troward tells us that the great lesson he learned from the airplane and wireless telegraphy is the triumph of principle over precedent, and the working of an idea to its logical conclusion in spite of accumulated testimony of all past experience.

With such an example before you, can you not realize that still greater secrets may be disclosed? Also "That you hold the key within yourself, with which to unlock the secret chamber that contains your heart's desire? All that is necessary in order that you may use this key and make your life exactly what you wish it to be, is a careful inquiry into the unseen causes which stand back of every external and visible condition. Then bring these unseen causes into harmony with your conception, and you will find that you can make practical working realities of possibilities which at present seem but fantastic dreams."

We all know that the balloon was the forefather of the airplane. In 1766 Henry Cavendish, an English nobleman, proved that hydrogen gas was seven times lighter than atmospheric air. From that discovery the balloon came into existence, and from the ordinary balloon the dirigible, a cigar-shaped airship, was evolved. Study of aeronautics and the laws of aerial locomotion of birds and projectiles led to the belief that mechanism could be evolved by which heavier-than-air machines could be made to travel from place to place and remain in the air by the maintenance of great speed which would overcome by propulsive force the ordinary law of gravitation.

Professor Langley of Washington who developed much of the theory which others afterward improved was subjected to much derision when he sent a model airplane up only to have it bury its nose in the muddy water of the Potomac. But the Wright Brothers, who experimented in the latter part of the Nineteenth Century, realized the possibility of traveling through the air in a machine that had no gas bag. They saw themselves enjoying this mode of transportation with great facility. It is said that one of the brothers would tell the other (when their varied experiments did not turn out as they expected): "It's all right, brother, I can see myself riding in that machine, and it travels easily and steadily." Those Wright Brothers knew what they wanted, and kept their pictures constantly before them.

In visualizing, or making a mental picture, you are not endeavoring to change the laws of Nature. You are fulfilling them. Your object in visualizing is to bring things into regular order both mentally and physically. When you realize that this method of employing the creative power brings your desires, one after another, into practical material accomplishment, your confidence in the mysterious but unfailing **law of attraction**, which has its central power station in the very heart of your word/picture, becomes supreme. Nothing can shake it. You never feel that it is necessary to take anything from anybody else. You have learned that asking and seeking have receiving and finding as their correlatives. You know that all you have to do is to start the plastic substance of the Universe flowing into the thought-molds your picture-desire provides.

Chapter 2 - How To Attract To Yourself The Things You Desire

The power within you which enables you to form a thought picture is the starting point of all there is. In its original state it is the undifferentiated formless substance of life. Your thought picture forms the mold (so to speak) into which this formless substance takes shape.

Visualizing, or mentally seeing things and conditions as you wish them to be, is the condensing, the specializing power in you that might be illustrated by the lens of a magic lantern. The magic lantern is one of the best symbols of this imaging faculty. It illustrates the working of the Creative Spirit on the plane of the initiative and selection (or in its concentrated specializing form) in a remarkably clear manner.

This picture slide illustrates your own mental picture -invisible in the lantern of your mind until you turn on the light of your will. That is to say, you light up your desire with absolute faith that the Creative Spirit of Life, in you, is doing the work. By the steady flow of light of the will on the Spirit, your desired picture is projected upon the screen of the physical world, an exact reproduction of the pictured slide in your mind.

Visualizing without a will sufficiently steady to inhibit every thought and feeling contrary to your picture would be as useless as a magic lantern without the light. On the other hand, if your will is sufficiently developed to hold your picture in thought and feeling, without any "ifs," simply realizing that your thought is the great attracting power, then your mental picture is as certain to be projected upon the screen of your physical world as any pictured slide put into the best magic lantern ever made.

Try projecting the picture in a magic lantern with a light that is constantly shifting from one side to the other, and you will have the effect of an uncertain will. It is as necessary that you should always stand back of your picture with a strong, steady will, as it is to have a strong steady light back of a picture slide.

The joyous assurance with which you make your picture is the very powerful magnet of Faith, and nothing can obliterate it. You are happier than you ever were, because you have learned to know where your source of supply is, and you rely upon its never-failing response to your given direction.

When all said and done, happiness is the one thing which every human being wants, and the study of visualization enables you to get more out of life than you ever enjoyed before. Increasing possibilities keep opening out, more and more, before you.

A business man once told me that since practicing visualization and forming the habit of devoting a few minutes each day to thinking about his work as he desired it to be in a large, broad way, his business had more than doubled in six months. His method was to go into a room every morning before breakfast and take a mental inventory of his business as he had left it the evening before, and then enlarge upon it. He said he expanded and expanded in this way until his affairs were in remarkably successful condition. He would see himself in his office doing everything that he wanted done. His occupation required him to meet many strangers every day. In his mental picture he saw himself meeting these people, understanding their needs and supplying them in just the way they wished. This habit, he said, had strengthened and steadied his will in an almost inconceivable manner. Furthermore, by thus mentally seeing things as he wished them to be, he had acquired the confident feeling that a certain creative power was exercising itself, for him and through him, for the purpose of improving his little world.

When you first begin to visualize seriously, you may feel, as many others do, that someone else may be forming the same picture you are, and that naturally would not suit your purpose. Do not give yourself any unnecessary concern about this. Simply try to realize that your picture is an orderly exercise of the Universal Creative Power specifically applied. Then you may be sure that no one can work in opposition to you. The universal law of harmony prevents this. Endeavor to bear in mind that your mental picture is Universal Mind exercising its inherent powers of initiative and selection specifically.

God, or Universal Mind, made man for the special purpose of differentiating Himself through him. Everything that is, came into existence in this same way, by this self-same law of self-differentiation, and for the same purpose. First the idea, the mental picture or the prototype of the thing, which is the thing itself in its incipiency or plastic form.

The Great Architect of the Universe contemplated Himself as manifesting through His polar opposite, matter, and the idea expanded and projected itself until we have a world -many worlds.

Many people ask, "But why should we have a physical world at all?" The answer is: Because it is the nature of originating substance to solidify, under directivity rather than activity, just as it is the nature of wax to harden when it becomes cold, or plaster of paris to become firm and solid when exposed to the air. Your picture in this same Divine substance in its fluent state taking shape through the individualized center of Divine operation, your mind; and there is no power to prevent this combination of spiritual substance from becoming physical form. It is the nature of Spirit to complete its work and an idea is not complete until it has made for itself a vehicle.

Nothing can prevent your picture from coming into concrete form except the same power that gave it birth - yourself. Suppose you wish to have a more orderly room. You look about your room and the idea of order suggests boxes, closets, shelves, hooks and so forth. The box, the closet, the hooks, all are concrete ideas of order. Vehicles through which order and harmony suggest themselves.

Chapter 9 - How I Attracted To Myself Twenty Thousand Dollars

In the laboratory of experience in which my newly revealed relation to Divine operation was to be tested, the first problem was a financial one. My income was a stipulated one, quite enough for my everyday needs. But it did not seem sufficient to enable me to go comfortably to England where Troward lived, and remain for an indefinite period to study with so great a teacher as he must be. So before inquiring whether Troward took pupils or whether I would be eligible in case he did, I began to use the paragraph I had memorized. Daily, in fact, almost hourly, the words were in my mind: "My mind is a center of Divine operation, and Divine operation means expansion into something better than has gone before."

From the Edinburgh Lectures I had read something about the **Law of Attraction**, and from the Chapter of "Causes and Conditions" I had gleaned a vague idea of visualizing. So every night, before going to sleep, I made a mental picture of the desired $20,000. Twenty $1,000 bills were counted over each night in my bedroom, and then, with the idea of more emphatically impressing my mind with the fact that this twenty thousand dollars was for the purpose of going to England and studying with Troward, I wrote out my picture, saw myself buying my steamer ticket, walking up and down the ship's deck from New York to London, and, finally, saw myself accepted as Troward's pupil.

This process was repeated every morning and every evening, always impressing more and more fully upon my mind Troward's memorized statement: "My mind is a center of Divine operations." I endeavored to keep this statement in the back part of my consciousness all the time with no thought in mind as how the money might be obtained. Probably the reason why there was no thought of the avenues through which the money might reach me was because I could not possibly imagine where the $20,000 would come from. So I simply held my thought steady and let the power of attraction find its own ways and means.

One day while walking on the street, taking deep breathing exercises, the thought came: "My mind is surely a center of Divine operation. If God fills all space, then God must be in my mind also; if I want this money to study with Troward that I may know the truth of Life, then both the money and the truth must be mine, though I am unable to feel or see the physical manifestations of either; still," I declared, "it must be mine."

While these reflections were going on in my mind, there seemed to come up from within me the thought: "I am all the substance there is." Then, from another channel in my brain the answer seemed to come, "Of course, that's it; everything must have its beginning in mind. The "I" the Idea, must be the only one and primary substance there is, and this means money as well as everything else." My mind accepted this idea, and immediately all the tension of mind and body was relaxed.

There was a feeling of absolute certainty of being in touch with all the power Life has to give. All thought of money, teacher, or even my own personality, vanished in the great wave of joy which swept over my entire being. I walked on and on with this feeling of joy steadily increasing and expanding until everything about me seemed aglow with resplendent light. Every person I passed was illuminated as I was. All consciousness of personality had disappeared, and in its place there came that great and almost overwhelming sense of joy and contentment.

That night when I made my picture of the twenty thousand dollars it was with an entirely changed aspect. On previous occasions, when making my mental picture, I had felt that I was waking up something within myself. This time there was no sensation of effort. I simply counted over the twenty thousand dollars. Then, in a most unexpected manner, from a source of which I had no consciousness at the time, there seemed to open a possible avenue through which the money might reach me.

At first it took great effort not to be excited. It all seemed so wonderful, so glorious to be in touch with supply. But had not Troward cautioned his readers to keep all excitement out of their minds in the first flush of realization of union with Infinite supply, and to treat this fact as a perfectly natural result that had been reached through our demand? This was even more difficult for me than it was to hold the thought that "all the substance there is, I am; I (idea) am the beginning of all form, visible or invisible."

Just as soon as there appeared a circumstance which indicated the direction through which the twenty thousand dollars might come, I not only made a supreme effort to regard the indicated direction calmly as the first sprout of the seed I had sown in the absolute, but left no stone unturned to follow up that direction by fulfilling my part. By so doing one circumstance seemed naturally to lead to another, until, step-by-step, my desired twenty thousand dollars was secured. To keep my mind poised and free from excitement was my greatest effort.

This first concrete fruition of my study of Mental Science as expounded by Troward's book had come by a careful following of the methods he had outlined. In this connection, therefore, I can offer to the reader no better gift than to quote Troward's book, "The Edinburgh Lectures," from which may be derived a complete idea of the line of action I was endeavoring to follow. In the chapter on Causes and Conditions he says: "To get good results we must properly understand our relation to the great impersonal power we are using. It is intelligent, and we are intelligent, and the two intelligences must co-operate.

"We must not fly in the face of the Law expecting it to do for us what it can only do through us; and we must therefore use our intelligence with the knowledge that it is acting as the instrument of a greater intelligence; and because we have this knowledge we may and should cease from all anxiety as to the final result.

"In actual practice we must first form the ideal conception of our object with the definite intention of impressing it upon the universal mind -it is this thought that takes such thought out of the region of mere casual fancies -and then affirm that our knowledge of the Law is sufficient reason for a calm expectation of a corresponding result, and that therefore all necessary conditions will come to us in due order. We can then turn to the affairs of our daily life with the calm assurance that the initial conditions are either there already or will soon come into view. If we do not at once see them, let us rest content with the knowledge that the spiritual prototype is already in existence and wait till some circumstance pointing in the desired direction begins to show itself.

"It may be a very small circumstance, but it is the direction and not the magnitude that is to be taken into consideration. As soon as we see it we should regard it as the first sprouting of the seed sown in the Absolute, and do calmly, and without excitement, whatever the circumstances seem to require, and then later on we shall see that this doing will in turn lead to a further circumstance in the same direction, until we find ourselves conducted, step by step, to the accomplishment of our object.

"In this way the understanding of the great principle of the Law of Supply will, by repeated experiences, deliver us more and more completely out of the region of anxious thought and toilsome labor and bring us into a new world where the useful employment of all our powers, whether mental or physical, will only be an unfolding of our individuality upon the lines of its own nature, and therefore a perpetual source of health and happiness; a sufficient inducement, surely, to the careful study of the laws governing the relation between the individual and the Universal Mind."

To my mind, then as now, this quotation outlines the core and center of the method and manner of approach necessary for coming in touch with Infinite supply. At least it, together with the previously quoted statement, "My mind is a center of Divine operation," etc., constituted the only apparent means of attracting to myself the twenty thousand dollars. My constant endeavor to get into the spirit of these statements, and to attract to myself this needed sum, was about six weeks, at the end of which time I had in my bank the required twenty thousand dollars. This could be made into a long story, giving all the details, but the facts, as already narrated, will give you a definite idea of the magnetic condition of my mind while the twenty thousand dollars was finding its way to me.

The complete text of the books behind these excerpts may be found in -

Law of Attraction: Your Invisible Power , and

The Complete Genevieve Behrend Collection

(Please see Bibliography for details.)

Henry Thomas Hamblin

When you look up the life of Hamblin, you see a man who "followed his bliss" in order to write his thoughts and publish them for others to use and improve their lives.

Truly one of the less known writers in our current age, he is nonetheless an incredible find. He was successful businessman before he became a bestselling author and publisher.

His works are continued today via the Hamblin Trust, which continued the magazine Hamblin founded and have maintained and expanded his legacy.

Our immediate use is to find how he treats the law of attraction – indeed, "The Law which keeps the Universe running so smoothly is the law of Attraction. It is this law that brought it together; it is this law that keeps it from falling apart."

Dynamic Thought

PART VII

TO the ordinary "man in the street" a thought is an "airy nothing "--a mere flash in the consciousness--it comes, it goes, and there is an end to it. To the student of Mind however, thought is known to be the power that is greater than any other power--a force that controls all other forces. An American writer speaking of Universal Mind says:

> "It thinks, and Suns spring into shape;
> It wills, and Worlds disintegrate;
> It loves and Souls are born."

It will thus be seen that thought is the origin of the visible Universe. All that we see around us is the result of thought. We may even go further, and say that all the invisible forces, which keep the wonderful machinery of the Universe working perfectly and smoothly, are but the thought-energies of the same Universal Mind.

As in the macrocosm so is it in the microcosm; the subliminal mind of man is the same in essence as the Universal Mind of the Universe; the difference is not one of kind but of degree.

In our world, our circumstances, our life, our bodies, we stand supreme, or rather we have within us the power, which properly directed, can make us supreme. This power is "Thought." Thought is so subtle, so elusive, that it has by the majority of men, been considered impossible of control, but the greatest philosophers, seers and leaders in the World's history have known differently. All that they achieved, they accomplished through the power of thought; and this was possible because they had learned the art of thought control.

"What man has done, man can do." This was never so true as it is today, because the science of Mind is now being spread abroad, and that it is possible for quite ordinary people to learn how to control their thoughts, is now known to be a scientific possibility.

Dr. Abrams in his epoch-making book entitled "New Concepts in Diagnosis and Treatment; The Practical Application of the Electrotonic Theory in the Interpretation and Treatment of Disease," describes how he has discovered the energy of thought and measured it by means of an instrument called the Bio-dynamometer.

With one subject in a room with closed doors, and another subject, in another room, forty or more feet away, it was found that one subject could affect the other by a definite exercise of thought. Anger and emotion yielded an energy which produced an effect at a distance of eighty feet. Dr. Abrams also found that there arts three great energy centers in the human body, the right and left side of the brain, called by him the right and left psychomotor areas; and the finger tips. When the brain is actively engaged in thought there is an increase in the discharge of energy from the psychomotor areas, and also from the finger tips.

It was also found that ordinary people discharged energy from one psychomotor area only, but a great thinker discharged energy from both. The amount of energy discharged in this way can be gaged by the fact that Edward Markham, the poet, discharged energy from his left psychomotor area alone equal to a resistance of sixty ohms. As the energy discharged from a giant magnet with a lifting capacity of 400 lbs. to the square inch is only thirty-two ohms, we can form some idea of the immense power of thought which man possesses.

The flow of energy from the finger tips is also suggestive. In all ages the laying on of hands has been recognized as a healing act, now it is proved by scientific means to have been simply the power or energy of thought.

You will therefore see that "thought" so far from being "an airy nothing" or a mere flash in the consciousness is a wonderful and potent force, the most wonderful and potent force of which we know.

A man is a small individualized part of the Universal Mind, alike in essence but infinitely less in degree. Just as the Universal Mind finds expression through all the Universe, so does man when awake to his own interior powers, express himself by the power of his thought, through his body, his work, his circumstances and his life. Thus far can he go and no farther. In himself he is an epitome of the Universe, outside of the miniature Universe he has no jurisdiction. By this I mean that man has the power to do what he likes with his own life, but he has no right to dominate other people or to interfere with their lives.

I mention this because there is a pernicious practice being taught today. It is known as "mind domination." People are being taught that by using what is called the "hypnotic gaze," by telepathy and hetero-suggestion they can dominate other people. It is quite true; it can be done and is being done. This is precisely the same method as that practiced by certain criminals in America. By this method people are being deprived of money and property--they sign documents they do not wish to sign, simply because they are compelled to do so by "mind domination."

No one is to be safe from these misguided people. While you sit in a public room or theater somebody may be behind you concentrating his "hypnotic gaze" upon the back of your neck. When you receive a visit from a traveling salesman he may be working some of his mind dominating black art upon you in order to coerce you into acting against your better judgment, simply and solely that he may reap a temporary benefit.

This sort of thing is not only being practiced, but is being taught, both in this country and America.

I mention this in order to put you on your guard against such practices; first, so that you can avoid being hypnotized by these people, and second, that you should never under any circumstances use your mind forces in order to dominate other people. Whoever prostitutes his mental powers in this way is hurrying to disaster. To so misuse the tremendous powers of the mind is to destroy oneself, body and soul. All who sink to these practices are deliberately creating for themselves an inferno of trouble. The powers of the mind are like electricity; for the latter, if used according to certain laws, produces beneficial results; if used in opposition to these laws, it burns, maims, and destroys. So it is with the powers of the Mind, used aright they lead to success, happiness and all accomplishment; if used wrongly they grind to powder.

Both Hypnotism and Mind Domination are being so largely used and taught that it is advisable to always work against them. These are really a revival of the "Black Magic" of bygone days. Sorcery, witchcraft, necromancy, thaumaturgy, they are all the practice of the same power, and all who use them bring destruction upon their own heads. Sorcery, black magic, or hypnotism, or whatever you like to call it, is accomplished by the lower mind of man. The higher self, the perfect mental or spiritual creature, the real Ego, has nothing to do with it. This is why hypnotic healing is always harmful. If a person is healed by hypnotic suggestion in about three months' time either the same disease will reappear, or a new and worse disease will manifest itself. But healing done by the higher perfect mind, that is one with, and forms part of, the Universal Infinite Mind, that is in turn one and part of the Infinite Principle of Good, such healing is permanent and can have no relapse.

By this we see that the higher mind is infinitely more powerful than the lower. Therefore Hypnotism and Mind Domination can be overcome and guarded against by the use of the higher Mental Powers.

To work against Hypnotism, it is necessary not only to live as much as possible in the atmosphere of your perfect World of Mind, but also to deny the power of Hypnotism to affirm the perfect power of the perfect Universal Mind of which you, your higher self, form a part. If you work in this way you will make yourself proof against all Hypnotism, Sorcery, Witchcraft and Malpractice of every kind.

The Law which keeps the Universe running so smoothly is the **law of Attraction**. It is this law that brought it together; it is this law that keeps it from falling apart.

Those who practice Mind domination are acting in direct opposition to this immutable law. They are trying to do by force that which should be accomplished by attraction, therefore they are encompassing their own mental, moral and physical disintegration.

All the Universe, in all its planes, is ruled by this law; in the Spiritual World it is called the Law of Love; in the Mental World the **Law of Attraction**; in the Material World it is known as the Law of Affinity. They all mean the same--in essence they are the same.

Just as the electrons are called together in the invisible aether, thus to form an atom so, in turn, are atoms brought together, and by vibrating at different rates of speed, create what we call form. Thus is matter (so-called) built up into all the beautiful forms we see, simply by the **Law of Attraction**.

It is this law that holds all matter together. If it failed, rocks would fly asunder and all things would disintegrate, because the power that attracted one atom to another would have ceased to operate.

It is the same in the Mental World, everything works according to this same law. It is because "like creates like" and "like attracts like" that it is possible to revolutionize our lives by the power of thought.

"Thoughts," said Prentice Mulford, "are things." "Thoughts," says T. Sharper Knowlson, "so far from being mere brain flashes, are, judging solely from their effects, real entities, apparently composed of spiritual substance, the nature of which is outside the range of discovery of our present faculties." "Thought," says Levy, "is not an event which dies in a world ethereal, super-sensible, imperceptible; it has continually its likeness and repercussion in our organism." "Thought is not," says Ralph Waldo Trine, "as is many times supposed, a mere indefinite abstraction, or something of a like nature. It is, on the contrary, a vital, living force, the most vital, subtle and irresistible force in the Universe."

In our very laboratory experiments we are demonstrating the great fact that thoughts are forces. They have form, and quality, and substance, and power, and we are beginning to find that there is what we may term a science of thought.

We are beginning to find also that through the instrumentality of our thought forces we have creative power in reality. Many more authorities could be quoted, but these will suffice to show that thoughts are just as much "things" as town halls or mountains are "things." It is a great mistake to imagine that because you can see a thing with your physical eyes, feel it with your hands, or hit it with a hammer, that it is for that reason more real than something you can neither see nor feel. On the contrary the "Unseen" is vastly more powerful, lasting and forceful than anything you can see with your physical eyes. What you see with your eyes is only the effect of greater causes which are invisible.

"Everything exists in the unseen before it is manifested in the seen, and in this sense it is true that the unseen things are real, while the things that are seen are the unreal. The unseen things are cause; the seen things are effect. The unseen things are eternal; the seen things are the changing, the transient."

Thoughts then are "entities," are "things," are "forces," are vital subtle "powers." They, like everything else, and every other force in the universe, are subject to law. This law is the **Law of Attraction**.

Whatever thoughts you think will attract to you thoughts of a similar nature. According as you create good or bad thoughts, so do you determine whether your life shall be blessed or cursed. If you think a good thought and dwell upon it, and, as it were, nourish it with your meditations, it will not only bless and enrich your life, but will attract hosts of other thoughts of equal power and beauty, which will hasten to minister to you. Thus, if you think "Success" thoughts, and affirm them, and cling to them in the face of apparent defeat and failure, you will attract to yourself such a wave of powerful, upbuilding and inspiring thoughts that you will be lifted right over your difficulty and carried, as by invisible forces, along the path of accomplishment.

On the other hand, it is equally true that if you think a weak thought, a low thought, a vile thought, or a thought of failure, there will be attracted to you a host of thoughts of like character, which by their nature will curse you and drag you down. "Unto him that hath shall be given, and from him that hath not shall be taken away that which he hath" is simply the working of the **Law of Attraction**. Think "Success" and thousands of invisible forces will fly to your aid. Think "failure" and innumerable forces will help to make your failure even more complete.

If thought is the "greatest power of all powers," "the most vital, subtle and irresistible force in the universe," and if your thoughts have the power to attract other thoughts of a like character, then the choice of your thoughts is the 'nose important act of your life.

By choosing your thoughts you choose either success or failure, happiness or misery, health or disease, hope or despair.

Says one of deep insight into the nature of things: "The things that we see, are but a very small fraction of the things that are. The real, vital forces at work in our own lives, and in the world about us, are not seen by the ordinary physical eye. Yet they are the causes of which all things we see are merely the effects. Thoughts are forces; like builds like, and like attract like. For one to govern his thinking then is to determine his life."

Therefore do not believe anyone who wants to teach you how to "overcome" other people, and to dominate them either by "will-power" or by Hypnotism. If you seek to get the better of other people and to influence them by mine domination, you are charging full tilt against the Law of the Universe, and this can only lead to the most disastrous results.

The "hypnotic gaze" and "suggestion" can never bring you success; it may bring a temporary, fleeting advantage, but this will be followed by disaster either in your business or profession, your body, your life, or your home.

By the right use of your thought-forces you can make yourself a magnet and attract to yourself all that you deserve. We each get what he or she deserves. As we improve the quality of our thoughts, so do we become deserving of better results; as we become deserving of better results, so do better things flow to us by the operation of Universal Law.

By the use of carefully graded denials and affirmations, we break the power of evil thought-habit, and in its place create a new mental attitude, hopeful, strong, cheerful, successful, confident, an attitude of mind that knows not failure, can never be discouraged; that stands firm and unafraid amid the changing scenes of life; an attitude of mind that overcomes, conquers and achieves. An attitude of mind that lives in a sea of positive, helpful, stimulating thoughts, that are the products of the best minds of all ages.

Thus it all comes down to this. It is by the use of denials and affirmations, and by persevering in their use, that the life can be changed, circumstances altered, and ambitious realized.

By denials and affirmations we can direct our thought-stream into the right channel; by denials and affirmations we can impress upon our sub-conscious mind thoughts which, becoming translated into actions, lead to success and all accomplishment. By denials and affirmations we can break down the force of evil habit, and in its place install habits that ennoble and enrich our lives. By denials and affirmations we can build up our characters, changing what was weak and vacillating into that which is powerful and stable. By denials and affirmations we can concentrate our consciousness upon thoughts of Power, Success and Courage and these, in turn, will attract to us multitudes of other thoughts of a similar nature. Do you realize, dear Reader, the extent of the wonderful power that you hold in your hands?

———————

Make denials and affirmations to suit your particular needs. Whatever you desire to do, affirm beforehand that you can do it, and that you will do it when the time for doing comes. Whatever disagreeable or difficult duty lies before you, deny failure, and affirm beforehand that you can and will do it, that already in your Mental World it is accomplished; then visualize yourself doing the thing calmly and without effort. Mentally see yourself dealing with a difficult or unpleasant matter, with calm dignity and ease. When the time for action arrives you will succeed.

MEDITATION

Concentrate your whole attention upon the meditations. If you find your thoughts wandering through lack of concentrative power make use of the following denial and affirmation. First of all cleanse the mind by the denial of evil and calm and strengthen it by the affirmation of good. You have by so doing raised yourself into your perfect Mental World, breathing the pure air of perfect mental freedom. Now say, "Mind wandering cannot affect me. I am a perfect MIND, part of the great Universal Mind that is everywhere and works in and through everything. Therefore my mental powers are perfect. It was a mistake that made me think I could not concentrate; it was simply a delusion of the physical senses. Now I know that this could never be, because I am a perfect Mind gifted with God-like powers." Now affirm as follows: "Now I know that I can concentrate on any subject I please. My potential powers are infinite, I have only to develop them, I have only to 'try' and I must succeed." Working in this way you will develop tremendous powers of Concentration.

MEDITATION VII

I send out my thoughts to all mankind and say: "Dear everybody, I love you." Like the beams of a searchlight my mental vision sweeps over all the continents and islands of the world, and visualizes all peoples, sending out to them a great beam of Love and Blessedness. Then it takes in all sky and sun and earth and sea, and the sweet breath of heaven. It embraces all animals and flowers and loveliness, it sweeps through a thousand sunsets and a million dew-washed fragrant dawns back to the one Source of all life--again affirming, "I love you, I love you." Then into my heart flows a great wave of divinest peace, a great inrush of the accumulated love-force of the invisible Universe, I become submerged in a sea of Infinite Blessedness. Thus in blessing others do I help to make the world a little better, and in return I am doubly blessed.

For this week's visualizing exercise take six small articles and examine them very carefully one at a time. For instance, if one article is a lead pencil, look at it and see in what respects it differs from other lead pencils. You notice its color; its shape, either round, hexagon or oval; its point, well sharpened or otherwise; the maker's name and trade-mark; what kind of lead, either BB, B or JIB; the name of the pencil itself; its condition, scratches on the surface of the polish; all these and many other points should be minutely noticed. Examine each article in turn and just as minutely. When you have examined them all, shut your eyes and visualize each article, and see every point and peculiarity in your mind's eye, just as you did with your physical sight. Change the articles for new ones from day to day.

APPENDIX

If you lack knowledge of a certain subject and desire to gain this knowledge, then tell your subliminal mind what it is that you require; it will then either supply direct the knowledge that you need or bring to your notice the very book or course of lessons that you require. Also in solving your problems your subliminal mind may bring a sentence to your notice, which, directly you read it, tells you that it is the answer to your riddle. The more you can quieten the senses and the objective mind and rely upon your subliminal mind the greater will be your wisdom and understanding.

In the letter I have sent you this week I speak of visualizing and affirming the success that you desire to demonstrate, fn the same way hold the picture of perfect health ever before your mind. Let it be a constant inspiration and source of radiant joy.

The complete text of the book behind these excerpts may be found in -

Law of Attraction: Dynamic Thought

(Please see Bibliography for details.)

William Walker Atkinson

A prolific author, Atkinson wrote under many pen names in order to publish his diverse writings.

Having become a very successful lawyer, he then had a complete physical and nervous breakdown – healing himself through study of New Thought materials.

Shortly after, he moved to Chicago and began his publishing career – where we see the bulk of his work being produced as articles and books.

In this volume, we see his thoughts from four of his books. Truly few have written as much on the Law of Attraction as Atkinson

Practical Mental Influence

Chapter 3 - Mental Induction

As we stated in the preceding chapter, the phenomena of Mental Influence bears a striking analogy to that of the electrical or magnetic energy. Not only is this so in the phase of wave motion and transmission, but also in the phase of induction, as we shall see presently.

In physical science the term Induction is used to indicate that quality in a manifestation of energy which tends to reproduce in a second object the vibrations manifesting in the first object, without direct contact between the two bodies. A magnet will induce magnetism in another object removed from its space. An electrified object will tend to produce similar vibrations in another object by induction, over great spaces. Heat waves travel along the ether, and tend to produce heat vibrations in objects far removed, notably in the case of the sun and the earth. Even sound waves will affect other objects in this way, as in the well-known instance of the glass or vase "singing" in response to the musical note sounded afar off. In fact, we see and hear by processes similar to those described.

And in this same manner that Thought-Waves carry the vibrations of the mind sending them forth to great distances, or lesser ones, tending to set up similar vibrations in the middle of other persons within their field force. Thus a person feeling a strong degree of anger will pour forth waves of that degree of mental vibration, which, coming in contact with the brains of other persons, tend to set up a similar feelings or emotions and thus cause the person to "feel cross" or "peevish" or even to manifest a similar angry state of mind. We all know how easily a fight is started by a very angry person in a room sending forth violent vibrations. One has but to remember the instances of mob violence to see how easily the "contagion of hate and anger" spread among people who allow themselves to be influenced. And not only is this true of undesirable emotions and feelings, but also of desirable ones. The influence of a good man who happens to be strong mentally spreads among those around him, influencing in them for good.

Orators, actors, preachers and teachers send forth strong within toll currents, which tend to produce mental conditions on the part of their hearers corresponding to the feeling held by the mind of the speaker. When you remember how this speaker swayed your feelings, or how that actor made you weep with pity, shiver with fear, or laugh with joy, you will see how Mental induction acts.

But not only is this true when we are in the actual presence of the person sending out the Thought-Waves, but it is equally true that we are influenced by persons far removed from us in space, often without their knowledge or intent, although sometimes (in the case of one who understands the principal most) with full knowledge and intent.

The ether with which space is filled carries these Thought-Waves in all directions, and the surface of the earth, particularly in the densely occupied portions, is filled with these waves. These waves, carrying the mental vibrations, coming in contact with each other, tend to set up combinations on one hand, or else neutralize each other on the other hand. That is to say, if two sets of waves of a similar nature meet there is likely to be a combination formed between them just as between two chemicals having an affinity for each other. In this way the "mental atmosphere" of places, towns, houses, etc., is formed. On the other hand if currents of opposing vibrations came in contact with each other, there will be manifested a conflict between the two, in which each will lose in proportion to its weakness, and the result will be either a neutralization of both or else a combination having vibrations of an average rate. For instance, if two currents of mental energy meet, one being a thought of Love and the other Hate, they will neutralize each other if they are equal, or if one is stronger than the other, it will persist but robbed of much of its strength. If it were not for this neutralizing effect we would be largely at the mercy of stray currents of thought. Nature protects us in this way, and also by rendering us immune to a considerable extent.

But nevertheless we are affected by these waves to a considerable extent, unless we have learned to throw them off by knowledge of the laws and an enforcement of them by practice. We all know how great waves of feeling spread over the town, city or country, sweeping people off their balance. Great waves of political enthusiasm, or War spirits, or prejudice for or against certain people, or groups of people, sweep over places and cause men to act in a manner that they will afterward regret when they come to themselves and consider their acts in cold blood. Demagogues will sway them or magnetic leaders who wish to gain their votes or patronage; and they will be led into acts of mob violence, or similar atrocities, by yielding to these waves of "contagious" thought. On the other hand we all know how great waves of religious feeling sweep over a community upon the occasion of some great "revival" excitement or fervor.

The effect of these Thought-Waves, so far as the power of induction is concerned, of course depends very materially upon the strength of the thought or feeling being manifested in the mind sending them forth. The majority of persons put but little force into the mental manifestations, but here and there is to be found a thinker whose Thought-Waves are practically "a stream of living will" and which of course have a very strong inductive effect upon the minds of others with whom the waves come in contact. But it likewise follows that a number of persons thinking along the same lines will produce a great volume of power by a combination of their thought currents into great streams of mental force.

Then again there is another feature of the case that we must not lose sight of, and that is the Attraction between minds, by virtue of which one draws to himself the Thought-Waves of others whose thoughts are in accord with his own. The contrary is true, for there is Repulsion between the minds of persons and the Thought-Waves of others whose thoughts are not in accord with his own. The contrary is true, for there is Repulsions between the minds of persons and the Thought-Waves of others antagonistic to their thoughts. To quote a well-worn and much-used expression to illustrate this truth, "Like attracts Like," and "Birds of a Feather flock together." There is ever in operation this marvelous **law of Attraction** and Repulsion of Mental Energy-Persons allowing their thoughts to run along certain lines, and permitting the feelings to be expressed in certain ways, draw to themselves the Thought-Waves and mental influences of others keyed to the same mental key-note. And likewise they repel the waves and influences of an opposing nature. This is an important fact to remember in one's everyday life. Good attracts Good and repels Evil. Evil attracts Evil and repels Good. The predominant Mental Attitude serves to attract similar influences and to repel the opposing ones. Therefore watch carefully the character and nature of your thoughts - cultivate the desirable ones and repress the undesirable ones. Verily "As a man thinketh in his heart, so is he."

Some Thought-Waves sent forth with but little strength travel slowly and do not proceed very far from their place of emanation, but creep along like some smoke or fog, lazily and yielding. Other thoughts charged with a greater intensity of desire or will, dart forth vigorously like an electric spark, and often travel great distances. The weak Thought-Waves do not last a very long time, but fade away or become neutralized or dissipated by stronger, forces. But the strong thoughts persist for a long time, retaining much of their vitality and energy.

In the same manner the Thought-Waves of a person will continue to vibrate around him wherever he goes, and those coming in contact with him will be impressed by the character of his vibrations in this way. Some men send forth gloomy vibrations in this way. Some men send forth gloomy vibrations, which you feel when you come in contact with them. Others radiate good-cheer, courage and happiness, which conditions are induced in those with whom they come in contact. Many people will manifest these qualities so strongly that one can notice the effect the moment such persons enter a room. They carry their atmosphere with them, and the same is induced in the minds of others around them.

In the same way some people carry with them vibrations of Will-Power and Masterfulness that beat upon the minds of others, making them feel the power of such persons and conquering their own will-power and changing their desires. Others manifest a strong power of Fascination or Attraction, in a similar manner which tends to draw others to them and to their desires and wishes. Not only does this principle operate in the phase of general mental atmospheres, but also in the phase of direct personal influence.

All forms of Mental influence operate along the lines of Mental induction, as herein described. The principle is the same in all cases and instances, although the manner of operation varies according to the particular phase of the phenomena manifested. Remember this as we proceed, and you will be able to understand the subject much better.

The Secret of Success

LESSON VII - THE LAW OF ATTRACTION

There is in Nature a great Law -- the **Law of Attraction** -- by the operations of which all things -- from atoms to men -- are attracted toward each other in the degree of the common affinity of common use. The reverse of this law -- which is merely another manifestation of its power -- is what is called Repulsion, which is but the other pole of Attraction, and by the operations of which things tend to repel each other in the degree that they are unlike, opposing, and of no use to each other. The **Law of Attraction** is Universal, on all the planes of life, from the physical to the spiritual. Its operations are uniform and constant, and we may take the phenomena of one plane and thereby study the phenomena of another plane, for the same rule applies in each case -- the same Law is in operation in the same way.

Beginning with the tiny corpuscles, electrons, or ions, of which the atoms are formed, we find manifested the **Law of Attraction** -- certain electrons attract each other, and repel others still, thereby causing to spring into existing groups, combinations and colonies of electrons which being in agreement and harmony manifest and constitute what are called atoms, which until recently were supposed to be the primal form of matter. Passing on the atoms themselves, we find many degrees of affinity and attraction existing between them which cause them to combine and form into molecules of which all masses of matter consists. For instance, every drop of water is composed of countless molecules of water. And each molecule is composed of two atoms of Hydrogen and one atom of Oxygen --the combination always being the same in every molecule of water. Now, why do these atoms combine in just this way --

with the same invariable grouping and proportion? Not by chance, surely, for there is no such thing in Nature -- there is a natural law back of every phenomenon. And in this case it is the **Law of Attraction** manifesting in the case of these atoms. And it is so in all chemical combinations --it is called Chemical Affinity. Sometimes an attached atom will come in contact with, or in proximity to, another atom, and then bang goes the explosion of the molecule as the atom flies away from its partners and into the arms of the other atom for which it has a greater affinity. There are marriages and divorces in the world of atoms, you will notice.

And in the cases of the molecules, it is found that certain molecules are attracted to others of the same kind, under what is called Cohesion, and thus masses of matter are composed. A piece of gold, silver, tin, glass, or other form of matter is composed of countless molecules held together tightly by Cohesion -- and this Cohesion is merely another form of the **Law of Attraction** -- the same that draws all things together. And, underlying the **Law of Attraction** is to be found our old Principle of Desire and Will. You may shrug your shoulders at this mention of desire and Will in connection with electrons, atoms, molecules -- all forms of matter, but just wait a bit and see what the leading scientific authorities have to say on the subject.

Prof. Hakel, one of the world's greatest scientists -- a materialist who would sneer at the teachings of Mental Science -- even this man, naturally prejudiced against mentalist theories, finds himself compelled to say: "The idea of chemical affinity consists in the fact that the various chemical elements perceive the qualitative differences in other elements -- experience pleasure of revulsion at contact with them, and execute specific movements on this ground." He also positively and distinctly states that in the atoms there must be something corresponding to Desire for contact and association with other atoms, and Will to enable the atom to respond to the Desire Law is constant throughout Nature, from atom to man --physical, mental and spiritual.

But what has all this to do with the Secret of Success you may ask? Simply, that the **Law of Attraction** is an important part in the Secret of Success, inasmuch as it tends to bring to us the things, persons and circumstances in accordance with our earnest Desire, Demand, and Will, just as it brings together the atoms and other particles of matter. Make yourself an atom of Living Desire and you will attract to yourself the person, things and circumstances fitting in with the accomplishment of your Desire. You will also get into rapport with those who are working along the same lines of thought, and will be attracted to them and they to you, and you will be brought into relations with persons, things and environments likely to work out the problem of your Desires -- you will get "next to" the right persons and things -- all by the operation of this great natural **Law of Attraction**. No Necromancy or Magic about it at all -- nothing supernatural or mysterious -- just the operations of a great Natural Law.

You can do little by yourself in Life, be you ever so strong and able. Life is a complex thing, and individuals are interdependent upon each other for the doings of things. One Individual, segregated from all the other Individuals, could accomplish little or nothing along the lines of outer activity. He must form combinations, arrangements, harmonies and agreements with others, and in accordance with environments and things, that is, he must create and use the proper environments and things, and draw to himself others with whom he must form combinations, in order to do things. And these persons, things and environments come to him -- and he to them -- by reason of this great **Law of Attraction**. And the way he sets into operation this great **Law of Attraction** is by the operation of his Desire, and along the lines of Mental Imagery. Do you see the connection now? So be careful to form, cultivate and manifest the right Desires --hold to them firmly, strongly and constantly, and you will set into operation this great Law, which forms an important part of the Secret of Success.

Desire-Force is the motive power leading the activities of Life. It is the basic vital power, which animates the minds of living things and urges them forth to action.

Without strong Desire no one accomplishes anything worthy of the name -- and the greater the desire the greater will be the amount of energy generated and manifested, everything else being equal. That is to say, that given a dozen men of equal intellect, physical health and mental activity -- equal in everything else except Desire, in short, the ones in whom the greatest Desire resides and is manifested will outstrip the others in attainment -- and of these winners the one in who Desire burns like an unquenchable flame will be the one who will Master the others by the force of his primitive elementary power.

Not only does Desire give to the man that inward motive which leads to the enfoldment of the power within himself, but it does more than this; it causes to radiate from him the finer and more subtle mental and vital forces of his nature, which, flowing forth in all directions like the magnetic waves from the magnet, or the electric waves from the dynamo, influencing all who come within the field of force. Desire-Force is a real, active, effective force of Nature, and serves to attract, draw and bring to a center that which is in line with the nature of the Desire. The much talked of **Law of Attraction**, of which so much is heard in Mental Science and the New Thought, depends largely upon the force and power of Desire. Desire-Force is at the center of the **Law of Attraction**. There is a tendency in Nature to attract and draw to the center of a Desire the things which are needed to fulfill that Desire. One's "own will come to him" by reason of his natural force, which lies behind and underneath the entire phenomena of Mental Influence. This being so, does it not become at once apparent why one who wishes to accomplish anything should be sure to create a strong Desire for it, and at the same time be sure to acquire the art of Visualization so as to form a clear Mental Picture of the thing Desired -- a clear mold in which the materialized reality may manifest? Have you ever come in contact with any of the great men of modern business life? If you have seen these people in action, you will have become conscious of a subtle, mysterious something about them -- a something that you could actually feel -- a something that seemed to draw you to fit in to their schemes, plans, and desires almost by an irresistible force. These people are all people of the strongest kind of Desire -- their Desire-Force manifests strongly and affects those with whom they come in contact. Not only this, but their Desire-Force flows from them in great waves, which occultists inform us soon manifests a circular, or whirlpool-like motion, swung round and around the center of the Desire -- these men become actual cyclones of Desire into which nearly everything that comes within its sweep is affected and swept into the vortex. Have we not evidences of this in the cases of all the great leaders of men -- can we not see the operation of that mighty **law of attraction** which brings to them their own? We are apt to call this Will-Power, and so it is in a way, back and under the Will in such cases is to be found the ardent, burning Desire that is the motive force of the attractive power.

This Desire-Force is a primitive, elemental thing. It is found in the animal kingdom, and among the lower races of men, perhaps more clearly than among the higher types of men, but only because in such instances it is seen stripped of the covering, sheaths, disguises and masks that surround the more civilized forms and planes of life. But remember this well, the same principle is manifested under and beneath the polished veneer of civilized life -- the Desire-Force of the cultured leader of men is as elemental as that animating the fierce and shaggy caveman or the wild Berserker who, naked and half-mad, rushed upon overwhelming hordes of his enemy, brushing them aside like flies -- that is, if you will but look beneath the polished surface. In the old wild days Desire manifested its force on the physical plane -- now it manifests on the Mental Plane -- that is the only difference, the Force is the same in both cases.

While we write, there has just been produced on stage a new play that illustrates this principle. The heroine, the daughter of an old New York family of high social standing and wealth, has a dream of her life in a former incarnation, in which she sees herself torn from the arms of her cave-dweller father by the mighty arms of a fierce savage chief, whose desire is manifested through the physical. She awakens from her dream, and to her horror soon discovers the face of her dream-captor on a man who comes into her father's life in New York. This man comes from the West, forceful, resourceful and desirous, beating down all before him in the game of finance. As of old, he places his foot not on the neck of his enemies -- but on the mental-plane, this time, instead of the physical. The same old Desire for power is strong within him -- the same old masterfulness manifests itself. This man says: "I have never quit; I have never been afraid." The same old Desire then flamed up in the savage now manifests in the Master of Wall Street, and between the force of its Attraction and the coupled and allied force of his Will, he repeats the performances of his previous incarnation -- but on the plane of mental forces and achievement this time -- mind, not muscle, being the instrument through which the Desire manifests.

We give the above example merely as an illustration of the fact that Desire is the motivating force that moves the Will into action, and which cause the varied activity of life, men and things. Desire-Force is a real power in life, and influences not only tracts, but influences and compels other persons and things to swing in toward the center of the Desire sending forth the currents. In the Secret of Success, Desire plays a prominent part. Without a Desire for Success, there is no Success, none. The **Law of Attraction** is set into motion by Desire.

The majority of the principles advanced in this book have been in the nature of Positive injunctions -- that is, you have been urged to do certain things rather than to not do the opposite or contrary. But here we come to a place in which the advice must be given along the negative lines -- we must urge you not to do a certain thing. We allude to that great poison of the mind and Will known as Fear.

We do not allude to physical fear -- important though physical courage may be, and as regrettable as physical cowardice may be considered, still it is not a part of the purpose of this book to preach against the latter and advise a cultivation of the former quality -- you will find much of that elsewhere. Our purpose here is to combat that subtle, insidious enemy of true Self-Expression which appears in the shape and guise of mental fear, forebodings which may be considered as Negative

Thought just as the other principles mentioned in this work may be considered as Positive Thought.

Fear thoughts is that condition of the mind in which everything is seen through blue glasses -- in which everything seems to bring a sense of the futility of endeavor -- the "I Can't" principle of mentality, as contrasted with the "I Can and I Will" mental attitude. It is the noxious weed in the mental garden, which tends to kill the valuable plants to be found therein. It is the fly in the ointment -- the spider in the cup of the Wine of Life. So far as we know the first person to use the word "Fear-Thought" -- which has now passed into common use -- was Horace Fletcher, the well-known writer, who coined it to supplant the use of the word "Worry" in a certain sense. He had pointed out that Anger and Worry were the two great hindrances to a well- balanced, advanced and progressive mentality, but many misunderstood him and urged that to abolish Worry meant to cease taking any consideration of the morrow -- a lack of common prudence and forethought. And so Fletcher coined the word "Fear-Thought" to express a phase of his idea of "Forethought without Worry," and he entitled his second book on the subject, "Happiness, as found in Forethought minus Fear-Thought," a very happy expression of a very happy idea.

Fletcher also was the first to advance the idea that Fear was not a thing-in-itself, but merely an expression of Fear-Thought -- a manifestation of the state of mind known as Fear-Thought. He and others who have written on the subject, have taught that Fear might be abolished by the practice of abolishing Fear-Thought from the mind -- by driving it out of the mental chamber -- and the best teachers have taught that the best way to drive out Fear (or any other undesirable mental state) was by cultivating the thought of the opposite quality of mind by compelling the mind to dwell upon the mental picture of the desirable quality, and by the appropriate auto-suggestions. The illustration has often been stated that the way to drive darkness from a room is not to shovel it out, but to throw open the shutters and let the sunlight stream in, and that is the best way to neutralize Fear-Thought.

The mental process has aptly been spoken of as "vibrations," a figure that has a full warrant in modern science. Then, by raising the vibration to the Positive pitch, the negative vibrations may be counteracted. By cultivating the qualities recommended in the other lessons of this book, Fear-Thought may be neutralized. The poison of Fear-Thought is insidious and subtle, but it slowly creeps through the veins until it paralyzes all useful efforts and action, until the heart and brain are affected and find it difficult to throw it off. Fear-Thought is at the bottom of the majority of failures and "going down" in life. As long as a man keeps his nerve and confidence in himself, he is able to rise to his feet after each stumble, and face the enemy resolutely -- but let him feel the effects of Fear-Thought to such an extent that he cannot throw it off and he will fail to rise and will perish miserable. "There is nothing to fear except Fear," has well been said.

We have spoken elsewhere about the **Law of Attraction**, which operates in the direction of attracting to us, that which we Desire. But there is a reverse side to this -- it is a poor rule that will not work both ways. Fear will set into motion the **Law of Attraction** just as well as Desire. Just as Desire draws to one the things he pictures in his mind as the Desired Thing, so will Fear draw to him the thing pictured in his mind as the Thing Feared. "The thing that I feared hath befallen me." And the reason is very simple, and the apparent contradiction vanishes when we examine the matter. What is the pattern upon which the **Law of Attraction** builds under the force of Desire? The Mental Image, of course. And so it is in the case of Fear -- the person carries about the Mental Image or haunting picture of the Feared Thing, and the **Law of Attraction** brings it to him just as it brings the Desired Thing. Did you ever stop to think that Fear was the negative pole of Desire? The same laws work in both cases.

So avoid Fear-Thought as you would the poisonous draught that you know would cause your blood to become black and thick, and your breathing labored and difficult. It is a vile thing, and you should not rest content until you have expelled it from your mental system. You can get rid of it by Desire and Will, coupled with the holding of the Mental

Image of Fearlessness. Drive it up by cultivating its opposite. Change your polarity. Raise your mental vibrations. Someone has said, "There is no Devil but Fear" -- then send that Devil back to the place where he properly belongs, for if you entertain him hospitably he will make your heaven a hell in order that he may feel at home. Use the mental Big Stick on him.

Thought Vibration

Chapter 1 - Law of Attraction in the Thought World

THE Universe is governed by Law - one great Law. Its manifestations are multiform, but viewed from the Ultimate there is but one Law. We are familiar with some of its manifestations, but are almost totally ignorant of certain others. Still we are learning a little more every day - the veil is being gradually lifted.

We speak learnedly of the Law of Gravitation, but ignore that equally wonderful manifestation, THE **LAW OF ATTRACTION** IN THE THOUGHT WORLD. We are familiar with that wonderful manifestation of Law which draws and holds together the atoms of which matter is composed - we recognize the power of the law that attracts bodies to the earth, that holds the circling worlds in their places, but we close our eyes to the mighty law that draws to us the things we desire or fear, that makes or mars our lives.

When we come to see that Thought is a force - a manifestation of energy - having a magnet-like power of attraction, we will begin to understand the why and wherefore of many things that have heretofore seemed dark to us. There is no study that will so well repay the student for his time and trouble as the study of the workings of this mighty law of the world of Thought - the **Law of Attraction**.

When we think we send out vibrations of a fine ethereal substance, which are as real as the vibrations manifesting light, heat, electricity, magnetism. That these vibrations are not evident to our five senses is no proof that they do not exist. A powerful magnet will send out vibrations and exert a force sufficient to attract to itself a piece of steel weighing a hundred pounds, but we can neither see, taste, smell, hear nor feel the mighty force. These thought vibrations, likewise, cannot be seen, tasted, smelled, heard nor felt in the ordinary way; although it is true there are on record cases of persons peculiarly sensitive to psychic impressions who have perceived powerful thought-waves, and very many of us can testify that we have distinctly felt the thought vibrations of others, both whilst in the presence of the sender and at a distance. Telepathy and its kindred phenomena are not idle dreams.

Light and heat are manifested by vibrations of a far lower intensity than those of Thought, but the difference is solely in the rate of vibration. The annals of science throw an interesting light upon this question. Prof. Elisha Gray, an eminent scientist, says in his little book, "The Miracles of Nature":

"There is much food for speculation in the thought that there exist sound-waves that no human ear can hear, and color-waves of light that no eye can see. The long, dark, soundless space between 40,000 and 400,000,000,000,000 vibrations per second, and the infinity of range beyond 700,000,000,000,000 vibrations per second, where light ceases, in the universe of motion, makes it possible to indulge in speculation."

M. M. Williams, in his work entitled "Short Chapters in Science," says:

"There is no gradation between the most rapid undulations or tremblings that produce our sensation of sound, and the slowest of those which give rise to our sensations of gentlest warmth. There is a huge gap between them, wide enough to include another world of motion, all lying between our world of sound and our world of heat and light; and there is no good reason whatever for supposing that matter is incapable of such intermediate activity, or that such activity may not give rise to intermediate sensations, provided there are organs for taking up and sensifying their movements."

I cite the above authorities merely to give you food for thought, not to attempt to demonstrate to you the fact that thought vibrations exist. The last-named fact has been fully established to the satisfaction of numerous investigators of the subject, and a little reflection will show you that it coincides with your own experiences.

We often hear repeated the well-known Mental Science statement, "Thoughts are Things," and we say these words over without consciously realizing just what is the meaning of the statement. If we fully comprehended the truth of the statement and the natural consequences of the truth back of it, we should understand many things which have appeared dark to us, and would be able to use the wonderful power, Thought Force, just as we use any other manifestation of Energy.

As I have said, when we think we set into motion vibrations of a very high degree, but just as real as the vibrations of light, heat, sound, electricity. And when we understand the laws governing the production and transmission of these vibrations we will be able to use them in our daily life, just as we do the better known forms of energy. That we cannot see, hear, weigh or measure these vibrations is no proof that they do not exist. There exist waves of sound which no human ear can hear, although some of these are undoubtedly registered by the ear of some of the insects, and others are caught by delicate scientific instruments invented by man; yet there is a great gap between the sounds registered by the most delicate instrument and the limit which man's mind, reasoning by analogy, knows to be the boundary line between sound waves and some other forms of vibration. And there are light waves which the eye of man does not register, some of which may be detected by more delicate instruments, and many more so fine that the instrument has not yet been invented which will detect them, although improvements are being made every year and the unexplored field gradually lessened.

As new instruments are invented, new vibrations are registered by them - and yet the vibrations were just as real before the invention of the instrument as afterward. Supposing that we had no instruments to register magnetism - one might be justified in denying the existence of that mighty force, because it could not be tasted, felt, smelt, heard, seen, weighted or measured. And yet the mighty magnet would still send out waves of force sufficient to draw to it pieces of steel weighing hundreds of pounds.

Each form of vibration requires its own form of instrument for registration. At present the human brain seems to be the only instrument capable of registering thought waves, although occultists say that in this century scientists will invent apparatus sufficiently delicate to catch and register such impressions. And from present indications it looks as if the invention named might be expected at any time. The demand exists and undoubtedly will be soon supplied. But to those who have experimented along the lines of practical telepathy no further proof is required than the results of their own experiments.

We are sending out thoughts of greater or less intensity all the time, and we are reaping the results of such thoughts. Not only do our thought waves influence ourselves and others, but they have a drawing power - they attract to us the thoughts of others, things, circumstances, people, "luck," in accord with the character of the thought uppermost in our minds. Thoughts of Love will attract to us the Love of others; circumstances and surroundings in accord with the thought; people who are of like thought. Thoughts of Anger, Hate, Envy, Malice and Jealousy will draw to us the foul brood of kindred thoughts emanating from the minds of others; circumstances in which we will be called upon to manifest these vile thoughts and will receive them in turn from others; people who will manifest inharmony; and so on. A strong thought or a thought long continued, will make us the center of attraction for the corresponding thought waves of others. Like attracts like in the Thought World - as ye sow so shall ye reap. Birds of a feather flock together in the Thought World - curses like chickens come home to roost, and bringing their friends with them.

The man or woman who is filled with Love sees Love on all sides and attracts the Love of others. The man with hate in his heart gets all the Hate he can stand. The man who thinks Fight generally runs up against all the Fight he wants before he gets through. And so it goes, each gets what he calls for over the wireless telegraphy of the Mind. The man who rises in the morning feeling "grumpy" usually manages to have the whole family in the same mood before the breakfast is over. The "nagging" woman generally finds enough to gratify her "nagging" propensity during the day.

This matter of Thought Attraction is a serious one. When you stop to think of it you will see that a man really makes his own surroundings, although he blames others for it. I have known people who understood this law to hold a positive, calm thought and be absolutely unaffected by the inharmony surrounding them. They were like the vessel from which the oil had been poured on the troubled waters - they rested safely and calmly whilst the tempest raged around them. One is not at the mercy of the fitful storms of Thought after he has learned the workings of the Law.

We have passed through the age of physical force on to the age of intellectual supremacy, and are now entering a new and almost unknown field, that of psychic power. This field of energy has its established laws, as well as have the others, and we should acquaint ourselves with them or we will be crowded to the wall as are the ignorant on the planes of effort. I will endeavor to make plain to you the great underlying principles of this new field of energy which is opening up before us, that you may be able to make use of this great power and apply it for legitimate and worthy purposes, just as men are using steam, electricity and other forms of energy today.

Chapter 7 - The Transmutation of Negative Thought

WORRY is the child of Fear - if you kill out Fear, Worry will die for want of nourishment. This advice is very old, and yet it is always worthy of repetition, for it is a lesson of which we are greatly in need. Some people think that if we kill out Fear and Worry we will never be able to accomplish anything. I have read editorials in the great journals in which the writers held that without Worry one can never accomplish any of the great tasks of life, because Worry is necessary to stimulate interest and work. This is nonsense, no matter who utters it. Worry never helped one to accomplish anything; on the contrary, it stands in the way of accomplishment and attainment.

The motive underlying action and "doing things" is Desire and Interest. If one earnestly desires a thing, he naturally becomes very much interested in its accomplishment, and is quick to seize upon anything likely to help him to gain the thing he wants. More than that, his mind starts up a work on the subconscious plane that brings into the field of consciousness many ideas of value and importance. Desire and Interest are the causes that result in success. Worry is not Desire. It is true that if one's surroundings and environments become intolerable, he is driven in desperation to some efforts that will result in throwing off the undesirable conditions and in the acquiring of those more in harmony with his desire. But this is only another form of Desire - the man desires something different from what he has; and when his desire becomes strong enough his entire interest is given to the task, he makes a mighty effort, and the change is accomplished. But it wasn't Worry that caused the effort. Worry could content itself with wringing its hands and moaning, "Woe is me," and wearing its nerves to a frazzle, and accomplishing nothing. Desire acts differently. It grows stronger as the man's conditions become intolerable, and finally when he feels the hurt so strongly that he can't stand it any longer, he says, "I won't stand this any longer - I will make a change," and lo! Then Desire springs into action. The man keeps on "wanting" a change the worst way (which is the best way) and his Interest and Attention being given to the task of deliverance, he begins to make things move. Worry never accomplished anything. Worry is negative and death producing. Desire and Ambition are positive and life producing. A man may worry himself to death and yet nothing will be accomplished, but let that man transmute his worry and discontent into Desire and Interest, coupled with a belief that he is able to make the change - the "I Can and I Will" idea - then something happens.

Yes, Fear and Worry must go before we can do much. One must proceed to cast out these negative intruders, and replace them with Confidence and Hope. Transmute Worry into keen Desire. Then you will find that Interest is awakened, and you will begin to think things of interest to you. Thoughts will come to you from the great reserve stock in your mind and you will start to manifest them in action. Moreover you will be placing yourself in harmony with similar thoughts of others, and will draw to you aid and assistance from the great volume of thought waves with which the world is filled. One draws to himself thought waves corresponding in character with the nature of the prevailing thoughts in his won mind - his mental attitude. Then again he begins to set into motion the great **Law of Attraction**, whereby he draws to him others likely to help him, and is, in turn, attracted to others who can aid him. This **Law of Attraction** is no joke, no metaphysical absurdity, but is a great live working principle of Nature, as anyone may learn by experimenting and observing.

To succeed in anything you must want it very much - Desire must be in evidence in order to attract. The man of weak desires attracts very little to himself. The stronger the Desire the greater the force set into motion. You must want a thing hard enough before you can get it. You must want it more than you do the things around you, and you must be prepared to pay the price for it. The price is the throwing overboard

of certain lesser desires that stand in the way of the accomplishment of
the greater one. Comfort, ease, leisure, amusements, and many other
things may have to go (not always, though). It all depends on what you
want. As a rule, the greater the thing desired, the greater the price to be
paid for it. Nature believes in adequate compensation. But if you really
Desire a thing in earnest, you will pay the price without question; for the
Desire will dwarf the importance of the other things.

You say that you want a thing very much, and are doing
everything possible toward its attainment? Pshaw! You are only playing
Desire. Do you want the thing as much as a prisoner wants freedom - as
much as a dying man wants life? Look at the almost miraculous things
accomplished by prisoners desiring freedom. Look how they work
through steel plates and stone walls with a bit of stone. Is your desire as
strong as that? Do you work for the desired thing as if your life depended
upon it? Nonsense! You don't know what Desire is. I tell you if a man
wants a thing as much as the prisoner wants freedom, or as much as a
strongly vital man wants life, then that man will be able to sweep away
obstacles and impediments apparently immovable. The key to attainment
is Desire, Confidence, and Will. This key will open many doors.

Fear paralyzes Desire - it scares the life out of it. You must get rid
of Fear. There have been times in my life when Fear would get hold of
me and take a good, firm grip on my vitals, and I would lose all hope; all
interest; all ambition; all desire. But, thank the Lord, I have always
managed to throw off the grip of the monster and face my difficulty like
a man; and lo! Things would seem to be straightened out for me
somehow. Either the difficulty would melt away or I would be given
means to overcome, or get around, or under or over it. It is strange how
this works. No matter how great is the difficulty, when we finally face it
with courage and confidence in ourselves, we seem to pull through
somehow, and then we begin to wonder what we were scared about. This
is not a mere fancy, it is the working of a mighty law, which we do not as
yet fully understand, but which we may prove at any time.

People often ask: "it's all very well for you New Thought people to say 'Don't worry,' but what's a person to do when he thinks of all the possible things ahead of him, which might upset him and his plans? Well, all that I can say is that the man is foolish to bother about thinking of troubles to come at some time in the future. The majority of things that we worry about don't come to pass at all; a large proportion of the others come in a milder form than we had anticipated, and there are always other things which come at the same time which help us to overcome the trouble. The future holds in store for us not only difficulties to be overcome, but also agents to help us in overcoming the difficulties. Things adjust themselves. We are prepared for any trouble which may come upon us, and when the time comes we somehow find ourselves able to meet it. God not only tempers the wind to the shorn lamb, but He also tempers the shorn lamb to the wind. The winds and the shearing do not come together; there is usually enough time for the lamb to get seasoned, and then he generally grows new wool before the cold blast comes.

It has been well said that nine-tenths of the worries are over things which never comes to pass, and that the other tenth is over things of little or no account. So what's the use in using up all your reserve force in fretting over future troubles, if this be so? Better wait until your troubles really come before you worry. You will find that by this storing up of energy you will be able to meet about any sort of trouble that comes your way.

What is it that uses up all the energy in the average man or woman, anyway? Is it the real overcoming of difficulties, or the worrying about impending troubles? It's always "Tomorrow, tomorrow," and yet tomorrow never comes just as we feared it would. Tomorrow is all right; it carries in its grip good things as well as troubles. Bless my soul, when I sit down and think over the things which I once feared might possibly descend upon me, I laugh! Where are those feared things now? I don't know - have almost forgotten that I ever feared them.

You do not need fight Worry - that isn't the way to overcome the habit. Just practice concentration, and then learn to concentrate upon something right before you, and you will find that the worry thought has vanished. The mind can think of but one thing at a time, and if you concentrate upon a bright thing, the other thing will fade away. There are better ways of overcoming objectionable thoughts than by fighting them. Learn to concentrate upon thoughts of an opposite character, and you will have solved the problem.

When the mind is full of worry thoughts, it cannot find time to work out plans to benefit you. But when you have concentrated upon bright, helpful thoughts, you will discover that it will start to work subconsciously; and when the time comes you will find all sorts of plans and methods by which you will be able to meet the demands upon you. Keep your mental attitude right, and all things will be added unto you. There's no sense in worrying; nothing has ever been gained by it, and nothing ever will be. Bright, cheerful and happy thoughts attract bright, cheerful and happy things to us - worry drives them away. Cultivate the right mental attitude.

Power of Concentration

LESSON XVI. HOW CONCENTRATION CAN FULFILL YOUR DESIRE

"It is a spiritual law that the desire to do necessarily implies the ability to do."

You have all read of "Aladdin's Lamp," which accomplished such wonderful things. This, of course, is only a fairy story, but it illustrates the fact that man has within him the power, if he is able to use it, to gratify his every wish.

If you are unable to satisfy your deepest longings it is time you learned how to use your God-given powers. You will soon be conscious that you have latent powers within capable when once developed of revealing to you priceless knowledge and unlimited possibilities of success.

Man should have plenty of everything and not merely substance to live on as so many have. All natural desires can be realized. It would be wrong for the Infinite to create wants that could not be supplied. Man's very soul is in his power to think, and it, therefore, is the essence of all created things. Every instinct of man leads to thought, and in every thought there is great possibility because true thought development, when allied to those mysterious powers which perhaps transcend it, has been the cause of all the world's true progress.

In the silence we become conscious of "that something" which transcends thought and which uses thought as a medium for expression. Many have glimpses of "that something," but few ever reach the state where the mind is steady enough to fathom these depths. Silent, concentrated thought is more potent than spoken words, for speech distracts from the focusing power of the mind by drawing more and more attention to the without.

Man must learn more and more to depend on himself; to seek more for the Infinite within. It is from this source alone that he ever gains the power to solve his practical difficulties. No one should give up when there is always the resources of Infinity. The cause of failure is that men search in the wrong direction for success, because they are not conscious of their real powers that when used are capable of guiding them.

The Infinite within is foreign to those persons who go through life without developing their spiritual powers. But the Infinite helps only he who helps himself. There is no such thing as a Special "Providence." Man will not receive help from the Infinite except to the extent that he believes and hopes and prays for help from this great source.

Concentrate on What You Want and Get It. The weakling is controlled by conditions. The strong man controls conditions. You can be either the conqueror or the conquered. By the law of concentration you can achieve your heart's desire. This law is so powerful that that which at first seems impossible becomes attainable.

By this law what you at first see as a dream becomes a reality.

Remember that the first step in concentration is to form a Mental Image of what you wish to accomplish. This image becomes a thought-seed that attracts thoughts of a similar nature. Around this thought, when it is once planted in the imagination or creative region of the mind, you group or build associated thoughts which continue to grow as long as your desire is keen enough to compel close concentration.

Form the habit of thinking of something you wish to accomplish for five minutes each day. Shut every other thought out of consciousness. Be confident that you will succeed; make up your mind that all obstacles that are in your way will be overcome and you can rise above any environment.

You do this by utilizing the natural laws of the thought world which are all powerful.

A great aid in the development of concentration is to write out your thoughts on that which lies nearest your heart and to continue, little by little, to add to it until you have as nearly as possible exhausted the subject.

You will find that each day as you focus your forces on this thought at the center of the stream of consciousness, new plans, ideas and methods will flash into your mind. There is a **law of attraction** that will help you accomplish your purpose. An advertiser, for instance, gets to thinking along a certain line. He has formed his own ideas, but he wants to know what others think. He starts out to seek ideas and he soon finds plenty of books, plans, designs, etc., on the subject, although when he started he was not aware of their existence.

The same thing is true in all lines. We can attract those things that will help us. Very often we seem to receive help in a miraculous way. It may be slow in coming, but once the silent unseen forces are put into operation, they will bring results so long as we do our part. They are ever present and ready to aid those who care to use them. By forming a strong mental image of your desire, you plant the thought-seed which begins working in your interest and, in time, that desire, if in harmony with your higher nature, will materialize.

It may seem that it would be unnecessary to caution you to concentrate only upon achievement that will be good for you and work no harm to another, but there are many who forget others and their rights, in their anxiety to achieve success. All good things are possible for you to have, but only as you bring your forces into harmony with that law that requires that we mete out justice to fellow travelers as we journey along life's road. So first think over the thing wanted and if it would be good for you to have; say, "I want to do this; I am going to work to secure it. The way will be open for me."

If you fully grasp mentally the thought of success and hold it in mind each day, you gradually make a pattern or mold which in time will materialize. But by all means keep free from doubt and fear, the destructive forces. Never allow these to become associated with your thoughts.

At last you will create the desired conditions and receive help in many unlooked-for ways that will lift you out of the undesired environment. Life will then seem very different to you, for you will have found happiness through awakening within yourself the power to become the master of circumstances instead of their slave.

To the beginner in this line of thought some of the things stated in this book may sound strange, even absurd, but, instead of condemning them, give them a trial. You will find they will work out.

The inventor has to work out his idea mentally before he produces it materially. The architect first sees the mental picture of the house he is to plan and from this works out the one we see. Every object, every enterprise, must first be mentally created.

I know a man that started in business with thirteen cents and not a dollar's worth of credit. In ten years he has built up a large and profitable business. He attributes his success to two things—belief that he would succeed and hard work. There were times when it did not look like he could weather the storm. He was being pressed by his creditors who considered him bankrupt. They would have taken fifty cents on the dollar for his notes and considered themselves lucky. But by keeping up a bold front he got an extension of time when needed. When absolutely necessary for him to raise a certain sum at a certain time he always did it. When he had heavy bills to meet he would make up his mind that certain people that owed him would pay by a certain date and they always did. Sometimes he would not receive their check until the last mail of the day of the extension, and I have known him to send out a check with the prospect of receiving a check from one of his customers the following day. He would have no reason other than his belief in the power of affecting the mind of another by concentration of thought for expecting that check, but rarely has he been disappointed.

Just put forth the necessary concentrated effort and you will be wonderfully helped from sources unknown to you.

Remember the mystical words of Jesus, the Master: "Whatsoever thing ye desire when ye pray, pray as if ye had already received and ye shall have."

The complete text of the books behind these excerpts may be found in -

, and

Law of Attraction: Thought Vibration

(Please see Bibliography for details.)

James Allen

Best known for his "As a Man Thinketh", James Allen has remained one of the most poetic of New Thought authors, due to his beautifully-crafted prose.

In this chapter from his "Byways of Blessedness", he reminds us that while we may choose to use the Law of Attraction to gain material things, there is also reciprocal action which comes from the way we think about others, too.

The lives of others around us may or may not affect us directly, however, the thoughts we have about them will change our relationships for better or for worse...

Byways of Blessedness

Forgiveness

"If men only understood All the emptiness and acting Of the sleeping and the waking Of the souls they judge so blindly, Of the hearts they pierce so unkindly, They, with gentler words and feeling, Would apply the balm of healing- If they only understood." "Kindness, nobler ever than revenge." - Shakespeare

The remembering of injuries is spiritual darkness; the fostering of resentment is spiritual suicide. To resort to the spirit and practice of forgiveness is the beginning of enlightenment; it is also the beginning of peace and happiness. There is no rest for him who broods over slights and injuries and wrongs; no quiet repose of mind for him who feels that he has been unjustly treated, and who schemes how best to act for the discomfiture of his enemy.

How can happiness dwell in a heart that is so disturbed by ill-will? Do birds resort to a burning bush wherein to build and sing? Neither can happiness inhabit in that breast that is aflame with burning thoughts of resentment. Nor can wisdom come and dwell where such folly resides.

Revenge seems sweet only to the mind that is unacquainted with the spirit of forgiveness; but when the sweetness of forgiveness is tasted then the extreme bitterness of revenge is known. Revenge seems to lead to happiness to those who are involved in the darkness of passion; but when the violence of passion is abandoned, and the mildness of forgiveness is restored to, then it is seen that revenge leads to suffering.

Revenge is a virus which eats into the very vitals of the mind, and poisons the entire spiritual being. Resentment is a mental fever which burns up the wholesome energies of the mind, and "taking offense" is a form of moral sickness which saps the healthy flow of kindliness and good-will, and from which men and women should seek to be delivered. The unforgiving and resentful spirit is a source of great suffering and sorrow, and he who harbors and encourages it, who does not overcome and abandon it, forfeits much blessedness, and does not obtain any measure of true enlightenment. To be hard-hearted is to suffer, is to be deprived of light and comfort; to be tender-hearted is to be serenely glad, is to receive light and be well comforted. It will seem strange to many to be told that the hard-hearted and unforgiving suffer most; yet it is profoundly true, for not only do they, by the **law of attraction**, draw to themselves the revengeful passions in other people, but their hardness of heart itself is a continual source of suffering. Every time a man hardens his heart against a fellow-being he inflicts upon himself five kinds of suffering - namely, the suffering of loss of love; the suffering of lost communion and fellowship; the suffering of a troubled and confused mind; the suffering of wounded passion or pride; and the suffering of punishment inflicted by others. Every act of unforgiveness entails upon the doer of that act these five sufferings; whereas every act of forgiveness brings to the doer five kinds of blessedness - the blessedness of love; the blessedness of increased communion and fellowship; the blessedness of a calm and peaceful mind; the blessedness of passion stilled and pride overcome; and the blessedness and kindness and good-will bestowed by others.

Numbers of people are today suffering the fiery torments of an unforgiving spirit, and only when they make an effort to overcome that spirit can they know what a cruel and exacting taskmaster they are serving. Only those who have abandoned the service of such a master for that of the nobler master of forgiveness can realize and know how grievous a service is the one, how sweet the other.

Let a man contemplate the strife of the world: how individuals and communities, neighbors and nations, live in continual retaliations towards each other; let him realize the heartaches, the bitter tears, the grievous partings and misunderstandings - yea, even the blood-shed and woe which spring from that strife - and, thus realizing, he will never again yield to ignoble thoughts of resentment, never again take offense at the actions of others, never again live in unforgiveness towards any being.

"Have good-will To all that lives, letting unkindness die And greed and wrath; so that your lives be made Like soft airs passing by."

When a man abandons retaliation for forgiveness he passes from darkness to light. So dark and ignorant is unforgiveness that no being who is at all wise or enlightened could descend to it; but its darkness is not understood and known until it is left behind, and the better and nobler course of conduct is sought and practiced. Man is blinded and deluded only by his own dark and sinful tendencies; and the giving up of all unforgiveness means the giving up of pride and certain forms of passion, the abandonment of the deeply-rooted idea of the importance of one-self and of the necessity for protecting and defending that self; and when that is done the higher life, greater wisdom, and pure enlightenment, which pride and passion completely obscured, are revealed in all their light and beauty.

Then there are petty offenses, little spites and passing slights, which, while of a less serious nature than deep-seated hatreds and revenges, dwarf the character and cramp the soul. They are due to the sin of self and self-importance and thrive on vanity. Whosoever is blinded and deluded by vanity will continually see something in the actions and the attitudes of others towards him at which to take offense, and the more there is of vanity the more greatly will the imaginary slight or wrong be exaggerated. Moreover, to live in the frequent indulgence of petty resentments increase the spirit of hatred, and leads gradually downward to greater darkness, suffering, and self-delusion. Don't take offense or allow your feelings to be hurt, which means - get rid of pride and vanity. Don't give occasion for offense or hurt the feelings of others, which means - be gently considerate, forgiving, and charitable towards all.

The giving up - the total uprooting - of vanity and pride is a great task; but it is a blessed task, and it can be accomplished by constant practice in non-resentment and by meditating upon one's thoughts and actions so as to understand and purify them; and the spirit of forgiveness is perfected in one in the measure that pride and vanity are overcome and abandoned.

The not-taking-offense and the not-giving-offense go together. When a man ceases to resent the actions of others he is already acting kindly towards them, considering them before himself or his own defense. Such a man will be gently in what he says and does, will arouse love and kindness in others, and not stir them up to ill-will and strife. He will also be free from all fear concerning the actions of others towards him, for he who hurts none fears none. But the unforgiving man, he who is eager to "pay back" some real or imaginary slight or injury, will not be considerate towards others, for he considers himself first, and is continually making enemies; he also loves in the fear of others, thinking that that they are trying to do towards him as he is doing towards them. He who contrives the hurt of others fears others.

That is a beautiful story of Prince Dhirgayu which was told by an ancient Indian teacher to his disciples in order to impress them with the truth of the sublime percept that "hatred ceases not by hatred at any time; hatred ceases by not-hatred." The story is as follows: Brahmadatta, a powerful king of Benares, made war upon Dirgheti, the king of Kosala, in order to annex his kingdom, which was much smaller than his own. Dirgheti, seeing that it was impossible for him to resist the greater power of bramhadatta, fled, and left his kingdom in his enemy's hands. For some time he wandered from place to place in disguise, and at last settled down with his queen in an artisan's cottage; and the queen gave birth to a son, whom they called Dirghayu.

Now, King Brahmadatta was anxious to discover the hiding-place of Dirgheti, in order to put to death the conquered king, for he thought, "Seeing that I have deprived him of his kingdom he may someday treacherously kill me If I do not kill him."

But many years passed away, and Dirgheti devoted himself to the education of his son,. who by diligent application, became learned and skillful and wise.

And after a time Dirgheti's secret became known, and he, fearing that brahmadatta would discover him and slay all three, and thinking more of the life of his son than his own, sent away the prince. Soon after the exile king fell into the hands of Brahmadatta, and was, along with his queen, executed.

Now Brahmadatta thought: I have got rid of Dirgheti and his queen, but their son , Prince Dirghayu, lives, and he will be sure to contrive some means of effecting my assassination; yet he is unknown to any, and I have no means of discovering him." So the king lived in great fear and continual distress of mind.

Soon after the execution of his parents, Dirghayu, under an assumed name, sought employment in the king's stables, and was engaged by the master of elephants.

Dirghayu quickly endeared himself to all, and his superior abilities came at last under the notice of the king, who had the young man brought before him, and was so charmed with him that he employed him in his own castle, and he proved to be so able and diligent that the king shortly placed him in a position of great trust under himself.

One day the king went on a long hunting expedition, and became separated from his retinue, Dirghayu alone remaining with him. And the king, being fatigued with his exertions, lay down, and slept with his head in Dirghayu's lap.

Then Dirghayu thought: This king has greatly wronged me. He robbed my father of his kingdom, and slew my parents, and he is now entirely in my power." And he drew his sword, thinking to slay Brahmadatta. But, remembering how his father had taught him never to seek revenge but to forgive to the uttermost, he sheathed his sword.

At last the king awoke out of a disturbed sleep, and the youth inquired of him why he looked so frightened. "My sleep", said the king "is always restless, for I frequently dream that I am in the power of young Dirghayu and that he is alone to slay me. While lying here I again dreamed that with greater vividness than ever before and it has filled me with dread and terror.

Then the youth, drawing his sword, said: "I am Prince Dirghayu, and you are in my power: the time of vengeance has arrived."

Then the king fell upon his knees and begged Dirghayu to spare his life. And Dirghayu said: "It is you, O King! who must spare my life. For many years you have wished to find me in order that you might kill me; and , now that you have found me, let me beg of you to grant me my life."

And there and then did Brahmadatta and Dirghayu grant each other life, took hands, and solemnly vowed never to harm each other. And so overcome was the king by the noble and forgiving spirit of Dirghayu that he gave him his daughter in marriage, and restored to him his father's kingdom.

Thus hatred ceases by not-hatred - by forgiveness, which is very beautiful, and is sweeter and more effective than revenge. It is the beginning of love, of that divine love that does not seek its own; and he who practices it, who perfects himself in it, comes at last to realize that blessed state wherein the torments of pride and vanity and hatred and retaliation are forever dispelled, and good-will and peace are unchanging and unlimited. In that state of calm, silent bliss, even forgiveness passes away, and is no longer needed, for he who has reached it sees no evil to resent but only ignorance and delusion on which to have compassion, and forgiveness is only needed so long as there is any tendency to resent, retaliate, and take offense. Equal love towards all is the perfect law, the perfect state in which all lesser states find their completion. Forgiveness is one of the doorways in the faultless temple of Love Divine.

The complete text of the book behind this excerpt may be found in -

Law of Attraction: Byways of Blessedness

(Please see Bibliography for details.)

Ernest Holmes

One of the most influential writers and lecturers of New Thought, Holmes wrote "Science of Mind" in 1926, which quickly became a handbook and textbook for many people studying in this field.

While he initially studied Christian Science, his wide-ranging mind soon took him beyond the scope of their teachings. He wrote numerous books on theology and founded a religious organization which continues to this day.

His work on the Law of Attraction is represented here in a single chapter, though his text continues to expand on this and other natural laws.

His book is a classic any serious or casual student should have for study and reference.

Science of Mind

Lesson One: Introduction

In presenting these lessons in Mental Science to the public, it is my desire to make it possible for any one, who cares to take the time to study them, to demonstrate the truths that will be discussed. It is, perhaps, hard to set down in writing a complete teaching in Mental Science that will not appear difficult to understand; but this could be said as well of any science, and the Science of Mind is no exception to the general rule.

SCIENCE

Science is knowledge of facts built around some proven principle. All that we know about any science is that certain things happen under certain conditions. Take electricity as an example; we know that there is such a thing as electricity; we have never seen it, but we know that it exists because we can use it; we know that it operates in a certain way and we have discovered the way it works. From this knowledge we go ahead and deduce certain facts about electricity; and, applying them to the general principle, we receive definite results. No one has ever seen the power or the energy that we call electricity; and the only proof we have that it really exists is that from it we receive light, heat and motive power.

No one has ever seen any of the great causes that lie back of the manifestations of life, and perhaps no one ever will; but we know that such principles exist because we can use them.

HOW LAWS ARE DISCOVERED

The discovery of a law is generally made more or less by accident, or by some one who, after careful thought and observation, has come to the conclusion that such a principle must exist. As soon as a law is discovered experiments are made with it, certain facts are proved to be true, and in this way a science is gradually formulated; for any science consists of the number of known facts about any given principle. As more and more facts are gathered and proven, the science expands and gradually becomes accepted by all and used by those who understand it. In this way all of our sciences have been evolved until to-day we have the use of powers and unseen forces of which our ancestors never even dreamed.

PROOF OF MIND

This is true of the Science of Mind. No one has ever seen Mind or Spirit, but who could possibly doubt their existence? Nothing is more self-evident than that we live; and since we live, we must have life; yet who has ever seen this life? The only proof of life we have is that we live; and the only proof we have of Mind is that we can think; so we are perfectly justified in believing that we have a mind and that we live.

WHERE OUR THOUGHTS GO

As we watch the processes of thought we find that we think consciously, and we also find that something happens to our thoughts after we have thought them; for instance, they become memory. This proves that we have a deeper aspect of mind, which is called subjective, lying just below the threshold of the conscious. This subjective mind is the place where our thoughts go and from whence they eventually return to us again as memory. Observation proves this to be true; for it always happens this way.

Observation has proven that the subjective mind is the seat of memory and that it contains mental pictures, or impressions, of all that has ever happened to the individual. As these mental impressions come to the surface of the conscious mind they are called memories.

Moreover observation has shown that the subjective mind is the builder of the body. It has proven that it is not only the seat of memory; it is also the avenue through which Instinctive

Man works. We mean by Instinctive Man that part of the individual which came with him when he was born--that inner something which makes him what he is. For instance, we do not have to consciously think to make the body function; so we say that the inner, or the Instinctive, Man, does this for us. This is true of most of the functions of the body; they appear to be automatic; they came with us and are nature's way of working through us. So we say that in the unconscious or the sub-conscious or the subjective, there is a silent process forever working away and always doing its duty, carrying on all of the unconscious activities of the body without effort on our part.

SUGGESTION BECOMES MEMORY

It has been observed that suggestions, planted in the subconscious, become memories, and eventually tend to externalize in the body. From this it has been deduced that the sub-conscious mind is the builder of the body and is the creative factor in man. It has also been proven that certain types of thought produce certain kinds of results. This shows that the subjective mind takes our suggestions and tends to act upon them, no matter what the suggestion may be.

While the Instinctive Man, or the Natural Man, must be perfect, it is known that the thoughts of the conscious man may hinder instinctive action, through adverse suggestion. That is, conscious thought, acting as memory, may build a false condition in the body, which condition we call disease. Conscious thought may also erase this memory and thereby heal the disease.

Through observations such as these, a science of the subjective mind has gradually been formulated, many facts have been put together; and, to-day, these facts constitute what we call the science of the subjective life in its relationship to mental healing.

MENTAL MEDIUM THROUGH ALL

It has also been proven that thought operates in such a manner as to make it possible to convey mental impressions from one person to another, showing that there is a mental medium between all people. When we think of it, how could we talk with each other unless there were some kind of a medium through which we talked? We could not; and so we know that there really is such a medium. While there is a place where our bodies begin and leave off, as form, there does not appear to be a place where our thought leaves off. Indeed, the observations made and the facts gathered show that the medium between men's minds is omnipresent; that is, it seems to be everywhere present. Radio also shows this, for messages are sent out through some kind of a universal medium, and all that we can say of it is that we know the medium is there. So it is with Mind; all that we can say is that everything happens just as though it were there. We have a perfect right, then, to say that such a medium exists.

This opens up a far-reaching theory, for it leads to the conclusion that we are surrounded by a Universal Mind which is the Medium of the communication of our thoughts. Perhaps this is the Mind of God! Who knows? That It is there, we cannot doubt.

READING THOUGHT

Other observations have shown even more wonderful possibilities. It is known that certain people can read our thoughts, even when we are not aware of the fact, showing that thought operates through a medium which is universal, or always present. This also shows that the medium is subjective; for it retains our thoughts and transmits them to others. This leads to the conclusion that what we call our subjective mind is really the use that we, as individuals, make of something which is universal. Perhaps, just as radio messages are operative through a universal medium, our thoughts are operative through the medium of a Universal Mind. Indeed, this has been believed for thousands of years by some of the deepest thinkers.

MENTAL LAW

As we think of the medium of radio transmission in terms of law, so we should think of the Mental Medium in terms of law; for it must be the law of mental action. While we might think of it as the Mind of God, we surely could not think of it as the Spirit of God; for the Mental Medium is automatic, while the Spirit must be Self-Knowing. We could not call the Universal Medium of Mind God, any more than we could call electricity God. It is but one of the many attributes of God or the Universe of Life. It is the avenue through which God operates as Law.

THE WORD OF GOD AS LAW

Since man has a self-conscious mind, a subconscious mind and a body, we know that he is threefold in his nature. First, he is conscious mind or spirit; next, he is subconscious mind or mental law; and then, he is body. The conscious mind controls the subconscious; and in its turn, the subconscious controls the body.

It is evident that man comes from God, Life or Nature, whichever we choose to call It. It is also evident that we can get from Life only that which is in It. Man must partake of the Divine Nature if he comes from It or is made out of It; for what is true of the Whole must also be true of any of Its parts. Something cannot come from nothing; something must come from something; for nothing comes from nothing and nothing is the result; but man is something, else he could not declare himself; and since he is something, he must be made from, or come out of, something; and that something must be what we call God.

THREEFOLD NATURE OF GOD

If we study the true nature of man, then, we shall have delved into the real nature of God, or First Cause, from which man springs; and as we have found that man is threefold in his nature, so we must also deduce that God is threefold in His

Nature; that is, God is Spirit, or Self-Knowingness; God is Law and action; and God is Result or Body. This is the inner meaning of the teaching of "the Trinity." But let us elaborate: God, as Self-Knowing Spirit, means the Divine Being Whom we have always thought of and believed in; the Being to Whom we have prayed and Whom we have adored. God, as Law, means the way in which the Spirit works; and Law in this sense, would be the servant of the Spirit. God, as Body, means the manifestation of the Spirit. We might put it in another form and say, there is the Thing, the way that It works and the result of Its work. Still another form would be to say, Cause, Medium and Effect.

TRINITY OF BEING

A trinity of being appears to run through all Nature and all Life; for instance, there is electricity, the way it works and its result, which is light or motive power. There is the seed, the creative medium of the soil and the plant. Turn it as we may, we are confronted with the necessity of a trinity of being. There must always be the thing, what it does and the way that it operates. Always a trinity runs through life and through everything in it. But through the Trinity of God and man there runs a Self-Conscious Spirit, and this is what distinguishes man from the brute, or from a purely mechanical creation; and is the only thing that could make God a Self-Knowing Power.

CONSCIOUS MIND IN GOD AND MAN

In God and in man there is a power that, while it may not transcend law, yet consciously uses it for definite purposes. In God this knowledge must be complete, but in man it is, of course, but dimly perceived. Jesus, the wisest Man who ever lived, said that God and man are One in real nature, and no doubt this understanding was what gave Him His marvelous power.

UNITY

It is well to remember that the enlightened in every age have taught that back of all things there is One Unseen Cause: In studying the teachings of the great thinkers we find that a common thread runs through all--the thread of Unity. There is no record of any deep thinker, of any age, who taught duality. One of the great teachings of Moses was, "Hear, O Israel, the Lord our God is One Lord"; and the saying, "I AM that I AM," was old when Moses was yet unborn; for it had been inscribed over the temple entrances for generations. We may go back much farther than Moses and find the same teaching, for it crops out from the literatures and sayings of the wise of all ages. Jesus taught this when He said, "I and the Father are One," and in the saying, "The Father that dwelleth in me."

This teaching of Unity is the chief cornerstone of the Sacred Scriptures of the East as well as of our own Sacred Writings. It is to-day the mainspring of the teachings of the modern philosophies, such as Christian Science, Divine Science, The Unity Teachings, The New Thought Movement, The Occult Teachings, The Esoteric or Inner Teachings, and even of much that is taught under the name of Psychology. Without this basic teaching of Unity these movements would have but little to offer. Science has found nothing to contradict this teaching, and it never will, for the teaching is self-evident.

WORSHIP OF GOD

That there is a God or First Cause no one can doubt. That the Being Whom we call God really exists from eternity to eternity is self-evident. In every age people have worshiped some kind of Deity. It is true that as the evolution of man has progressed the idea of God has expanded, and the more that people have realized of life, and of nature and her laws, the clearer has been the concept of Deity, for this is the logical result of an unfolding mentality.

MANY GODS

The first stages of human thought brought out the idea that there were many gods, the natural outcome of a life which experienced many kinds of misfortune and difficulties. As there were many gods so there were many devils or evil powers; but as the understanding of man grew he began to realize that there could not be so many powers, since the Cause back of everything must be a Unity, else It could not exist. More than one power would indicate a universe divided against itself, and this kind of a universe could not hold together. However, it has taken a long time to come to this conclusion, and in the stages between many weird ideas have been formulated and believed in. At first there were many gods and many devils; but as thought progressed, this was narrowed down to One God and one devil or evil power. Duality has been believed in since time immemorial, and, indeed, is still believed in by many. By duality we mean a belief in more than One Power back of all things.

BELIEF IN DUALITY--ITS RESULTS

The belief in duality has robbed theology of power and has polluted philosophy with untruths; it has divided science against itself and has made countless thousands go through life with saddened hearts.

DUALITY IN THEOLOGY

The belief in duality has given rise in theology to the idea of a God and a devil, each with equal power to impose upon man a blessing or a curse, and men have worshiped a devil just as truly as they ever worshiped God. Even to-day this monstrous thought is robbing men of their birthright to happiness and a sense of security. Even to-day, and openly, men still teach that there is an evil power in the universe, that there is damnation to the souls of those who do not fall down and worship--they know not what. But the time is rapidly coming when such teachings will be thrown on the scrap heap and numbered among the delusions of a frantic mentality. It has been the habit of many religious teachers of all times to hold the crowd in awe before a mighty throne of condemnation and utter destruction, till the poor, ignorant population have rent the air with their lamentations of complete despair. This, indeed, was a good method to compel the attention with the hope of salvation through some sacred rites to be performed by those whom God had appointed. In justice to such an awful performance, we would better give to these religious teachers the benefit of the doubt and say that they themselves have believed in the atrocious teachings which they have so unhesitatingly given out.

Be this as it may, the time has now come for a clearer understanding of the true nature of the Deity, in Whom we all believe, and Whom we all seek to know and to understand. That there is a God no sane person would deny; that there could be a God of vengeance and hate, having all the characteristics of a huge man in a terrible rage, no person can well believe and keep his sanity. We will say, then, and without mincing matters in the least, that the most we had better believe about such a God is that there is no such being.

DUALITY IN PHILOSOPHY

As the belief in duality has robbed theology of its greater message, so it has robbed much of the philosophy of the ages of a greater truth; for in philosophy the belief in duality has created a confusion that is almost as great as that in theology. It has made a philosophy of good and evil in which men have come to believe. True philosophy in every age, however, has perceived that the Power back of all things must be One Power; and the clearer the thought of Unity, the greater has been the philosophy. It has shone forth as a beacon light toward which weary souls have traveled, hoping to find reality. To the great philosophers of all times we owe the advancement of the world; for they have been the great way-showers and helpers of mankind. In reverence, we humbly bow before them as Messengers of the Most High; for God has spoken through their lips and has told us that we are not creatures of the dust but that we are Divine Beings, made in the image of Perfection and with an endless destiny.

DUALITY AND SCIENCE

The belief in duality has robbed science, in that it has created Spirit and matter; i.e., a dual universe. However, modern science is rapidly giving out a different idea of the universe; for with the passing of matter into a hypothetical and theoretical ether there is but little left on which to hang any belief in materialism. We now are told that all matter is in a constant state of flow; that it all comes from one source; and that it will eventually return to that source.

AN AWAKENING

The world is waking up to the fact that things are not at all what they appear to be; that matter and form are but the one substance appearing and disappearing; and that form is simply used to express something which is formless, but self-conscious life. What this life is, science does not attempt to explain. This has been left to theology, and whether or not it has been delegated to those competent to handle the problem time alone will tell.

PHILOSOPHY LEADS MAN'S THOUGHT

Philosophy has always transcended science and always will; for philosophy deals with causes while science deals with effects. A scientist observes the result of nature's work while a philosopher speculates as to its cause. Many things which philosophy has taught for thousands of years are to-day being demonstrated by science. The two should really go hand in hand; for one deals with causes and the other with effects. True philosophy and true science will some day meet on a common basis; and, working together, will give to the world a theology of reality. Then, indeed, will "God go forth anew into Creation."

A DEEP INQUIRY

The deep thinkers of antiquity as well as the philosophers of all ages have meditated long and earnestly on the nature of the Divine Being. Knowing that there could be but One Ultimate Reality back of all things, they have pondered deeply upon the nature of that Reality; and it is a significant fact that all of the greatest thinkers have come to about the same conclusion.

THE GREAT DIFFICULTY

The difficulty that has beset the path of true philosophy has been the necessity of explaining a multiplied Creation with a Unitary Cause. Nothing is more evident than that we live in a world of constant change. Things and forms come and go continuously; forms appear only to disappear; things happen only to stop happening; and it is no wonder that the average person, unused to trying to discover causes, is led to feel and to believe that there is a multiple cause back of the world of things.

The philosophers of all times have had to meet the difficulty of explaining how One Cause could manifest Itself in a multiplicity of forms without dividing or breaking up the One. This has not been easy, yet, when understood, the explanation becomes very apparent.

THE VOICE OF GOD IN CREATION

The argument has been something after this manner: The Ultimate Cause back of all things must be One, since Life cannot be divided against Itself; the Infinite must be One, for there could not be two Infinites. Whatever change takes place must take place within the One; but the One must be Changeless; for, being One and Only, It cannot change into anything but Itself. All seeming change, then, is really only the play of Life upon Itself; and all that happens must happen by and through It. How do these things happen through It? By some inner action upon Itself. What would be the nature of this inner action? It could not be physical, as we understand physics, but would have to be by the power of the inner Word of Life; that is, the Voice of God, God standing for the First great and Only Cause of all that Is.

THE WORD OF GOD

It is impossible to conceive of anything other than the Word of God being that which sets power in motion. This is why the Scriptures announce that, "In the beginning was the Word, and the Word was with God and the Word was God. All things were made by Him, and without Him was not anything made that was made." God speaks and it is done.

It is evident that First Cause must be Self-Existent; that is, It must be Causeless. Nothing came before That Which was First; and, while it may be a little hard to understand this, yet we can all grasp the fact that whatever the Being is Whom we call God, It must be Self-Existent.

SPIRIT KNOWS ITSELF

God speaks and it is done; but if God speaks, His Word must be Law. The Word of God is also the Law of God. God is Word, God is Law and God is Spirit; this is self-evident. We arrive at the conclusion that God, as Spirit, is Self-Conscious Life. That Spirit is conscious is proven by the fact that we have evidence of this consciousness strewn through all time and space. God must know that God Is. This is the inner meaning of the teaching of the "I AM," handed down from antiquity. "The Spirit is the Power that knows Itself," is one of the oldest sayings of time.

LAW, SERVANT OF THE WORD

Spirit knows Itself, but the Law is the servant of the Spirit and is set in motion through Its Word. It is known that all law is some form of universal force or energy. Law does not know itself; law only knows to do; it is, therefore, the servant of the Spirit. It is the way that the Spirit works; and is the medium through which It operates to fulfill Its purpose.

Did God make law? As it is not possible to conceive a time when law did not operate, it is impossible to conceive that it was ever created; therefore, law must be coexistent and coeternal with Spirit. We might say that law is one of the attributes of Spirit.

The Spirit operated through law which is some part of Its own Nature; therefore, all action must be some action of Spirit as Law. The Word of Spirit sets Its purposes in motion through the law; and since the law must be as Infinite as the Spirit, we could not think of a time when it was not, or a time when it would cease to be; neither can we imagine the law ever failing to operate when set in motion.

We have, then, an Infinite Spirit and an Infinite Law; Intelligence and the way that It works; God, working through Law, which is unfailing and certain.

FORMS OF SPIRIT OR CREATION

Next, we come to the forms of Spirit, which forms we call matter. But what is matter? Science tells us that matter is eternal and indestructible; that, at first, it is an invisible cosmic stuff; and that it gradually takes form through some law working within it. The worlds were formed by the power of His Word. We know that right now worlds are being formed in the vast reaches of space, and worlds are also ceasing to be; that is, they are gradually losing their form. In this way Creation is eternally going on. This proves a definite purposefulness, a definite law set in motion to work out this purposefulness, and a definite form as the result of the operation of this purposefulness. In other words, it shows that there is an Intelligence inherent in the universe which knows what It is doing, and how to do it, and which knows why It does it; and that there is a law obeying Its will. It also shows that there is something upon which It operates. This "something" we will call matter in its unformed state. Perhaps this is "the ether" of science; it is impossible to say; but surely there is something upon which the Spirit works.

The teaching of the great thinkers of all times is that we live in a threefold universe of Spirit, Soul and Body--of Intelligence, Substance and Form.

MEANING OF CREATION

With this in mind, we shall be better able to realize that Creation does not mean making something out of nothing, but means the passing of Substance into form through a law which is set in motion by the Word of Spirit. Creation is eternally going on; for we could not imagine a time when the activity of Spirit would cease. It is "the same yesterday, to-day and forever."

The whole action of Spirit must be within Itself, upon the Law, which is also within Itself, and upon the Universal Stuff, or matter, which is also within Itself. The three must in reality be One; hence, "The Trinity."

THE WORD ALONE IS CONSCIOUS

One of the main facts to bear in mind is, that, of the three attributes of Spirit, the Word alone is conscious of Itself. The Law is force, and matter is simply stuff ready to take form. Since law or energy is proven to be timeless, that is, not added to or taken from; and since matter is known to be of the same nature, we have a right to suppose that both matter and law are coexistent and coeternal with Spirit. But Spirit alone is Conscious. Law, of itself, is only a force, and matter has no mind of its own. Law is not a thinker but is a doer, while matter cannot think but is thought upon.

THE THOUGHT OF GOD

Just what is meant by the Word of God? This must mean the Inner Consciousness, or Self-Knowingness, of Spirit; the Thought of God. The word "thought" seems to mean more to us than any other word; it seems to cover the meaning better, for we know that thought is an inner process or consciousness.

The Thought of God must be back of all that really exists, and, as there are many things that really exist, there must be many thoughts in the Mind of the Infinite. This is logical to suppose; for an Infinite Mind can think of an infinite number of ideas. Hence the world of multiplicity or many things. But the world of multiplicity does not contradict the world of Unity; for the many live in the One.

ETERNAL CREATION

There may be confusion in the minds of men but not in the Thought of God; and so we have a universe expressing the limitless Ideas of a Limitless Mind, and without confusion. We have, then, a Cosmic World, and an infinite and endless Creation. This is the inner meaning of those mystic words, "World without end." Creation always was and always will be. Things may come and things may go, but Creation goes on forever; for It is the Thought of God coming into expression. This is, indeed, a wonderful concept, for it means that there will always be a manifestation of the Divine Ideas. We need not worry about whether it will ever cease; it cannot cease so long as God exists; and since God will be forever, there will forever be some kind of manifestation.

THE UNIVERSE IS ALIVE

The universe is alive with action and power, with energy and life. We touch it only in parts, but from these parts we do catch a glimpse of the nature of the Whole. "He hath not left Himself without a witness."

Modern science is revealing many things that the great thinkers of the ages have announced. One of them is that matter is in a constant state of flow; it is like a river flowing in, out and on; it is operated upon by an unseen force or law and takes its form through some agency which science supposes to be the Will and Purpose of Spirit. This we call the Word. All things were made by the Word.

CONCLUSION

To sum up: There is a power in the universe which acts as though It were Intelligent and we may assume that It is. There is an activity in the universe which acts as law. We know this to be true. And there is a formless stuff in the universe, forever taking form, and forever changing its form; this also is self-evident. We have every right, then, to assume that there is a threefold nature of Being which we will call Spirit, Soul and Body. We will think of the Spirit as the great Actor, the Soul as the medium of Its action, and the Body as the result of this action. We will think of Spirit as the only Conscious Actor, the only Power that knows Itself. We will think of Soul as a blind force, obeying the Will of Spirit; and we will think of Body as the effect of the Spirit, working through law, thus producing form. We will say that neither the Law nor the stuff from which form comes has any conscious intelligence, but must, because of its nature, take the form of the Word. This simplifies the whole matter and enables us to see that in the entire universe One Power Alone really acts, the Power of the Word of God.

The complete text of the book behind this excerpt may be found in -

Law of Attraction: Science of Mind

(Please see Bibliography for details.)

Charles Fillmore

Truly a success story for those who wish to follow that "voice within" and achieve their dreams.

He and his wife healed themselves of their physical ailments through New Thought teachings. Intrigued by these new teachings, Charles soon began to form his vision of what he would accomplish. While he first formed a prayer group, he soon began publishing and quickly owned his own publishing house.

While he published many authors through his magazines (such as W. W. Atkinson above), his "Daily Word" is still one of the highest circulation magazines today.

He founded the Unity School of Christianity, which has one of the largest congregations worldwide.

Here we have an excerpt from his work "Prosperity" - where he gives us helpful lessons in how to apply the Law of Attraction to attain all the prosperity you can stand in your life...

Prosperity

Chapter 4 - Man, the Inlet and Outlet of Divine Mind

THE POSSESSIONS of the Father are not in stocks and bonds but in the divine possibilities implanted in the mind and soul of every man. Through the mind of man ideas are brought into being. Through the soul of man God's wealth of love finds its expression.

It is well said that the mind is the crucible in which the ideal is transmuted into the real. This process of transformation is the spiritual chemistry we must learn before we are ready to work intelligently in the great laboratory of the Father's substance. There is no lack of material there to form what we will, and we can all draw on it as a resource according to our purpose. Wealth of consciousness will express itself in wealth of manifestation.

One who knows Principle has a certain inner security given him by the understanding of God-Mind. Our affirmations are for the purpose of establishing in our consciousness a broad understanding of the principles on which all life and existence depend. Our religion is based on a science in which ideas are related to Principle and to other ideas in a great universal Mind that works under mental laws. It is not a new religion nor a religious fad but points out the real and the true in any religion. If you know Principle, you are able to know at once whether a religion is founded on facts or has a basis of man-made ideas.

In order to demonstrate Principle we must keep establishing ourselves in certain statements of the law. The more often you present to your mind a proposition that is logical and true the stronger becomes that inner feeling of security to you. The mind of man is built on Truth and the clearer your understanding of Truth is the more substantial your mind becomes. There is a definite and intimate relation between what we call Truth and this universal substance of Being. When the one Mind is called into action in your mind by your thinking about it, it lays hold of the substance by the **law of attraction** or sympathy of thought. Thus the more you know about God the more successful you will be in handling your body and all your affairs. The more you know about God the healthier you will be, and of course the healthier you are the happier, more beautiful, and better you will be in every way. If you know how to take hold of the universal substance and mold it to your uses, you will be prosperous. Mind substance enters into every little detail of your daily life whether you realize the Truth or not. However, to establish yourself in a certain security in the possession and use of universal life, love, intelligence, and substance, you must get a consciousness of it by first mentally seeing the Truth.

All true action is governed by law. Nothing just happens. There are no miracles. There is no such thing as luck. Nothing comes by chance. All happenings are the result of cause and can be explained under the law of cause and effect. This is a teaching that appeals to the innate logic of our mind, yet we sometimes feel like doubting it when we see things happen that have no apparent cause. These happenings that seem miraculous are controlled by laws that we have not yet learned and result from causes that we have not been able to understand. Man does not demonstrate according to the law but according to his knowledge of the law, and that is why we must seek to learn more of it. God is law and God is changeless. If we would bring forth the perfect creation, we must conform to law and unfold in our mind, body, and affairs as a flower unfolds by the principle of innate life, intelligence, and substance.

The United States Congress establishes laws that rule the acts of all American citizens. Those who keep the laws are rewarded by the protection of the law. Congress does not see to it that men obey the laws. That is left to the executive department of the government. The same thing is true of the universal law. God has ordained the law but does not compel us to follow it. We have free will, and the manner of our doing is left entirely to us. When we know the law and work with it, we are rewarded by its protection and use it to our good. If we break the universal law, we suffer limitations, just as a convicted lawbreaker is limited to a cell or prison. The Holy Spirit is the executive official through whom Divine Mind enforces its laws.

You can see from this consideration that God has bestowed the power of Divine Mind on every man. You are using your organism, body, mind, and soul, to carry out a law that God established as a guide for all creation. If you righteously fulfill this mission, you cannot fail to get the righteous results. If you fail to live in accordance with the law-- well, that is your affair. God cannot help it if you are not following the law and by it demonstrating health, happiness, prosperity, and all good. Blackstone said that law is a rule of action. So with God's law: if you follow the rules of action, you will demonstrate Truth. You will have all that God has prepared for you from the foundation of the world.

What are the rules of the law? First, God is good and all His creations are good. When you get that firmly fixed in your mind, you are bound to demonstrate good and nothing but good can come into your world. If you let in the thought that there is such a thing as evil and that you are as liable to evil as to good, then you may have conditions that conform to your idea of evil. But remember, evil and evil conditions are not recognized by Divine Mind. If you have thought of evil as a reality or as having any power over you, change your thought at once and begin to build up good brain cells that never heard about anything but good. Pray thus: I am a child of the absolute good. God is good, and I am good. Everything that comes into my life is good, and I am going to have only the good. Establish this consciousness and only the good will be attracted to you and your life will be a perpetual joy. I cannot tell you why this is true but I know that it is and that you can prove it for yourself to your satisfaction.

If you will start right now with the idea of universal and eternal goodness uppermost in your mind, talk only about the good, and see with the mind's eye everything and everybody as good, then you will soon be demonstrating all kinds of good. Good thoughts will become a habit, and good will manifest itself to you. You will see it everywhere. And people will be saying of you, "I know that that man is good and true. I have confidence in him. He makes me feel the innate goodness of all men." That is the way in which the one Mind expresses itself through man. It is the law. Those who live in accordance with the law will get the desired results. Those who fail to do so will get the opposite results.

The law also applies to our demonstrations of prosperity. We cannot be very happy if we are poor, and nobody needs to be poor. It is a sin to be poor. You may ask whether Jesus cited any example of poverty's being a sin? Yes. You will find it in the story of the prodigal son. That is often used as a text to preach to moral sinners, but a close study of it shows that Jesus was teaching the sin of lack and how to gain plenty. It is a wonderful prosperity lesson.

The prodigal son took his inheritance and went into a far country, where he spent it in riotous living and came to want. When he returned to his father's house he was not accused of moral shortcoming, as we should expect. Instead the father said, "Bring forth quickly the best robe and put it on him." That was a lesson in good apparel. It is a sin to wear poor clothes. This may seem to some to be rather a sordid way of looking at the teaching of Jesus, but we must be honest. We must interpret it as He gave it, not as we think it ought to be.

The next act of the father was to put a gold ring on the prodigal's finger, another evidence of prosperity. The Father's desire for us is unlimited good, not merely the means of a meager existence. The ring symbolizes the unlimited, that to which there is no end. It also represents omnipresence and omnipotence in the manifest world. When the father gave that ring to the son, he gave him the key to all life activity. It was the symbol of his being a son and heir to all that the father had. "All that is mine is thine." The Father gives us all that He has and is, omnipotence, omniscience, all love, and all substance when we return to the consciousness of His house of plenty.

"Put ... shoes on his feet" was the father's next command to the servants. Feet represent that part of our understanding that comes into contact with earthly conditions. In the head or "upper room" we have the understanding that contacts spiritual conditions, but when we read in Scripture anything about the feet, we may know that it refers to our understanding of things of the material world.

The next thing the father did for his returned son was to proclaim a feast for him. That is not the way we treat moral sinners. We decree punishment for them; we send them to jail. But the Father gives a feast to those who come to Him for supply. He does not dole out only a necessary ration but serves the "fatted calf," universal substance and life in its fullness and richness.

The parable is a great lesson on prosperity, for it shows us that people who are dissipating their substance in sense ways are sinners and eventually fall into a consciousness of lack. It also proves that they may become lawful and prosperous again by returning to the Father-Mind. When there are so many lessons in the Bible for moral delinquents, there is no need to twist the meaning of this parable to that purpose. It is so plainly a lesson on the cause of lack and want. Jesus expressly states that the youth wasted his substance in a "far country," a place where the divine law of plenty was not realized. There is a very close relation between riotous living and want. Persons who waste their substance in sensation come to want in both physical and financial ways. If we would make the right use of the divine substance and the divine law, we must come back to the consciousness of the Father and conserve our body substance. Then health and prosperity will become naturally manifest. If we are not resourceful or secure in our use of the one divine substance, we are not secure in anything. Substance is a very important thing in our world, in fact the foundation of it. Therefore we should be secure in our understanding of it and use it according to God's law.

Then let us enter into the very Truth of Being and observe the divine law. Let us realize that our Father is always here and that we are in a "far country" only when we forget His presence. He is constantly giving us just what we will acknowledge and accept under His law. We can take our inheritance and divorce ourselves in consciousness from the Father, but we shall suffer the results, for then we shall not do things in divine wisdom and divine order, and there will be a "famine" in that land. Let us rather seek the divine wisdom to know how to handle our substance and the law of prosperity will be revealed to us. To come into this realization, declare with faith and all assurance: The all-providing Mind is my resource, and I am secure in my prosperity.

Primitive men did not contend for the products of nature so long as they could easily pick the fruits from the trees and sleep beneath the branches. When they began to live in caves contention arose over the best places, and the strongest were usually the victors. "Success leads to success." Those who were able to take the best did so and proved the law that "whosoever hath, to him shall be given, and he shall have abundance." This seems at first thought to be an unjust law, but it has always prevailed in the affairs of the world. Jesus, the greatest of metaphysicians, taught it as a divine law and gave it His commendation. He could not have done otherwise, for it is a righteous law that man shall have what he earns, that industry, effort, and ability be rewarded and laziness discouraged.

This law operates in every department of being. Those who seek the things that the material realm has to offer usually find them. Those who strive for moral excellence usually attain that goal. Those who aspire to spiritual rewards are also rewarded. The law is that we get what we want and work for, and all experience and history have proved it a good law. If this law were removed, world progress would cease and the race become extinct. Where there is no reward for effort, there will be no effort and society will degenerate. We may talk wisely about the inner urge, but when it has no outer field of action it eventually becomes discouraged and ceases to act.

When men evolve spiritually to a certain degree, they open up inner faculties that connect them with cosmic Mind, and attain results that are sometimes so startling that they seem to be miracle workers. What seems miraculous is the action of forces on planes of consciousness not previously understood. When a man releases the powers of his soul, he does marvels in the sight of the material-minded, but he has not departed from the law. He is merely functioning in a consciousness that has been sporadically manifested by great men in all ages. Man is greater than all the other creations of God-Mind because he has the ability to perceive and to lay hold of the ideas inherent in God-Mind and through faith bring them into manifestation. Thus evolution proceeds by man's laying hold of primal spiritual ideas and expressing them in and through his consciousness.

In the exercise of his I AM identity man needs to develop certain stabilizing ideas. One of them is continuity or loyalty to Truth. In the Scriptures and in life we have many examples of how love sticks to the thing on which it has set its mind. Nothing so tends to stabilize and unify all the other faculties of mind as love. That is why Jesus gave as the greatest commandment that we love God.

When you first begin to think of God as everywhere present substance, your mind will not adhere continuously to the idea. You will drop your attention after a while and think, "I haven't enough to meet all our bills." There you have made a break and have lost momentum in your ongoing, and you must patch it up quickly. Affirm, "I am not going to be led astray. The old ideas are error and they are nothing. They have no power over me. I am going to stick to this proposition. God is love, the substance of my supply."

Ruth, the Moabitish woman, became so attached to Naomi (spiritual thought) that she would not leave her but accompanied her back to Palestine. She was loyal and steadfast because of her love. What was the result of her stick-to-itiveness? She was at first a gleaner; then became the wife of a very rich man and was immortalized as one of the ancestresses of David. This lesson of abiding in our highest ideals is one that we must understand. Nothing is so important as sticking to the ideal and never giving up the work we have set out to accomplish. Affirm the law continuously and be loyal to it and you will become successful in its demonstration.

You have doubtless found that there is a spiritual law that brings into manifestation the thoughts we concentrate our attention on, a divine universal law of mind activity that is unfailing. Some adverse condition of your own thought has prevented a full demonstration. Do not let this swerve you from your loyalty to the law. You may seem to attain results very slowly, but that is the best reason for sticking closely to your ideal and not changing your mind. Be loyal to Principle and the adverse condition will break up. Then the true light will come and the invisible substance you have been faithfully affirming will begin to reveal itself to you in all its fullness of good.

Jesus stressed the idea that God has made abundant provision for all His children, even to the birds of the air and the lilies of the field. The Lord has clothed you with soul substance as gloriously as He did Solomon. But you must have faith in this all-providing substance of good and by your continuity of imagination set it to forming the things you desire. If you are persistent in working this idea in your conscious mind, it will eventually drop down into your subconscious mind and continue to work there where things take form and become manifest. Invisible substance, when your subconsciousness becomes filled with it to the overflowing point, will ooze out, as it were, into all your affairs. You will become more prosperous and successful so gradually, simply, and naturally that you will not realize that it derives from a divine source and in answer to your prayers. We must realize all the while however that whatever we put as seed into the subconscious soil will eventually bring forth after its kind and we must exercise the greatest caution so that we do not think or talk about insufficiency or allow others to talk to us about it. As we sow in mind so shall we reap in manifestation.

Some of our well-meaning friends have a way of loading us up with "hard-times" ideas that disperse this prosperity substance that we have accumulated. Sometimes even one adverse thought will cause it to escape; then we must go back and patch up the broken reservoir of substance thinking. We have to hold it in our mind in all its fullness and we should not let go of it for a minute lest the work of demonstration be delayed. When you retire at night, let your last thought be about the abundance of spiritual substance. See it filling all the house and the minds of all the people in the house. That potent thought will then sink into your subconsciousness and continue to work whether you are asleep or awake.

The law of supply is a divine law. This means that it is a law of mind and must work through mind. God will not go to the grocery and bring food to your table. But when you continue to think about God as your real supply, everything in your mind begins to awaken and to contact the divine substance, and as you mold it in your consciousness, ideas begin to come which will connect you with the visible manifestation. You first get the ideas in consciousness direct from their divine source, and then you begin to demonstrate in the outer. It is an exact law and it is scientific and unfailing. "First the blade, then the ear, then the full grain in the ear."

When you work in harmony with this universal law, every needed thing is abundantly supplied. Your part is simply to fulfill the law; that is, to keep your mind filled with mind substance, to store up spiritual substance until the mind is filled with it and it cannot help but manifest in your affairs in obedience to the law "Whosoever hath, to him shall be given." But you are not fulfilling the law when you allow poverty-stricken thoughts to dwell in your mind. They draw other like thoughts, and your consciousness will have no room for the truth that prosperity is for you.

Poverty or prosperity, it all depends on you. All that the Father has is yours, but you alone are responsible for the relationship of the Father's good to your life. Through conscious recognition of your oneness with the Father and His abundance you draw the living substance into visible supply.

Do not hesitate to think that prosperity is for you. Do not feel unworthy. Banish all thoughts of being a martyr to poverty. No one enjoys poverty, but some people seem to enjoy the sympathy and compassion they can excite because of it. Overcome any leaning in that direction and every belief that you were meant to be poor. No one is ever hopeless until he is resigned to his imagined fate. Think prosperity, talk prosperity, not in general but in specific terms, not as something for the other fellow but as your very own right. Deny every appearance of failure. Stand by your guns and affirm supply, support, and success in the very face of question and doubt, then give thanks for plenty in all your affairs, knowing for a certainty that your good is now being fulfilled in Spirit, in mind, and in manifestation.

A Prosperity Treatment

Twenty-Third Psalm (Revised)

The Lord is my banker; my credit is good.
He maketh me to lie down in the consciousness of
omnipresent abundance;
He giveth me the key to His strongbox.
He restoreth my faith in His riches;
He guideth me in the paths of prosperity for His name's sake.
Yea, though I walk in the very shadow of debt,
I shall fear no evil, for Thou art with me;
Thy silver and Thy gold, they secure me.
Thou preparest a way for me in the presence of the collector;
Thou fillest my wallet with plenty; my measure runneth over.

Surely goodness and plenty will follow me all the days of my life,
And I shall do business in the name of the Lord forever.

The complete text of the book behind this excerpt may be found in -

Law of Attraction: Prosperity

(Please see Bibliography for details.)

Prentice Mulford

While he literally rubbed shoulders with the likes of Bret Harte and Mark Twain, as well as fellow miners in the gold-fever-stricken California, Prentice Mulford made his real legacy through the skills he learned in writing.

But the gold prospected in the soul was more his bent, and he is known for founding the philosophy of New Thought. His greatest work, "The White Cross Library" was produced during a 17-year sojourn in the New Jersey swamps.

Our excerpt is from those pages, where he tells about "some laws of health and beauty"...

Thoughts are Things

Chapter Seven - SOME LAWS OF HEALTH AND BEAUTY

YOUR thoughts shape your face, and give it its peculiar expression. Your thoughts determine the attitude, carriage, and shape of your whole body.

The law for beauty and the law for perfect health is the same. Both depend entirely on the state of a your mind; or, in other words, on the kind of thoughts you most put out and receive.

Ugliness of expression comes of unconscious transgressions of a law, be the ugliness in the young or the old.

Any form of decay in a human body, any form of weakness, anything in the personal appearance of a man or woman which makes them repulsive to you, is because their prevailing mood of mind has made them so.

Nature plants in us what some call "instinct," what we call the higher reason, because it comes of the exercise of a finer set of senses than our outer or physical senses, to dislike everything that is repulsive or deformed, or that shows signs of decay. That is the inborn tendency in human nature to shun the imperfect, and seek and like the relatively perfect. Your higher reason is right in disliking wrinkles or decrepitude, or any form or sign of the body's decay, for the same reason you are right in disliking a soiled or torn garment. Your body is the actual clothing, as well as the instrument used by your mind or spirit. It is the same instinct, or higher reason making you like a well-formed and beautiful body, that makes you like a new and tasteful suit of clothes.

You and generations before you, age after age, have been told it was an inevitable necessity, that it was the law and in the order of nature for all times and all ages, that after a certain period in life your body must wither and become unattractive, and that even your minds must fail with increasing years. You have been told that your mind had no power to repair and recuperate your body--to make it over again, and make it newer and fresher continually.

It is no more in the inevitable order of Nature, that human bodies should decay as peoples' bodies have decayed in the past, than that man should travel only by stagecoach as he did sixty years ago; or that messages could be sent only by letter as they were fifty years ago, before the use of the electric telegraph; or that your portraits could be taken only by the painter's brush as they were half a century ago, before the discovery that the sun could imprint an image of yourself, an actual part of yourself, on a sensitive surface prepared for it.

It is the impertinence of a dense ignorance for any of us to say what is in or what is to be in the order of nature.

It is a stupid blunder to look back at the little we know of the past, and say that it is the unerring index finger telling us what is to be in the future.

If this planet has been what geology teaches it has been,--a planet fuller of coarser, cruder, and more violent forces than now; abounding in forms of coarser vegetable, animal, and even human life and organization than now; of which its present condition is a refinement and improvement as regards vegetable, animal, and man,--is not this the suggestion, the hint, the proof, of a still greater refinement and improvement for the future; a refinement and improvement going on now? Does not refinement imply greater power, as the greater power of the crude iron comes out in steel; and are not these greater and as yet almost unrecognized powers to come out of the highest and most complex form of known organization, man; and are all of man's powers yet known?

Internally, secretly, among the thinking thousands of this and other lands, is this and many other questions now being asked: "Why must we so wither and decay, and lose the best that life is worth living for, just as we have gained that experience and wisdom that best fits us to live?" The voice of the people is always at first a whispered voice. The prayer or demand or desire of the masses is always at first a secret prayer, demand, wish, or desire, which one man at first dare scarcely whisper to his neighbor for fear of ridicule. But it is a law of Nature, that every demand, silent or spoken, brings its supply of the thing wished for in proportion to the intensity of the wish, and the growing numbers so wishing; who, by the action of their minds upon some one subject, set in motion that silent force of thought, not as yet heeded in the world's schools of philosophy, which brings the needed supply.

Millions so wished in silence for means to travel more rapidly, to send intelligence more rapidly; and this brought steam and the electric telegraph. Soon other questions and demands are to be answered, questions ever going out in silence from multitudes; and, in answering them, in at first attempting to carry out and prove the answers and the means shown to accomplish or realize many things deemed impossible or visionary, there will be mistake and stupidity, and blunder and silliness, and breakdowns and failures, and consequent ridicule; just as there were ten smashes on railways, and ten bursted boilers in the earlier era of the use of steam, to one of today. But a truth always goes straight ahead despite mistake and blunder, and proves itself at last.

There are two kinds of age,--the age of your body, and the age of your mind. Your body in a sense is but a growth, a construction, of today, and for the use of today. Your mind is another growth or construction millions of years old. It has used many bodies in its growth. It has grown from very small beginnings to its present condition, power, and capacity in the use of these many bodies. You have, in using these bodies, been far ruder and coarser than you are now. You have lived as now you could not live at all, and in forms of life or expression very different from the form you are now using; and each new body or young body you have worn has been a new suit of clothes for your mind; and what you call "death" has been and is but the wearing out of this suit through ignorance of the means, not so much of keeping it in repair, as of building it continually into a newer and newer freshness and vitality.

You are not young relatively. Your present youth means that your body is young. The older your spirit, the better can you preserve the youth, vigor, and elasticity of your body. Because the older your mind, the more power has it gathered from its many existences. You can use that power for the preservation of beauty, of health, of vigor, of all that can make you attractive to others. You can also unconsciously use the same power to make you ugly, unhealthy, weak, diseased, and unattractive. The more you use this power in either of these directions, the more will it make you ugly or beautiful, healthy or unhealthy, attractive or unattractive; that is, as regards unattractiveness for this one existence. Ultimately you must, if not in this in some other existence, be symmetrical; because the evolution of the mind, of which the evolution of our bodies from coarser to higher forms is but a crude counterpart, is ever toward the higher, finer, better, and happier.

That power is your thought. Every thought of yours is a thing as real, though you cannot see it with the physical, or outer eye, as a tree, a flower, a fruit. Your thoughts are continually molding your muscles into shapes and manner of movement in accordance with their character.

If your thought is always determined and decided, your step in walking will be decided. If your thought is permanently decided, your whole carriage, bearing, and address will show that if you say a thing you mean it.

If your thoughts are permanently undecided, you will have a permanently undecided gesture, address, carriage, or manner of using your body; and this, when long continued, will make the body grow decidedly misshapen in some way, exactly as when you are writing in a mood of hurry, your hurried thought makes misshapen letters, and sometimes misshapen ideas; while your reposeful mood or thought makes well-formed letters and graceful curves as well as well-formed and graceful ideas.

You are every day thinking yourself into some phase of character and facial expression, good or bad. If your thoughts are permanently cheerful, your face will look cheerful. If most of the time you are in a complaining, peevish, quarrelsome mood, this kind of thought will put ugly lines on your face; they will poison your blood, make you dyspeptic, and ruin your complexion; because then you are in your own unseen laboratory of mind, generating an unseen end poisonous element, your thought; and as you put it out or think it, by the inevitable Law of nature it attracts to it the same kind of thought-element from others. You think or open your mind to the mood of despondency or irritability, and you draw more or less of the same thought-element from every despondent or irritable man or woman in your town or city. You are then charging your magnet, your mind, with its electric thought-current of destructive tendency, and the law and property of thought connects all the other thought-currents of despondency or irritability with your mental battery, your mind. If we think murder or theft, we bring ourselves by this law into spiritual relationship and rapport with every thief or murderer in the world.

Your mind can make your body sick or well, strong or weak, according to the thought it puts out, and the action upon it of the thought of others. Cry "Fire!" in a crowded theater, and scores of persons are made tremulous, weak, paralyzed by fear. Perhaps it was a false alarm. It was only the thought of fire, a horror acting on your body, that took away its strength.

The thought or mood of fear has in cases so acted on the body as to turn the hair white in a few hours.

Angered, peevish, worried, or irritable thought effects injuriously the digestion. A sudden mental shock may lose one's whole appetite for a meal, or cause the stomach to reject such meal when eaten. The injury so done the body suddenly, in a relatively few cases, by fear or other evil state of mind, works injury more gradually on millions of bodies all over the planet.

Dyspepsia does not come so much of the food we eat, as of the thoughts we think while eating it. We may eat the healthiest bread in the world; and if we eat it in a sour temper, we will put sourness in our blood, and sourness in our stomachs, and sourness on our faces. Or if we eat in an anxious frame of mind, and are worrying all the time about how much we should eat or should not eat, and whether it may not hurt us after all, we are consuming anxious, worried, fretful thought-element with our food and it will poison us. If we are cheerful and chatty and lively and jolly while eating, we are putting liveliness and cheer into ourselves, and making such qualities more and more a part of ourselves. And if our family group eat in silence, or come to the table with a sort of forced and resigned air, as if saying, each one to him or herself, "Well, all this must be gone over again;" and the head of the family buries himself in his business cares, or his newspaper, and reads all the murders and suicides and burglaries and scandals for the last twenty-four hours; and the queen of the household buries herself in sullen resignation or household cares, then there are being literally consumed at that table, along with the food, the thought-element of worry and murder and suicide and the morbid element, which loves to dwell on the horrible and ghastly; and, as a result, dyspepsia, in some of its many forms, will be manufactured all the way down the line, from one end of the table to the other.

If the habitual expression of a face be a scowl, it is because the thoughts behind that face are mostly scowls.

If the corners of a mouth are turned down, it is because most of the time the thoughts which govern and shape that mouth are gloomy and despondent. If a face does not invite people, and make them desire to get acquainted with its wearer, it is because that face is a sign advertising thoughts behind it which the wearer may not dare to speak to others, possibly may not dare to whisper to himself.

The continual mood of hurry, that is, of being in mind or spirit in a certain place long before the body is there, will cause the shoulders to stoop forward; because in such mood you do literally send your thought, your spirit, your real though invisible self, to the place toward which your power, your thought, is dragging your body head first and through such life-long habit of mind does the body grow as the thought shapes it. A "self-contained" man is never in a hurry; and a self-contained man keeps or contains his thought, his spirit, his power, mostly on the act or use he is making at the present moment with the instrument his spirit uses, his body; and the habitually self-possessed woman will be graceful in every movement, for the reason that her spirit has complete possession and command of its tool, the body; and is not a mile or ten miles away from that body in thought, and fretting or hurrying or dwelling on something at that distance from her body.

When we form a plan for any business, any invention, any undertaking, we are making something of that unseen element, our thought, as real, though unseen, as any machine of iron or wood. That plan or thought begins, as soon as made, to draw to itself, in more unseen elements, power to carry itself out, power to materialize itself in physical or visible substance. When we dread a misfortune, or live in fear of any ill, or expect ill luck, we make also a construction of unseen element, thought,--which, by the same **law of attraction**, draws to it destructive, and to you damaging, forces or elements. Thus the law for success is also the law for misfortune, according as it is used; even as the force of a man's arm can save another from drowning, or strike a dagger to his heart. Of whatever possible thing we think, we are building, in unseen substance, a construction which will draw to us forces or elements to aid us or hurt us, according to the character of thought we think or put out.

If you expect to grow old, and keep ever in your mind an image or construction of yourself as old and decrepit, you will assuredly be so. You are then making yourself so.

If you make a plan in thought, in unseen element, for yourself, as helpless, and decrepit, such plan will draw to you of unseen thought-element that which will make you weak, helpless, and decrepit. If, on the contrary, you make for yourself a plan for being always healthy, active, and vigorous, and stick to that plan, and refuse to grow decrepit, and refuse to believe the legions of people who will tell you that you must grow old, you will not grow old. It is because you think it must be so, as people tell you, that makes it so.

If you in your mind are ever building an ideal of yourself as strong, healthy, and vigorous, you are building to yourself of invisible element that which is ever drawing to you more of health, strength, and vigor. You can make of your mind a magnet to attract health or weakness. If you love to think of the strong things in Nature, of granite mountains and heaving billows and resistless tempests, you attract to you their elements of strength.

If you build yourself in health and strength today, and despond and give up such thinking or building tomorrow, you do not destroy what in spirit and of spirit you have built up. That amount of element so added to your spirit can never be lost but you do, for the time, in so desponding, that is, thinking weakness, stop the building of your health-structure; and although your spirit is so much the stronger for that addition of element, it may not be strong enough to give quickly to the body what you may have taken from it through such despondent thought.

Persistency in thinking health, in imagining or idealizing yourself as healthy, vigorous, and symmetrical, is the cornerstone of health and beauty. Of that which you think most, that you will be, and that you will have most of. You say "No." But your bed-ridden patient is not thinking, "I am strong;" he or she is thinking, "I am so weak." Your dyspeptic man or woman is not thinking, "I will have a strong stomach." They are ever saying, "I can't digest anything;" and they can't, for that very reason.

We are apt to nurse our maladies rather than nurse ourselves. We want our maladies petted and sympathized with, more than ourselves. When we have a bad cold, our very cough sometimes says to others, unconsciously, "I am this morning an object for your sympathy. I am so afflicted!" It is the cold, then, that is calling out for sympathy. Were the body treated rightly, your own mind and all the minds about you would say to that weak element in you, "Get out of that body!" and the silent force of a few minds so directed would drive that weakness out. It would leave as Satan did when the man of Nazareth imperiously ordered him. Colds and all other forms of disease are only forms of Satan, and thrive also by nursing. Vigor and health are catching also as well as the measles.

What would many grown-up people give for a limb or two limbs that had in them the spring and elasticity of those owned by a boy twelve years old; for two limbs that could climb trees, walk on rail fences, and run because they loved to run, and couldn't help running? If such limbs so full of life could be manufactured and sold, would there not be a demand for them by those stout ladies and gentlemen who get in and out of their carriages as if their bodies weighed a ton? Why is it that humanity resigns itself with scarcely a protest to the growing heaviness, sluggishness, and stiffness that comes even with middle age? I believe, however, we compromise with this inertia, and call it dignity. Of course a man and a father and a citizen and a voter and a pillar of the State--of inertia--shouldn't run and cut up and kick up like a boy, because he can't. Neither should a lady who has grown to the dignity of a waddle run as she did when a girl of twelve, because she can't, either. Actually we put on our infirmities as we would masks, and hobble around in them, saying, "This is the thing to do, because we can't do anything else." Sometimes we are even in a hurry to put them on; like the young gentleman who sticks an eyeglass to his eye, and thereby the sooner ruins the sight of a sound organ, in order to look tony or bookish.

There are more and more possibilities In Nature, in the elements, and in man and out of man; and they come as fast as man sees and knows how to use these forces in Nature and in himself. Possibilities and miracles mean the same thing.

The telephone sprung suddenly on "our folks" of two hundred years ago would have been a miracle, and might have consigned the person using it to the prison or the stake: all unusual manifestations of Nature's powers being then attributed to the Devil, because the people of that period had so much of the Devil, or cruder element, in them as to insist that the universe should not continually show and prove higher and higher expressions of the higher mind for man's comfort and pleasure.

The complete text of the book behind this excerpt may be found in -

Law of Attraction: Thoughts Are Things

(Please see Bibliography for details.)

Ralph Waldo Trine

Probably one of the most influential of all New Thought writers after Troward, Trine lived simply his entire life. This simplicity shows in his writings.

Henry Ford attributed his success to Trine's "In Tune with the Infinite" and ordered bulk copies of it to distribute freely to high profile industrialists. This single book has sold over two million copies.

I include here an excerpt from that book...

In Tune With the Infinite

Chapter 5 - The Supreme Fact Of Human Life

From the great central fact of the universe in regard to which we have agreed? namely, this Spirit of Infinite Life that is behind all and from which all comes, we are led to inquire as to what is the great central fact in human life. From what has gone before, the question almost answers itself.

The great central fact in human life, in your life and mine, is the coming into a conscious, vital realization of our oneness with this Infinite Life, and the opening of ourselves fully to this divine inflow.

This is the great central fact in human life, for in this all else is included, all else follows in its train. In just the degree that we come into a conscious realization of our oneness with the Infinite Life, and open ourselves to this divine inflow, do we actualize in ourselves the qualities and powers of the Infinite Life.

And what does this mean? It means simply this: that we are recognizing our true identity, that we are bringing our lives into harmony with the same great laws and forces, and so opening ourselves to the same great inspirations, as have all the prophets, seers, sages, and saviors in the world's history, all men of truly great and mighty power. For in the degree that we come into this realization and connect ourselves with this Infinite Source, do we make it possible for the higher powers to play, to work, to manifest through us.

We keep closed to this divine inflow, to these higher forces and powers, through ignorance, as most of us do, and thus hinder or even prevent their manifesting through us. Or we can intentionally close ourselves to their operations and thus deprive ourselves of the powers to which, by the very nature of our being, we are rightful heirs. On the other hand, we can come into so vital a realization of the oneness of our real selves with this Infinite Life, and can open ourselves so fully to the incoming of this divine inflow, and so the operation of these higher forces, inspirations, and powers, that we can indeed and in truth become what we may well term, God-men.

And what is a God-man? One in whom the powers of God are manifesting, though yet a man. No one can set limitations to a man of this type, for the only limitations he can have are those set by the self. Ignorance is the most potent factor in setting limitations to the majority of mankind, and so the great majority of people continue to live their little, dwarfed, and stunted lives simply by virtue of the fact that they do not realize the larger life to which they are heirs. They have never as yet come into a knowledge of the real identity of their true selves.

Mankind has not yet realized that the real self is one with the life of God. Through its ignorance it has never yet opened itself to the divine inflow, and so has never made itself a channel through which the infinite powers and forces can manifest. When we know ourselves merely as men, we live accordingly, and have the powers of men. When we come into the realization of the fact that we are God-men, then again we live accordingly, and have the powers of God-men. In the degree that we open ourselves to this divine inflow are we changed from mere men into God-men.

A friend has a beautiful lotus pond. A natural basin on his estate -- his farm as he always calls it -- is supplied with water from a reservoir in the foothills some distance away. A gate regulates the flow of the water from the main that conducts it from the reservoir to the pond. It is a spot of transcendent beauty. There, through the days of the perfect summer weather, the lotus flowers lie full blown upon the surface of the clear, transparent water. The June roses and other wild flowers are continually blooming upon its banks. The birds come here to drink and bathe, and from early until late one can hear the melody of their song. The bees are continually at work in this garden of wild flowers. A beautiful grove, in which many kinds of wild berries and many varieties of brakes and ferns grow, stretches at the back of the pond as far as the eye can reach.

Our friend is a man, nay more, a God-man, a lover of his kind, and as a consequence no notice bearing such words as 'Private rounds, no trespassing allowed,' or Trespassers will be prosecuted,' stands on his estate. But at the end of a beautiful by-way that leads through the wildwood up to this enchanting spot, stands a notice bearing the words 'All are welcome to the Lotus Pond.' All love our friend. Why? They can't help it. He so loves them, and what is his is theirs.

Here one may often find merry groups of children at play. Here many times tired and weary-looking men come, and somehow, when they go their faces wear a different expression -the burden seems to be lifted, and now and then I have heard them when leaving, sometimes in a faint murmur, as if uttering a benediction, say, 'God bless our brother-friend.' Many speak of this spot as the Garden of God. My friend calls it his Soul Garden, and he spends many hours in quiet here. Often have I seen him after the others have gone, walking to and fro, or sitting quietly in the clear moonlight on an old rustic bench, drinking in the perfume of the wild flowers. He is a man of a beautifully simple nature. He says that here his greatest and most successful plans, many times as by a flash of inspiration, suggest themselves to him.

Everything in the immediate vicinity seems to breathe a spirit of kindliness, comfort, goodwill, and good cheer. The very cattle and sheep as they come to the old stone-fence at the edge of the grove and look across to this beautiful spot seem, indeed, to get the same enjoyment that the people are getting. They seem almost to smile in the realization of their contentment and enjoyment, or perhaps it seems so to the looker-on, because he can scarcely help smiling as he sees the manifested evidence of their contentment and pleasure.

The gate of the pond is always open wide enough to admit a supply of water so abundant that it continually overflows a quantity sufficient to feed a stream that runs through the fields below, giving the pure mountain water in drink to the cattle and flocks that are grazing there. The stream then flows on through the neighbor's fields.

Not long ago our friend was absent for a year. He rented his estate during his absence to a man who, as the world goes, was of a very 'practical' turn of mind. He had no time for anything that did not bring him direct practical returns. The gate connecting the reservoir with the lotus pond was shut down, and no longer had the crystal mountain water the opportunity to feed and overflow it. The notice of our friend, 'All are welcome to the Lotus Pond,' was removed, and no longer were the gay companies of children and of men seen at the pond. A great change came over everything. On account of the lack of the life-giving water the flowers in the pond wilted, and their long stems lay stretched upon the mud in the bottom. The fish that formerly swam in its clear water soon died and gave off an offensive odor to all who came near. The flowers no longer bloomed on its banks. The birds no longer came to drink and to bathe. No longer was heard the hum of the bees, and more, the stream that ran through the fields below dried up, so that the cattle and the flocks no longer got their supply of clear mountain water.

The difference between the spot now and the lotus pond when our friend gave it his careful attention was caused, as we readily see, by the shutting of the gate to the pond, thus preventing the water from the reservoir in the hills, which was the source of its life, from entering it. And when this, the source of its life, was shut off, not only was the appearance of the lotus pond entirely changed, but the surrounding fields were deprived of the stream to whose banks the flocks and cattle came for drink.

In this do we not see a complete parallel so far as human life is concerned? In the degree that we recognize our oneness, our connection with the Infinite Spirit which is the life of all, and in the degree that we open ourselves to this divine inflow, do we come into harmony with the highest, the most powerful, and the most beautiful everywhere. And in the degree that we do this do we overflow, so that all who come in contact with us receive the effects of this realization on our part. This is the lotus pond of our friend, he who is in love with all that is truest and best in the universe. And in the degree that we fail to recognize our oneness with this Infinite Source, and so close, shut ourselves to this divine inflow, do we come into that state where there seems to be with us nothing of good, nothing of beauty, nothing of power, and when this is true, those who come in contact with us receive not good, but harm. This is the spot of the lotus pond while the farm was in the hands of a tenant.

There is this difference between the lotus pond and your life and mine. It has no power in itself of opening the gate to the inflow of the water from the reservoir which is its source. In regard to this it is helpless, and dependent upon an outside agency. You and I have the power, the power within us, to open or close ourselves to this divine inflow exactly as we choose. This we have through the power or mind through the operation of thought.

There is the soul of life, direct from God. This it is that relates us to the Infinite. There is, then, the physical life. This it is that relates us to the material universe about us. The thought life connects the one with the other. It is this that plays between the two.

Before we proceed further let us consider very briefly the nature of thought. Thought is not, as is many times supposed, a mere indefinite abstraction, or something of a like nature. It is, on the contrary, a vital, living force, the most vital, subtle, and irresistible force there is in the universe.

In our very laboratory experiments we are demonstrating the great fact that thoughts are forces. They have form, and quality, and substance, and power, and we are beginning to find that there is what we may term a science of thought. We are beginning also to find that through the instrumentality of our thought forces we have creative power not merely in a figurative sense, but creative power in reality.

Everything in the material universe about us, everything the universe has ever known, had its origin first in thought. From this it took its form. Every castle, every statue, every painting, every piece of mechanism, everything had its birth, its origin, first in the mind of the one who formed it before it received its material expression or embodiment. The very universe in which we live is the result of the thought energies of God, the Infinite Spirit that is behind all. And if it is true, as we have found, that we in our true selves are in essence the same, and in this sense are one with the life of this Infinite Spirit, do we not then see that in the degree that we come into a vital realization of this stupendous fact, we, through the operation of our interior, spiritual, thought forces, have in like sense creative power?

Everything exists in the unseen before it is manifested or realized in the seen, and in this sense it is true that the unseen things are the real, while the things that are seen are the unreal. The unseen things are the cause, the seen things are effect. The unseen things are the eternal the seen things are the changing, the transient. The 'power of the word' is a literal scientific fact. Through the operation of our thought forces we have creative power. The spoken word is nothing more or less than the outward expression of the workings of these interior forces. The spoken word is then, in a sense, the means whereby the thought forces are focused and directed along any particular line, and this concentration, this giving them direction, is necessary before any outward or material manifestation of their power can become evident.

Much is said in regard to building castles in the air, and one who is given to this building is not always looked upon with favor. But castles in the air are always necessary before we can have castles on the ground, before we can have castles in which to live. The trouble with the one who gives himself to building castles in the air is not that he builds them in the air, but that he does not go farther and actualize in life, in character, in material form, the castles he thus builds. He does a part of the work, a very necessary part, but another equally necessary part remains still undone.

There is in connection with the thought forces what we may term the drawing power of mind, and the great law operating here is one with the great law of the universe, that like attracts like. We are continually attracting to us, from both the seen and the unseen side of life, forces and conditions most akin to those of our own thoughts.

This law is continually operating whether we are conscious of it or not. We are all living, so to speak, in a vast ocean of thought, and the very atmosphere around us is continually filled with the thought forces that are being continually sent or that are continually going out in the form of thought waves. We are all affected, more or less, by these thought forces, either consciously or unconsciously and in the degree that we are more or less sensitively organized, or in the degree that we are negative and so are open to outside influences, rather than positive, thus determining what influences shall enter into our realm of thought, and hence into our lives.

There are those among us who are much more sensitively organized than others. As an organism their bodies are more finely, more sensitively constructed. These, generally speaking, are people who are always more or less affected by the mentalities of those with whom they come in contact, or in whose company they are. A friend, the editor of one of our great journals, is so sensitively organized that it is impossible for him to attend a gathering, such as a reception, talk and shake hands with a number of people during the course of the evening, without taking on, to a greater or less extent, their various mental and physical conditions. These affect him to such an extent that he is scarcely himself, and in his best condition for work, until some two or three days afterwards.

Some think it unfortunate for one to be sensitively organized. By no means. It is a good thing, for one may thus be more open and receptive to the higher impulses of the soul within, and to all higher forces and influences from without. It may, however, be unfortunate and extremely inconvenient to be so organized unless one recognize and gain the power of closing themselves, of making themselves positive to all detrimental or undesirable influences. This power everyone, however sensitively organized they may be, can acquire.

This they can acquire through the mind's action. And, moreover, there is no habit of more value to anyone, be they sensitively or less sensitively organized, than that of occasionally taking and holding themselves continually in the attitude of mind - I close myself, I make myself positive to all things below, and open and receptive to higher influences, to all things above. By taking this attitude of mind consciously now and then it soon becomes a habit, and if one is deeply in earnest in regard to it, it puts into operation silent but subtle and powerful influences in effecting the desired results. In this way all lower and undesirable influences from both the seen and the unseen side of life are closed out, while all higher influences are invited, and in the degree that they are invited will they enter.

And what do we mean by the unseen side of life? First, the thought forces, the mental and emotional conditions in the atmosphere about us that are generated by those manifesting on the physical plane through the agency of physical bodies. Second, the same forces generated by those who have dropped the physical body, or from whom it has been struck away, and who are now manifesting through the agency of bodies of a different nature.

The individual existence of man begins on the sense plane of the physical world, but rises through successive gradations of ethereal and celestial spheres, corresponding with his ever unfolding deific life and powers, to a destiny of unspeakable grandeur and glory. Within and above every physical planet is a corresponding ethereal planet, or soul world, as within and above every physical organism is a corresponding ethereal organism, or soul body, of which the physical is but the external counterpart and materialized expression.

From this etherealized or soul planet, which is the immediate home of our arisen humanity, there rises or deepens in infinite gradations spheres within and above spheres, to celestial heights of spiritualized existence utterly inconceivable to the sense of man. Embodiment, accordingly, is two-fold -the physical being but the temporary husk, so to speak, in and by which the real and permanent ethereal organism is individualized and perfected, somewhat as 'the full corn in the ear' is reached by means of its husk, for which there is no further use. By means of this indestructible ethereal body the corresponding ethereal spheres of environment with the social life and relations in the spheres, the individuality and personal life is preserved forever.'

The fact of life in whatever form means the continuance of life, even though the form be changed. Life is the one eternal principle of the universe and so always continues, even though the form of the agency through which it manifests be changed. 'In My Father's house are many mansions.' And, surely, because the individual has dropped, has gone out of the physical body, there is no evidence at all that the life does not go right on the same as before, not commencing for there is no cessation but commencing in the other form exactly where it has left off here, for all life is a continuous evolution, step by step, there one neither skips nor jumps.

There are in the other form, then, mentalities and hence lives of all grades and influences, just as there are in the physical form. If, then, the great law that like attracts like is ever operating, we are continually attracting to us from this side of life influences and conditions most akin to those of our own thoughts and lives. A gruesome thought that we should be so influenced, says one. By no means, all life is one, we are all bound together in the one common and universal life. Especially not so when we take into consideration the fact that we have it entirely in our own hands to determine the order of thought we entertain, and consequently the order of influences we attract, and are not mere willowy creatures of circumstance, unless indeed we choose to be.

In our mental lives we can either keep hold of the rudder and so determine exactly what course we take, what points we touch, or we can fail to do this, and failing, we drift, and are blown hither and thither by every passing breeze. And so, on the contrary, welcome should be the thought, for thus we may draw to us the influence and the aid of the greatest, the noblest, and the best who have lived on the earth, whatever the time, wherever the place.

We cannot rationally believe other than that those who have labored in love and with uplifting power here are still laboring in the same way, and in all probability with more earnest zeal, and with still greater power.

'And Elisha prayed, and said, Lord, I pray thee, open his eyes, that he may see. And the Lord opened the eyes of the young man, and he saw: and, behold, the mountain was full of horses and chariots of fire round about Elisha.'

While riding with a friend a few days ago, we were speaking of the great interest people are everywhere taking in the more vital things of life, the eagerness with which they are reaching out for a knowledge of the interior forces, their ever-increasing desire to know themselves and to know their true relations with the Infinite. And in speaking of the great spiritual awakening that is so rapidly coming all over the world, the beginnings of which we are so clearly seeing during the closing years of this, and whose ever-increasing proportions we are to witness during the early years of the coming century, I said, 'How beautiful if Emerson, the illumined one so far in advance of his time, who labored so faithfully and so fearlessly to bring about these very conditions, how beautiful if he were with us today to witness it all! how he would rejoice!' 'How do we know', was the reply, 'that he is not witnessing it all? and more, that he is not having a hand in it all -a hand even greater, perhaps, than when we saw him here?' Thank you, my friend, for this reminder. And, truly, 'are they not all ministering spirits sent forth to minister to those who shall be heirs of salvation?'

As science is so abundantly demonstrating today, the things that we see are but a very small fraction of the things that are. The real, vital forces at work in our own lives and in the world about us are not seen by the ordinary physical eye. Yet they are the causes of which all things we see are merely the effects. Thoughts are forces, like builds like, and like attracts like. For one to govern their thinking, then, is to determine their life.

Says one of deep insight into the nature of things, 'The law of correspondences between spiritual and material things is wonderfully exact in its workings. People ruled by the mood of gloom attract to them gloomy things. People always discouraged and despondent do not succeed in anything, and live only by burdening someone else. The hopeful, confident, and cheerful attract the elements of success. A man's front or back garden will advertise that man's ruling mood in the way it is kept. A woman at home shows her state of mind in her dress.

A slattern advertises the ruling mood of hopelessness, carelessness, and lack of system. Rags, tatters, and dirt are always in the mind before being on the body. The thought that is most put out brings its corresponding visible element to crystallize about you as surely and literally as the visible bit of copper in solution attracts to it the invisible copper in that solution. A mind always hopeful, confident, courageous, and determined on its set purpose, and keeping itself to that purpose, attracts to itself out of the elements things and powers favorable to that purpose.

'Every thought of yours has a literal value to you in every possible way. The strength of your body, the strength of your mind, your success in business, and the pleasure your company brings others, depends on the nature of your thoughts...... In whatever mood you set your mind does your spirit receive of unseen substance in correspondence with that mood. It is as much a chemical law as a spiritual law. Chemistry is not confined to the elements we see. The elements we do not see with the physical eye outnumber ten thousand times those we do see.

The Christ injunction, "Do good to those who hate you," is based on a scientific fact and a natural law. So, to do good is to bring to yourself all the elements in nature of power and good. To do evil is to bring the contrary destructive elements. When our eyes are opened, self-preservation will make us stop all evil thought. Those who live by hate will die of hate: that is, "those who live by the sword will die by the sword." Every evil thought is as a sword drawn on the person to whom it is directed. If a sword is drawn in return, so much the worse for both.'

And says another who knows full well whereof he speaks: 'The **law of attraction** works universally on every plane of action, and we attract whatever we desire or expect. If we desire one thing and expect another, we become like houses divided against themselves, which are quickly brought to desolation. Determine resolutely to expect only what you desire, then you will attract only what you wish for. . . . Carry any kind of thought you please about with you, and so long as you retain it, no matter how you roam over land or sea, you will unceasingly attract to yourself, knowingly or inadvertently, exactly and only what corresponds to your own dominant quality of thought. Thoughts are our private property, and we can regulate them to suit our taste entirely by steadily recognizing our ability so to do.'

We have just spoken of the drawing power of mind. Faith is nothing more nor less than the operation of the thought forces in the form of an earnest desire, coupled with expectation as to its fulfillment. And in the degree that faith, the earnest desire thus sent out, is continually held to and watered by firm expectation, in just that degree does it either draw to itself, or does it change from the unseen into the visible, from the spiritual into the material, that for which it is sent.

Let the element of doubt or fear enter in, and what would otherwise be a tremendous force will be so neutralized that it will fail of its realization. Continually held to and continually watered by firm expectation, it becomes a force, a drawing power, that is irresistible and absolute, and the results will be absolute in direct proportion as it is absolute.

We shall find, as we are so rapidly beginning to find today, that the great things said in regard to faith, the great promises made in connection with it, are not mere vague sentimentalities, but are all great scientific facts, and rest upon great immutable laws. Even in our very laboratory experiments we are beginning to discover the laws underlying and governing these forces. We are now beginning, some at least, to use them understandingly and not blindly, as has so often and so long been the case.

Much is said today in regard to the will. It is many times spoken of as if it were a force in itself. But will is a force, a power, only in so far as it is a particular form of the manifestation of the thought forces, for it is by what we call the 'will' that thought is focused and given a particular direction, and in the degree that thought is thus focused and given direction, is it effective in the work it is sent out to accomplish.

In a sense there are two kinds of will the human and the divine. The human will is the will of what, for convenience sake, we may term the lower self. It is the will that finds its life merely in the realm of the mental and the physical "the sense will". It is the will of the one who is not yet awake to the fact that there is a life that far transcends the life of merely the intellect and the physical senses, and which, when realized and lived, does not do away with or minify these, but which, on the contrary, brings them to their highest perfection and to their powers of keenest enjoyment. The divine will is the will of the higher self, the will of the one who recognizes their oneness with the Divine, and who consequently brings their will to work in harmony, in conjunction with the divine a will. 'The Lord thy God in the midst of thee is mighty.'

The human will has its limitations. So far and no farther, says the law. The divine will has no limitations. It is supreme. All things are open and subject to you, says the law, and so, in the degree that the human will is transmuted into the divine, in the degree that it comes into harmony with, and so acts in conjunction with the divine, does it become supreme. Then it is that 'Thou shalt decree a thing and it shall be established unto thee.' The great secret of life and power, then, is to make and to keep one's conscious connection with this Infinite Source.

The power of every life, the very life itself, is determined by what it relates itself to. God is immanent as well as transcendent. He is creating, working, ruling in the universe today, in your life and in mine, just as much as He ever has been. We are apt to regard Him after the manner of an absentee landlord, one who has set into operation the forces of this great universe, and then taken Himself away.

In the degree, however, that we recognized Him as immanent as well as transcendent, are we able to partake of His life and power. For in the degree that we recognize Him as the Infinite Spirit of Life and Power that is today, at this very moment, working and manifesting in and through all, and then, in the degree that we come into realization of our oneness with this life, do we become partakers of, and so do we actualize in ourselves the qualities of His Life. In the degree that we open ourselves to the inflowing tide of this immanent and transcendent life, do we make ourselves channels through which the Infinite Intelligence and Power can work.

It is through the instrumentality of the mind that we are enabled to connect the real soul life with the physical life, and so enable the soul life to manifest and work through the physical. The thought life needs continually to be illumined from within. This illumination can come in just the degree that through the agency of the mind we recognize our oneness with the Divine, of which each soul is an individual form of expression.

This gives us the inner guiding which we call intuition. 'Intuition is to the spiritual nature and understanding practically what sense perception is to the sensuous nature and understanding. It is an inner spiritual sense through which man is opened to the direct revelation and knowledge of God, the secrets of nature and life, and through which he is brought into conscious unity and fellowship with God, and made to realize his own deific nature and supremacy of being as the son of God. Spiritual supremacy and illumination, thus realized through the development and perfection of intuition under divine inspiration, gives the perfect inner vision and direct insight into the character, properties, and purpose of all things to which the attention and interest are directed.....

It is we repeat, a spiritual sense opening inwardly, as the physical senses open outwardly, and because it has the capacity to perceive, grasp and know the truth at first hand, independent of all external sources of information, we call it intuition. All inspired teaching and spiritual revelations are based upon the recognition of this spiritual faculty of the soul, and its power to receive and appropriate them..... Conscious unity of man in spirit and purpose with the Father, born out of his supreme desire and trust, opens his soul through this inner sense to immediate inspiration and enlightenment from the Divine Omniscience, and the co-operative energy of the Divine Omnipotence, under which he becomes a seer and a master.

'On this higher plane of realized spiritual life in the flesh the mind holds the impersonal attitude and acts with unfettered freedom and unbiased vision, grasping truth at first hand, independent of all external sources of information. Approaching all beings and things from the divine side, they are seen in the light of the divine Omniscience. God's purpose in them, and so the truth concerning them, as it rests in the mind of God, are thus revealed by direct illumination from the Divine Mind, to which the soul is opened inwardly through this spiritual sense we call intuition.' Some call it the voice of the soul, some call it the voice of God, some call it the sixth sense. It is our inner spiritual sense.

In the degree that we come into the recognition of our own true selves, into the realization of the oneness of our life with the Infinite Life, and in the degree that we open ourselves to this divine inflow, does this voice of intuition, this voice of the soul, this voice of God, speak clearly, and in the degree that we recognize, listen to, and obey it, does it speak ever more clearly, until by-and-by there comes the time when it is unerring, absolutely unerring, in its guidance.

The complete text of the book behind this excerpt may be found in -

Law of Attraction: In Tune With The Infinite

(Please see Bibliography for details.)

Christian D. Larson

Another key influence in New Thought circles was Christian Larson. Not only a prolific writer, he also had considerable influence of Ernest Holmes in his early career.

While he founded and published a magazine later known as Science of Mind, he also brought New Thought to Cincinnati, Ohio. Larson is also known as the author of the "Optimist's Creed", which was later adopted by Optimist International in 1922.

Here I've excerpted from his "Ideal Made Real" to give you a sample of his work – where he tells us, "If we wish to make the real the ideal, we must live the ideal in the real. When you want good things, make yourself better, and better things will naturally be attracted to you..."

Ideal Made Real

THE IDEAL AND THE REAL MADE ONE.

When the elements of the ideal are blended harmoniously with the elements of the real the two become one; the ideal becomes real and the real gives expression to the qualities of the ideal. To be in harmony with everything at all times and under all circumstances is therefore one of the great essentials in the living of that life that is constantly making real a larger and larger measure of the ideal; and so extremely important is continuous harmony that nothing should be permitted to produce confusion or discord for the slightest moment. Discord wastes energy, while harmony accumulates energy. If we wish to be strong in mind and body and do the best possible work, harmony is absolutely necessary and we must be in the best possible condition to make real the ideal. The person who lives in perpetual harmony with everything will accomplish from ten to one hundred per cent more than the average during any given period of time; a fact that gives the elements of harmony a most important place in life. When harmony is absent there is always a great deal of mental confusion, and a confused mind can never think clearly, therefore makes mistakes constantly. To establish complete and continuous mental harmony will reduce mistakes to a minimum in any mind; another fact that makes the attainment of harmony one of the great attainments.

The mind that is living in continuous harmony is realizing a great measure of heaven upon earth regardless of his personal attainments or external possessions. He has made real that ideal something that makes existence thoroughly worth while, and he is rich indeed. To live in harmony is to gain the joy everlasting, the contentment that is based upon the real value of life, and that satisfaction that grows larger and better for every day that passes by. On the other hand, to live in discord is to live in perpetual torment, even though our personal attainments may be great and our personal possessions as large as any mind could wish.

To live the good life, the ideal life, the beautiful life, we must be at peace with all things, including ourselves, and every thought, word and deed must be harmonious. Whatever we wish to do or be it is wisdom to make any sacrifice necessary for the sake of harmony, although that which we sacrifice for the sake of harmony is not a sacrifice. When we enter into harmony we will regain everything that we were willing to lose in order that we might possess harmony. When we establish ourselves in perfect harmony we shall be reunited with everything that we hold near and dear and the new unity will be far sweeter, far more beautiful than the one we had before. "My own shall come to me" is a favorite expression among all those who believe that every ideal can be made real, and many of these are waiting and watching for their own to come, wondering in the meantime what can be done to hasten that coming. There are many things to be done, however, but one of the most important is the attainment of harmony. No person who lives in perpetual harmony will be deprived very long of his own, whatever that own may be. Whatever you deserve, whatever you are entitled to, whatever belongs to you will soon appear in your world, if you are living in perfect harmony.

To enter harmony is to enter a new world where everything is better, where opportunities are greater and more numerous, and where persons, conditions and things are more agreeable. You will not only enter a better world, however, but the attitude of harmony will relate your life so perfectly to the good things in all worlds that may exist about you, that the best from every source will naturally gravitate towards your sphere of existence. But harmony will not only cause the good things of life to gravitate towards you; it will also cause you to radiate the good qualities in your own being and thus become a perpetual benediction to everybody. To be in the presence of a person who dwells serenely in the beautiful calm is, indeed, a privilege, especially to those who can appreciate the finer elements of a truly harmonious life. Whenever we are in touch with real harmony, whether it comes from the music of human life, the music of nature or the music of the spheres, we are one step nearer the Beautiful. We can therefore realize the great value of being able to actually live in perfect harmony at all times. The life of harmony is the foundation of happiness and health and is one of the greatest essentials to achievement and real success. When we look into the past we can always find that our failures originated in confusion; likewise our troubles and ills. On the other hand, all the good things that have happened to us in the past, or that are happening in the present, had their origin and their growth in the elements of continuous harmony; the ideal and the real were made one, and we consequently reached the goals we had in view.

The mind that works in perpetual harmony does more work and far better work than is possible in any other condition; besides, harmonious work is invariably conducive to higher development and growth. To work in harmony is to promote increase and development in all the qualities and powers of the personality; while to work in confusion is to weaken the entire system and thus originate causes that will terminate in failure. The majority state that they have no time for self development, but to live in harmony and work in harmony is to promote self development every moment, and this development will not be confined simply to those muscles or faculties that we use directly, but will express itself throughout the entire system; and the mind especially will, under such conditions, steadily gain both in power and in worth. In the presence of these facts we can realize readily that no person can afford to permit discord, disturbance or confusion at any time. The many declare, however, that they cannot help it, but we must help it and we can. There is no reason why our minds should be excited or our nerves upset at any time. We can prevent this just as easily as we can refuse to eat what we do not want.

To proceed, we must apply exact reason to this great subject. We should learn to understand that no wrong will be righted because we permit ourselves to "fly to pieces;" also that the act of becoming nervous over a trouble will never drive that trouble away. To live in a constant strain will not promote our purpose nor arrange matters the way we want them. This is a fact that we should impress deeply upon our minds, and then impress our minds to take another and a better course. The average person feels that it is a religious duty to be as excited as possible, and to string up all his nerves as high as possible, whenever he is passing through some exceptional event; in consequence, he spoils all or practically all of that which might have been gained; besides, he places his system in a condition where all sorts of ills may gain a foothold. There are many reasons why such a large number of undertakings fail, but one of the principal reasons is found in the fact that few people have learned to retain perfect harmony under all kinds of circumstances. Discord and confusion are usually present to a great degree, and in consequence, something almost invariably goes wrong. But when a person is in perfect harmony and does his very best, he will succeed at least in a measure every time, and he will thus prepare himself for the greater opportunities that are sure to follow: To believe that intelligent, well educated people almost daily break down over mere trifles is not mere simplicity, but the fact that it is the truth leads us to question why. Intelligence and education should give those who possess it the power to know better. Modern education, however, does not teach us how to use ourselves. We have learned how to mix material substances so as to satisfy every imaginable taste, and we have learned how to use the tangible forces of nature so as to construct almost anything we like in the physical world, but we have not learned how to combine the elements of mind so as to produce health, happiness, strength, brilliancy and harmony whenever we may so desire. A few, however, have made the attempt, but the elements of the mind will not combine for greater efficiency and higher states of expression unless the mind is in perfect harmony.

We have all learned to remember, but few have learned to think. To repeat verbatim what others have thought and said is counted knowledge and with such borrowed knowledge the majority imagine they are satisfied, the reason being they have not discovered the art of thinking thoughts of their own. This is an art that every person must learn; the sooner the better, if the ideal is to be made real. Original thinking is the secret of all greatness, all high attainments, all extraordinary achievements and all superior states of being; but no mind can create original thought until a high state of mental harmony is attained. To produce mental harmony we must first bear in mind the great fact that it is not what happens that disturbs us, but the way we think about that which happens; and our thought about anything depends upon our point of view. The way we look at things will determine whether the experience will produce discord or harmony, and it is in our power to look at things in any way that we may desire. When we are face to face with those things that usually upset the mind we should immediately turn our attention upon the life and the power that is back of the disturbing element, having the desire to find the better side of that life and power constantly in view. Everything has its better side, its ideal side, its calm and undisturbed side, and a mere desire to gain a glimpse of that better side will turn the mind away from confusion and cause attention to be centered upon that calm state that is being sought. This will decrease discord at once, and if applied the very moment we are aware of confusion we will entirely prevent any mental disturbance whatever. To meet all circumstances and events in this way is to develop in ourselves a harmonious attitude towards all things, and when we are established in this harmonious attitude nothing whatever disturbs us; no matter what may happen we will continue to remain in harmony, and will consequently be able to deal properly with whatever may happen.

The mind that is upset by confused circumstances will lose ground and fail, but the mind that continues calmly in harmony with everything, no matter what the circumstances may be, will master every occasion and steadily rise in the scale. He will continue to make real the ideal, because he is living in that harmonious state of being where the ideal and the real are harmoniously blended into one. To promote the highest and most perfect state of continuous harmony we must learn to meet those persons, things and events, with which we come in daily contact, in the right mental attitude. The result of such an attitude is determined directly by the nature of our own attitude of mind, and as we can express ourselves through any attitude we desire, it is in our power either to spoil the most promising prospects, or convert the most unpromising conditions into the greatest success. We should train ourselves to meet everything in that attitude of mind that expects all things to work out right. When we deeply and continually expect all things to work out right we relate ourselves more perfectly with that with which we come in contact; we take things, so to speak, the way they ought to be taken, and we thereby promote harmony and cooperation among all things concerned.

Though this be extremely important, it is insignificant, however, in comparison with another great fact in this connection; that is, the way things respond to the leading desires of the ruling mind; whether it is the exercise of the mysteries of mental force or the application of a mental law not generally understood, does not concern us just now; but it is a fact that things will do, as a rule what we persistently expect them to do. To understand why this is so may require some study of the great laws of mind and body, and everybody should seek to understand these laws perfectly; but in the meantime anyone can demonstrate the fact that things will work out right if we constantly expect them to do so. No matter what may happen we should continue in the faith that all things will come right, and as our faith is so it shall be. To place ourselves in perfect harmony with all things, the domineering attitude of mind must be eliminated completely. The mind that tries to domineer over things will not only lose control of things, but will lose control of its own faculties and forces. At first it may seem that the domineering mind gains ground, but the gain is only temporary. When the reaction comes, as it will, the loss will be far greater than the temporary gain. When you try to domineer over persons and things you gain possession and control of those things only that are too weak to control themselves. That is, you gain a temporary control over negatives, and negatives have no permanent value in your life; in fact, they soon prove themselves to be wholly detrimental. Occasionally a domineering mind may attract the attention of better things, but as soon as his domineering qualities are discovered those better things will part company with him at once. The **law of attraction** is at the foundation of all natural constructive processes; therefore, to promote construction, growth, advancement and real success we must work in harmony with that law. If we wish to attain the superior, we must become superior, because it is only like that attracts like. If we wish to gain the ideal, we must become ideal. If we wish to make real the ideal, we must live the ideal in the real. When you want good things, make yourself better, and better things will naturally be attracted to you; but good things do not submit to force. Therefore, to try to secure better things through forceful methods, or through the domineering attitude can only result in failure; such methods gain only the inferior, those things that can add neither to the welfare nor the happiness of any one. This fact holds good, not only among individuals, but also among nations and institutions. The more domineering an institution is the more inferior are its members, and the more autocratic the nation the weaker its subjects. On the other hand, we find the best minds where the individual is left free to govern himself and where he is expected to act wisely, to be true to the best that is within him. In order that the individual may advance he must steadily grow in the mastery of himself, and must so relate himself to the best things in life that he will naturally attract the best things; but these two essentials are wholly interfered with by the domineering attitude. Such an attitude repels everything and everybody that has any worth. It spoils the forces of mind, thus weakening all the mental faculties, and it steadily undermines whatever self control a person might possess. Never try to control anything or domineer over anything, but aim to live in perpetual harmony with the highest, the truest and the best that is in everything.

Whatever happens we should approach that event in that attitude that believes it is all right. We should never permit the attitude that condemns, not even when the things concerned have proved themselves to be wrong. The attitude that condemns is detrimental to our own minds, because it invariably produces discord. When you meet all things in the expectation of finding them right, you always find something about them that is right. This something you may appropriate and thus gain good from everything that happens. That person, however, who expects to find most things wrong will fail to see the good that may exist among the things that come his way; therefore, he gains far less from life than his wiser neighbor. But what is equally important, the man who expects to find everything right wherever he may go, will gradually gravitate towards those people and circumstances that are right. The man who expects to find everything wrong usually finds what he expects. The effect of these two attitudes upon mind and character is even more important, because the man is as his mind and character, and as the man is so is his destiny. The man who expects to find most things wrong and meets the world in that attitude is constantly impressing the wrong upon his mind, and as we gradually grow into the likeness of that which we think of the most, he is building upon sinking sand. The mind that is constantly looking for the wrong cannot be wholesome. Such a mind is not in harmony with the law of growth, power, and ability; therefore, can never do its best. Unwholesome thoughts will steadily undermine the finest character and mind, and the world is full of illustrations. There is always something wrong in the life of that person who constantly expects to find things wrong, and the reason why is simple. His own expectations are reacting upon himself; by thinking about the wrong he is creating the wrong and thus bringing forth the wrong in every part of his life.

The man, however, who expects to find everything right and meets the world in that attitude is daily nourishing his mind with right thoughts, wholesome thoughts and constructive thoughts; he thinks the most of that which is right, and is therefore steadily growing more and more into the likeness of that which is right, perfect, worthy and good; he is daily changing for the better, and through this constant change he steadily rises in the scale and thereby meets the better and the better at every turn. By expecting to find everything right he finds more and more of that which is right, and as he is becoming stronger in mind, character and soul, he is affected less and less by those few things that may not be as they should be. When you meet a disappointment meet it in the conviction that it is all right, because through this attitude you enter into harmony with the power that is back of the event at hand, and you thus convert the disappointment into a channel through which greater good may be secured. Those who doubt this should try it.; they will find that it is based upon exact scientific facts Transcend disappointment, and all the powers of adversity will begin to rise with you and will begin to work with you and help you reach the goal you have in view. You will thus find that, it is all for the best, because through the right mental attitude you made everything work out in such a way that the best transpired as a final result.

To live in what may be termed the "all right" attitude, that is, in that attitude that expects to find everything all right and that constantly affirms that everything is all right, is to press on to the realization and the possession of those things that are as you wish them to be. Disappointments and failures, when met in this attitude, simply become open doors to new worlds where you find better opportunities and greater possibilities than you ever knew before. When the average person meets disappointment he usually declares, "Just my luck;" in other words, he enters that mental attitude that faces ill luck; he thus fails to see anything else but misfortune in that which has happened; and so long as that person, consciously or unconsciously expects misfortune, into more and more misfortune he will go. He who believes that he is fated to have bad luck will have bad luck in abundance. The reason is he lives in that mental attitude that places his mind in constant contact with those confused elements in the world that never create anything else but bad luck. That person, however, who thoroughly believes that everything that happens is simply a step to greater good, higher attainments and greater achievements, will steadily rise into those greater things that he expects to realize; the reason being that he is living in that mental attitude that places his mind in contact with the building power of life. Those powers will always build for greater things to those with whom they are in harmony, and we all can place ourselves in harmony with those powers; therefore, we can all move upward and onward forever, eternally making real more and more of that which is ideal.

What we expect comes if our expectation is filled with all the power of life and soul, and what we believe our fate to be, that is the kind of a fate we will create for ourselves. To meet ill luck in the belief that it is your luck, your particular kind of luck, and that it is natural for you to have that kind of luck is to stamp your own mind as an unlucky mind. This will produce chaotic thinking, which will cause you to do everything at the wrong time, and all your energies will be more or less misdirected; in consequence, bad luck and misfortune must necessarily follow. Bad luck comes from doing the wrong thing, or from being your worst; while good luck comes from being your best and from doing the right thing at the right time. It is therefore mere simplicity to create good luck at any time and in the measure that we may desire. The person that fears misfortune or expects misfortune and faces life in that attitude is concentrating attention upon misfortune; he thereby creates a world of misfortune in his own mind; and he who lives in mental misfortune will produce misfortune in his external life. Like causes produce like effects; and this explains why the things we fear always come upon us. We create mental causes for those things, and corresponding tangible effects always follow. Train the mind to expect the right and the best, regardless of present circumstances, conditions or events. Call everything good that is met. Declare that everything that happens, happens for the best. Meet everything in that frame of mind, and no matter how wrong or adverse conditions seem to be, you cause them all to work out right.

When the mind expects the best, has the faith that the right will prevail, and constantly faces the superior, the true mental attitude has been gained. Through that attitude all the forces of mind and all the powers of will become constructive, and will build for man the very thing that he expects or desires while his mind is fixed upon the ideal. He relates himself harmoniously to the best that is in all things and thus unites the ideal with the real in all things; and when the ideal becomes one with the real, the ideal desired becomes an actual fact in the real; and this is the goal every true idealist has in view. He takes those elements that have been revealed to him through the vision of the soul and blends them harmoniously with the actions of daily life. He thus brings the ideal down to earth and causes the real of every day life to express the ideal in everything that he may undertake to do. His life, his thought, his action, his attainments, his achievements, all contain that happy state where the ideal and the real are made one. His dreams have become true. The visions of the soul are actually realized, and the tangible is animated with that ideal something that makes personal existence all that any one could wish it to be.

The complete text of the book behind this excerpt may be found in -

Law of Attraction: Ideal Made Real

(Please see Bibliography for details.)

Napoleon Hill

Best known for his "Think and Grow Rich", Napoleon Hill had concluded the bulk of his 20-year research program only a few years prior.

Commissioned by Andrew Carnegie, this study was to distill the successful programs and policies of the rich and successful – 500 of them – into a simple, understandable format the common man-on-the-street could use. That study culminated in the 16-volume "Law of Success".

From this massive set, I've selected a single (if long) selection where Hill is most descriptive about the Law of Attraction. Example after example is given – which you can use to change your own life with...

Law of Success

Lesson Three: SELF-CONFIDENCE
"You Can Do It if You Believe You Can!"

BEFORE approaching the fundamental principles upon which this lesson is founded it will be of benefit to you to keep in mind the fact that it is practical - that it brings you the discoveries of more than twenty-five years of research-that it has the approval of the leading scientific men and women of the world who have tested every principle involved.

Skepticism is the deadly enemy of progress and self-development. You might as well lay this book aside and stop right here as to approach this lesson with the feeling that it was written by some long-haired theorist who had never tested the principles upon which the lesson is based.

Surely this is no age for the skeptic, because it is an age in which we have seen more of Nature's laws uncovered and harnessed than had been discovered in all past history of the human race. Within three decades we have witnessed the mastery of the air; we have explored the ocean; we have all but annihilated distances on the earth; we have harnessed the lightning and made it turn the wheels of industry; we have made seven blades of grass grow where but one grew before; we have instantaneous communication between the nations of the world. Truly, this is an age of illumination and unfoldment, but we have as yet barely scratched the surface of knowledge. However, when we shall have unlocked the gate that leads to the secret power which is stored up within us it will bring us knowledge that will make all past discoveries pale into oblivion by comparison.

Thought is the most highly organized form of energy known to man, and this is an age of experimentation and research that is sure to bring us into greater understanding of that mysterious force called thought, which reposes within us. We have already found out enough about the human mind to know that a man may throw off the accumulated effects of a thousand generations of fear, through the aid of the principle of Auto-suggestion. We have already discovered the fact that fear is the chief reason for poverty and failure and misery that takes on a thousand different forms. We have already discovered the fact that the man who masters fear may march on to successful achievement in practically any undertaking, despite all efforts to defeat him.

The development of self-confidence starts with the elimination of this demon called fear, which sits upon a man's shoulder and whispers into his ear, "You can't do it - you are afraid to try - you are afraid of public opinion - you are afraid that you will fail - you are afraid you have not the ability."

This fear demon is getting into close quarters. Science has found a deadly weapon with which to put it to flight, and this lesson on self-confidence has brought you this weapon for use in your battle with the world-old enemy of progress, fear.

THE SIX BASIC FEARS OF MANKIND: Every person falls heir to the influence of six basic fears. Under these six fears may be listed the lesser fears. The six basic or major fears are here enumerated and the sources from which they are believed to have grown are described.

The six basic fears are:

a. The fear of Poverty

b. The fear of Old Age

c. The fear of Criticism

d. The fear of Loss of Love of Someone.

e. The fear of Ill Health

f. The fear of Death.

Study the list, then take inventory of your own fears and ascertain under which of the six headings you can classify them.

Every human being who has reached the age of understanding is bound down, to some extent, by one or more of these six basic fears. As the first step in the elimination of these six evils let us examine the sources from whence we inherited them.

PHYSICAL AND SOCIAL HEREDITY

All that man is, both physically and mentally, he came by through two forms of heredity. One is known as physical heredity and the other is called social heredity.

Through the law of physical heredity man has slowly evolved from the amoeba (a single-cell animal form), through stages of development corresponding to all the known animal forms now on this earth, including those which are known to have existed but which are now extinct.

Every generation through which man has passed has added to his nature something of the traits, habits and physical appearance of that generation. Man's physical inheritance, therefore, is a heterogeneous collection of many habits and physical forms.

There seems little, if any, doubt that while the six basic fears of man could not have been inherited through physical heredity (these six basic fears being mental states of mind and therefore not capable of transmission through physical heredity), it is obvious that through physical heredity a most favorable lodging place for these six fears has been provided.

For example, it is a well known fact that the whole process of physical evolution is based upon death, destruction, pain and cruelty; that the elements of the soil of the earth find transportation, in their upward climb through evolution, based upon the death of one form of life in order that another and higher form may subsist. All vegetation lives by "eating" the elements of the soil and the elements of the air. All forms of animal life live by "eating" some other and weaker form, or some form of vegetation.

The cells of all vegetation have a very high order of intelligence. The cells of all animal life likewise have a very high order of intelligence.

Undoubtedly the animal cells of a fish have learned, out of bitter experience, that the group of animal cells known as a fish hawk are to be greatly feared.

By reason of the fact that many animal forms (including that of most men) live by eating the smaller and weaker animals, the "cell intelligence" of these animals which enter into and become a part of man brings with it the FEAR growing out of their experience in having been eaten alive.

This theory may seem to be far-fetched, and in fact it may not be true, but it is at least a logical theory if it is nothing more. The author makes no particular point of this theory, nor does he insist that it accounts for any of the six basic fears. There is another, and a much better explanation of the source of these fears, which we will proceed to examine, beginning with a description of social heredity.

By far the most important part of man's make-up comes to him through the law of social heredity, this term having reference to the methods by which one generation imposes upon the minds of the generation under its immediate control the superstitions, beliefs, legends and ideas which it, in turn, inherited from the generation preceding.

The term "social heredity" should be understood to mean any and all sources through which a person acquires knowledge, such as schooling of religious and all other natures; reading, word of mouth conversation, story telling and all manner of thought inspiration coming from what is generally accepted as one's "personal experiences."

Through the operation of the law of social heredity anyone having control of the mind of a child may, through intense teaching, plant in that child's mind any idea, whether false or true, in such a manner that the child accepts it as true and it becomes as much a part of the child's personality as any cell or organ of its physical body (and just as hard to change in its nature).

REMEMBER that when you make an appointment with another person you assume the responsibility of punctuality, and that you have not the right to be a single minute late.

It is through the law of social heredity that the religionist plants in the child mind dogmas and creeds and religious ceremonies too numerous to describe, holding those ideas before that mind until the mind accepts them and forever seals them as a part of its irrevocable belief.

The mind of a child which has not come into the age of general understanding, during an average period covering, let us say, the first two years of its life, is plastic, open, clean and free. Any idea planted in such a mind by one in whom the child has confidence takes root and grows, so to speak, in such a manner that it never can be eradicated or wiped out, no matter how opposed to logic or reason that idea may be.

Many religionists claim that they can so deeply implant the tenets of their religion in the mind of a child that there never can be room in that mind for any other religion, either in whole or in part. The claims are not greatly overdrawn.

With this explanation of the manner in which the law of social heredity operates the student will be ready to examine the sources from which man inherits the six basic fears. Moreover, any student (except those who have not yet grown big enough to examine truth that steps upon the "pet corns" of their own superstitions) may check the soundness of the principle of social heredity as it is here applied to the six basic fears, without going outside of his or her own personal experiences.

Fortunately, practically the entire mass of evidence submitted in this lesson is of such a nature that all who sincerely seek the truth may ascertain, for themselves, whether the evidence is sound or not.

For the moment at least, lay aside your prejudices and preconceived ideas (you may always go back and pick them up again, you know) while we study the origin and nature of man's Six Worst Enemies, the six basic fears, beginning with:

THE FEAR OF POVERTY: It requires courage to tell the truth about the origin of this fear, and still greater courage, perhaps, to accept the truth after it has been told. The fear of poverty grew out of man's inherited tendency to prey upon his fellow man economically. Nearly all forms of lower animals have instinct but appear not to have the power to reason and think; therefore, they prey upon one another physically. Man, with his superior sense of intuition, thought and reason, does not eat his fellow men bodily; he gets more satisfaction out of eating them FINANCIALLY!

Of all the ages of the world of which we know anything, the age in which we live seems to be the age of money worship. A man is considered less than the dust of the earth unless he can display a fat bank account. Nothing brings man so much suffering and humiliation as does POVERTY. No wonder man FEARS poverty. Through a long line of inherited experiences with the man-animal man has learned, for certain, that this animal cannot always be trusted where matters of money and other evidences of earthly possessions are concerned.

Many marriages have their beginning (and oftentimes their ending) solely on the basis of the wealth possessed by one or both of the contracting parties.

It is no wonder that the divorce courts are busy!

"Society" could quite properly be spelled "$ociety," because it is inseparably associated with the dollar mark. So eager is man to possess wealth that he will acquire it in whatever manner he can; through legal methods, if possible, through other methods if necessary.

The fear of poverty is a terrible thing!

A man may commit murder, engage in robbery, rape and all other manner of violation of the rights of others and still regain a high station in the minds of his fellow men, PROVIDING always that he does not lose his wealth. Poverty, therefore, is a crime-an unforgivable sin, as it were.

No wonder man fears it!

Every statute book in the world bears evidence that the fear of poverty is one of the six basic fears of mankind, for in every such book of laws may be found various and sundry laws intended to protect the weak from the strong. To spend time trying to prove either that the fear of poverty is one of man's inherited fears, or that this fear has its origin in man's nature to cheat his fellow man, would be similar to trying to prove that three times two are six. Obviously no man would ever fear poverty if he had any grounds for trusting his fellow men, for there is food and shelter and raiment and luxury of every nature sufficient for the needs of every person on earth, and all these blessings would be enjoyed by every person except for the swinish habit that man has of trying to push all the other "swine" out of the trough, even after he has all and more than he needs.

The second of the six basic fears with which man is bound is:

THE FEAR OF OLD AGE: In the main this fear grows out of two sources. First, the thought that Old Age may bring with it POVERTY. Secondly, and by far the most common source of origin, from false and cruel sectarian teachings which have been so well mixed with "fire and brimstone" and with "purgatories" and other bogies that human beings have learned to fear Old Age because it meant the approach of another, and possibly a much more HORRIBLE, world than this one which is known to be bad enough.

In the basic fear of Old Age man has two very sound reasons for his apprehension: the one growing out of distrust of his fellow men who may seize whatever worldly goods he may possess, and the other arising from the terrible pictures of the world to come which were deeply planted in his mind, through the law of social heredity, long before he came into possession of that mind.

Is it any wonder that man fears the approach of Old Age?

The third of the six basic fears is:

THE FEAR OF CRITICISM: Just how man acquired this basic fear it would be hard, if not impossible, definitely to determine, but one thing is certain, he has it in well developed form.

Some believe that this fear made its appearance in the mind of man about the time that politics came into existence. Others believe its source can be traced no further than the first meeting of an organization of females known as a "Woman's Club." Still another school of humorists charges the origin to the contents of the Holy Bible, whose pages abound with some very vitriolic and violent forms of criticism. If the latter claim is correct, and those who believe literally all they find in the Bible are not mistaken, then God is responsible for man's inherent fear of Criticism, because God caused the Bible to be written.

This author, being neither a humorist nor a "prophet," but just an ordinary workaday type of person, is inclined to attribute the basic fear of Criticism to that part of man's inherited nature which prompts him not only to take away his fellow man's goods and wares, but to justify his action by CRITICISM of his fellow man's character.

The fear of Criticism takes on many different forms, the majority of which are petty and trivial in nature, even to the extent of being childish in the extreme.

Bald-headed men, for example, are bald for no other reason than their fear of Criticism. Heads become bald because of the protection of hats with tight fitting bands which cut off the circulation at the roots of the hair. Men wear hats, not because they actually need them for the sake of comfort, but mainly because "everybody's doing it," and the individual falls in line and does it also, lest some other individual CRITICIZE him.

Women seldom have bald heads, or even thin hair, because they wear hats that are loose, the only purpose of which is to make an appearance.

But it must not be imagined that women are free from the fear of Criticism associated with hats. If any woman claims to be superior to man with reference to this fear, ask her to walk down the street wearing a hat that is one or two seasons out of style!

IN every soul there has been deposited the seed of a great future, but that seed will never germinate, much less grow to maturity, except through the rendering of useful service.

The makers of all manner of clothing have not been slow to capitalize this basic fear of Criticism with which all mankind is cursed. Every season, it will be observed, the "styles" in many articles of wearing apparel change. Who establishes the "styles"? Certainly not the purchaser of clothes, but the manufacturer of clothes. Why does he change the styles so often? Obviously this change is made so that the manufacturer can sell more clothes.

For the same reason the manufacturers of automobiles (with a few rare and very sensible exceptions) change styles every season.

The manufacturer of clothing knows how the man-animal fears to wear a garment which is one season out of step with "that which they are all wearing now."

Is this not true? Does not your own experience back it up?

We have been describing the manner in which people behave under the influence of the fear of Criticism as applied to the small and petty things of life. Let us now examine human behavior under this fear when it affects people in connection with the more important matters connected with human intercourse. Take, for example, practically any person who has reached the age of "mental maturity" (from thirty-five to forty-five years of age, as a general average), and if you could read his or her mind you would find in that mind a very decided disbelief of and rebellion against most of the fables taught by the majority of the religionists.

Powerful and mighty is the fear of CRITICISM!

The time was, and not so very long ago at that, when the word "infidel" meant ruin to whomsoever it was applied. It is seen, therefore, that man's fear of CRITICISM is not without ample cause for its existence.

The fourth basic fear is that of:

THE FEAR OF LOSS OF LOVE OF SOMEONE: The source from which this fear originated needs but little description, for it is obvious that it grew out of man's nature to steal his fellow man's mate; or at least to take liberties with her, unknown to her rightful "lord" and master. By nature all men are polygamous, the statement of a truth which will, of course, bring denials from those who are either too old to function in a normal way sexually, or have, from some other cause, lost the contents of certain glands which are responsible for man's tendency toward the plurality of the opposite sex.

There can be but little doubt that jealousy and all other similar forms of more or less mild dementia praecox (insanity) grew out of man's inherited fear of the Loss of Love of Someone.

Of all the "sane fools" studied by this author, that represented by a man who has become jealous of some woman, or that of a woman who has become jealous of some man, is the oddest and strangest. The author, fortunately, never had but one case of personal experience with this form of insanity, but from that experience he learned enough to justify him in stating that the fear of the Loss of Love of Someone is one of the most painful, if not in fact the most painful, of all the six basic fears. And it seems reasonable to add that this fear plays more havoc with the human mind than do any of the other six basic fears, often leading to the more violent forms of permanent insanity.

The fifth basic fear is that of:

THE FEAR OF ILL HEALTH: This fear has its origin, to considerable extent also, in the same sources from which the fears of Poverty and Old Age are derived.

The fear of Ill Health must needs be closely associated with both Poverty and Old Age, because it also leads toward the border line of "terrible worlds" of which man knows not, but of which he has heard some discomforting stories.

The author strongly suspects that those engaged in the business of selling good health methods have had considerable to do with keeping the fear of Ill Health alive in the human mind.

For longer than the record of the human race can be relied upon, the world has known of various and sundry forms of therapy and health purveyors. If a man gains his living from keeping people in good health it seems but natural that he would use every means at his command for persuading people that they needed his services. Thus, in time, it might be that people would inherit a fear of Ill Health.

The sixth and last of the six basic fears is that of:

THE FEAR OF DEATH: To many this is the worst of all the six basic fears, and the reason why it is so regarded becomes obvious to even the casual student of psychology.

The terrible pangs of fear associated with DEATH may be charged directly to religious fanaticism, the source which is more responsible for it than are all other sources combined.

So-called "heathen" are not as much afraid of DEATH as are the "civilized," especially that portion of the civilized population which has come under the influence of theology.

For hundreds of millions of years man has been asking the still unanswered (and, it may be, the unanswerable) questions, "WHENCE?" and "WHITHER?" "Where did I come from and where am I going after death?"

The more cunning and crafty, as well as the honest but credulous, of the race have not been slow to offer the answer to these questions. In fact the answering of these questions has become one of the so-called "learned" professions, despite the fact that but little learning is required to enter this profession.

Witness, now, the major source of origin of the fear of DEATH!

"Come into my tent, embrace my faith, accept my dogmas (and pay my salary) and I will give you a ticket that will admit you straightway into heaven when you die," says the leader of one form of sectarianism. "Remain out of my tent," says this same leader, "and you will go direct to hell, where you will burn throughout eternity."

While, in fad, the self-appointed leader may not be able to provide safe-conduct into heaven nor, by lack of such provision, allow the unfortunate seeker after truth to descend into hell, the possibility of the latter seems so terrible that it lays hold of the mind and creates that fear of fears, the fear of DEATH!

In truth no man knows, and no man has ever known, what heaven or hell is like, or if such places exist, and this very lack of definite knowledge opens the door of the human mind to the charlatan to enter and control that mind with his stock of legerdemain and various brands of trickery, deceit and fraud.

The truth is this - nothing less and nothing more - That NO MAN KNOWS NOR HAS ANY MAN EVER KNOWN WHERE WE COME FROM AT BIRTH OR WHERE WE GO AT DEATH. Any person claiming otherwise is either deceiving himself or he is a conscious impostor who makes it a business to live without rendering service of value, through play upon the credulity of humanity.

Be it said, in their behalf, however, the majority of those engaged in "selling tickets into heaven" actually believe not only that they know where heaven exists, but that their creeds and formulas will give safe passage to all who embrace them.

This belief may be summed up in one word - CREDULITY!

Religious leaders, generally, make the broad, sweeping claim that the present civilization owes its existence to the work done by the churches. This author, as far as he is personally concerned, is willing to grant their claims to be correct, if, at the same time he be permitted to add that even if this claim be true the theologians haven't a great deal of which to brag.

But, it is not - cannot be - true that civilization has grown out of the efforts of the organized churches and creeds, if by the term "civilization" is meant the uncovering of the natural laws and the many inventions to which the world is the present heir.

If the theologians wish to claim that part of civilization which has to do with man's conduct toward his fellow man they are perfectly welcome to it, as far as this author is concerned; but, on the other hand, if they presume to gobble up the credit for all the scientific discovery of mankind the author begs leave to offer vigorous protest.

YOU are fortunate if you have learned the difference between temporary defeat and failure; more fortunate still, if you have learned the truth that the very seed of success is dormant in every defeat that you experience.

It is hardly sufficient to state that social heredity is the method through which man gathers all knowledge that reaches him through the five senses. It is more to the point to state HOW social heredity works, in as many different applications as will give the student a comprehensive understanding of that law.

Let us begin with some of the lower forms of animal life and examine the manner in which they are affected by the law of social heredity.

Shortly after this author began to examine the major sources from which men gather the knowledge which makes them what they are, some thirty-odd years ago, he discovered the nest of a ruffed grouse. The nest was so located that the mother bird could be seen from a considerable distance when she was on the nest. With the aid of a pair of field glasses the bird was closely watched until the young birds were hatched out. It happened that the regular daily observation was made but a few hours after the young birds came out of the shell. Desiring to know what would happen, the author approached the nest. The mother bird remained near by until the intruder was within ten or twelve feet of her, then she disarranged her feathers, stretched one wing over her leg and went hobbling away, making a pretense of being crippled. Being somewhat familiar with the tricks of mother birds, the author did not follow, but, instead, went tote nest to take a look at the little ones. Without the slightest signs of fear they turned their eyes toward him, moving their heads first one way and then another. He reached down and picked one of them up. With no signs of fear it stood in the palm of his hand. He laid the bird back in the nest and went away to a safe distance to give the mother bird a chance to return.

The wait was short. Very soon she began cautiously to edge her way back toward the nest until she was within a few feet of it, when she spread her wings and ran as fast as she could, uttering, meanwhile, a series of sounds similar to those of a hen when she has found some morsel of food and wishes to call her brood to partake of it.

She gathered the little birds around and continued to quiver in a highly excited manner, shaking her wings and ruffling her feathers. One could almost hear her words as she gave the little birds their first lesson in self-defense, through the law of SOCIAL HEREDITY:

"You silly little creatures! Do you not know that men are your enemies? Shame on you for allowing that man to pick you up in his hands. It's a wonder he didn't carry you off and eat you alive! The next time you see a man approaching make yourselves scarce. Lie down on the ground, run under leaves, go anywhere to get out of sight, and remain out of sight until the enemy is well on his way."

The little birds stood around and listened to the lecture with intense interest. After the mother bird had quieted down the author again started to approach the nest. When within twenty feet or so of the guarded household the mother bird again started to lead him in the other direction by crumpling up her wing and hobbling along as if she were crippled. He looked at the nest, but the glance was in vain. The little birds were nowhere to be found! They had learned rapidly to avoid their natural enemy, thanks to their natural instinct.

Again the author retreated, awaited until the mother bird had reassembled her household, then came out to visit them, but with similar results. When he approached the spot where he last saw the mother bird not the slightest signs of the little fellows were to be found.

When a small boy the author captured a young crow and made a pet of it. The bird became quite well satisfied with its domestic surroundings and learned to perform many tricks requiring considerable intelligence. After the bird was big enough to fly it was permitted to go wherever it pleased. Sometimes it would be gone for many hours, but it always returned home before dark.

One day some wild crows became involved in a fight with an owl in a field near the house where the pet crow lived. As soon as the pet heard the "caw, caw, caw" of its wild relatives it flew up on top of the house, and with signs of great agitation, walked from one end of the house to the other. Finally it took wing and flew in the direction of the "battle." The author followed to see what would happen. In a few minutes he came up with the pet. It was sitting on the lower branches of a tree and two wild crows were sitting on a limb just above, chattering and walking back and forth, acting very much in the same fashion that angry parents behave toward their offspring when chastising them.

As the author approached, the two wild crows flew away, one of them circling around the tree a few times, meanwhile letting out a terrible flow of most abusive language, which, no doubt, was directed at its foolish relative who hadn't enough sense to fly while the flying was good.

The pet was called, but it paid no attention. That evening it returned home, but would not come near the house. It sat on a high limb of an apple tree and talked in crow language for about ten minutes, saying, no doubt, that it had decided to go back to the wild life of its fellows, then flew away and did not return until two days later, when it came back and did some more talking in crow language, keeping at a safe distance meanwhile. It then went away and never returned.

Social heredity had robbed the author of a fine pet!

The only consolation he got from the loss of his crow was the thought that it had shown fine sportsmanship by coming back and giving notice of its intention to depart. Many farm hands had left the farm without going to the trouble of this formality.

It is a well known fact that a fox will prey upon all manner of fowl and small animals with the exception of the skunk. No reason need be stated as to why Mr. Skunk enjoys immunity. A fox may tackle a skunk once, but never twice! For this reason a skunk hide, when nailed to a chicken roost, will keep all but the very young and inexperienced foxes at a safe distance.

The odor of a skunk, once experienced, is never to be forgotten. No other smell even remotely resembles it. It is nowhere recorded that any mother fox ever taught her young how to detect and keep away from the familiar smell of a skunk, but all who are informed on "fox lore" know that foxes and skunks never seek lodgment in the same cave.

But one lesson is sufficient to teach the fox all it cares to know about skunks. Through the law of social heredity, operating via the sense of smell, one lesson serves for an entire life-time.

A bullfrog can be caught on a fish-hook by attaching a small piece of red cloth or any other small red object to the hook and dangling it in front of the frog's nose. That is, Mr. Frog may be caught in this manner, provided he is hooked the first time he snaps at the bait, but if he is poorly hooked and makes a get-away, or if he feels the point of the hook when he bites at the bait but is not caught, he will never make the same mistake again. The author spent many hours in stealthy attempt to hook a particularly desirable specimen which had snapped and missed, before learning that but one lesson in social heredity is enough to teach even a humble "croaker" that bits of red flannel are things to be let alone.

The author once owned a very fine male Airedale dog which caused no end of annoyance by his habit of coming home with a young chicken in his mouth.

IS it not strange that we fear most that which never happens? That we destroy our initiative by the fear of defeat, when in reality, defeat is a most useful tonic and should be accepted as such.

Each time the chicken was taken away from the dog and he was soundly switched, but to no avail; he continued in his liking for fowl.

For the purpose of saving the dog, if possible, and as an experiment with social heredity, this dog was taken to the farm of a neighbor who had a hen and some newly hatched chickens. The hen was placed in the barn and the dog was turned in with her. As soon as everyone was out of sight the dog slowly edged up toward the hen, sniffed the air in her direction a time or two (to make sure she was the kind of meat for which he was looking), then made a dive toward her. Meanwhile Mrs. Hen had been doing some "surveying" on her own account, for she met Mr. Dog more than halfway; moreover, she met him with such a surprise of wings and claws as he had never before experienced. The first round was clearly the hen's. But a nice fat bird, reckoned the dog, was not to slip between his paws so easily; therefore he backed away a short distance, then charged again. This time Mrs. Hen lit upon his back, drove her claws into his skin and made effective use of her sharp bill! Mr. Dog retreated to his corner, looking for all the world as if he were listening for someone to ring the bell and call the fight off until he got his bearings. But Mrs. Hen craved no time for deliberation; she had her adversary on the run and showed that she knew the value of the offensive by keeping him on the run.

One could almost understand her words as she flogged the poor Airedale from one corner to another, keeping up a series of rapid-fire sounds which for all the world resembled the remonstrations of an angry mother who had been called upon to defend her offspring from an attack by older boys.

The Airedale was a poor soldier! After running around the barn from corner to corner for about two minutes he spread himself on the ground as flat as he could and did his best to protect his eyes with his paws. Mrs. Hen seemed to be making a special attempt to peck out his eyes.

The owner of the hen then stepped in and retrieved her - or, more accurately stating it, he retrieved the dog - which in no way appeared to meet with the dog's disapproval.

The next day a chicken was placed in the cellar where the dog slept. As soon as he saw the bird he tucked his tail between his legs and ran for a corner! He never again attempted to catch a chicken. One lesson in social heredity, via the sense of "touch," was sufficient to teach him that while chicken-chasing may offer some enjoyment, it is also fraught with much hazard.

All these illustrations, with the exception of the first, describe the process of gathering knowledge through direct experience. Observe the marked difference between knowledge gathered by direct experience and that which is gathered through the training of the young by the old, as in the case of the ruffed grouse and her young.

The most impressive lessons are those learned by the young from the old, through highly colored or emotionalized methods of teaching. When the mother grouse spread her wings, stood her feathers on end, shook herself like a man suffering with the palsy and chattered to her young in a highly excited manner, she planted the fear of man in their hearts in a manner which they were never to forget.

The term "social heredity," as used in connection with this lesson, has particular reference to all methods through which a child is taught any idea, dogma, creed, religion or system of ethical conduct, by its parents or those who may have authority over it, before reaching the age at which it may reason and reflect upon such teaching in its own way; estimating the age of such reasoning power at, let us say, seven to twelve years.

There are myriads of forms of fear, but none are more deadly than the fear of poverty and old age. We drive our bodies as if they were slaves because we are so afraid of poverty that we wish to hoard money for –what - old age! This common form of fear drives us so hard that we overwork our bodies and bring on the very thing we are struggling to avoid.

What a tragedy to watch a man drive himself when he begins to arrive along about the forty-year mile post of life-the age at which he is just beginning to mature mentally. At forty a man is just entering the age in which he is able to see and understand and assimilate the handwriting of Nature, as it appears in the forests and flowing brooks and faces of men and little children, yet this devil fear drives him so hard that he becomes blinded and lost in the entanglement of a maze of conflicting desires. The principle of organized effort is lost sight of, and instead of laying hold of Nature's forces which are in evidence all around him, and permitting those forces to carry him to the heights of great achievement, he defies them and they become forces of destruction.

Perhaps none of these great forces of Nature are more available for man's unfoldment than is the principle of Auto-suggestion, but ignorance of this force is leading the majority of the human race to apply it so that it acts as a hindrance and not as a help.

Let us here enumerate the facts which show just how this misapplication of a great force of Nature takes place:

Here is a man who meets with some disappointment; a friend proves false, or a neighbor seems indifferent. Forthwith he decides (through self-suggestion) all men are untrustworthy and all neighbors unappreciative. These thoughts so deeply embed themselves in his subconscious mind that they color his whole attitude toward others. Go back, now, to what was said in Lesson Two, about the dominating thoughts of a man's mind attracting people whose thoughts are similar.

Apply the **Law of Attraction** and you will soon see and understand why the unbeliever attracts other unbelievers.

Reverse the Principle:

Here is a man who sees nothing but the best there is in all whom he meets. If his neighbors seem indifferent he takes no notice of that fact, for he makes it his business to fill his mind with dominating thoughts of optimism and good cheer and faith in others. If people speak to him harshly he speaks back in tones of softness. Through the operation of this same eternal **Law of Attraction** he draws to himself the attention of people whose attitude toward life and whose dominating thoughts harmonize with his own.

Tracing the principle a step further:

Here is a man who has been well schooled and has the ability to render the world some needed service. Somewhere, sometime, he has heard it said that modesty is a great virtue and that to push himself to the front of the stage in the game of life savors of egotism. He quietly slips in at the back door and takes a seat at the rear while other players in the game of life boldly step to the front. He remains in the back row because he fears "what they will say."

Public opinion, or that which he believes to be public opinion, has him pushed to the rear and the world hears but little of him. His schooling counts for naught because he is afraid to let the world know that he has had it. He is constantly suggesting to himself (thus using the great force of Auto-suggestion to his own detriment) that he should remain in the background lest he be criticized, as if criticism would do him any damage or defeat his purpose.

Here is another man who was born of poor parents. Since the first day that he can remember he has seen evidence of poverty. He has heard talk of poverty. He has felt the icy hand of poverty on his shoulders and it has so impressed him that he fixes it in his mind as a curse to which he must submit. Quite unconsciously he permits himself to fall victim of the belief "once poor always poor" until that belief becomes the dominating thought of his mind. He resembles a horse that has been harnessed and broken until it forgets that it has the potential power with which to throw off that harness. Auto-suggestion is rapidly relegating him to the back of the stage of life.

Finally he becomes a quitter. Ambition is gone. Opportunity comes his way no longer, or if it does he has not the vision to see it. He has accepted his FATE! It is a well established fact that the faculties of the mind, like the limbs of the body, atrophy and wither away if not used. Self-confidence is no exception. It develops when used but disappears if not used.

One of the chief disadvantages of inherited wealth is the fact that it too often leads to inaction and loss of Self-confidence. Some years ago a baby boy was born to Mrs. E. B. McLean, in the city of Washington. His inheritance was said to be around a hundred million dollars. When this baby was taken for an airing in its carriage it was surrounded by nurses and assistant nurses and detectives and other servants whose duty was to see that no harm befell it. As the years passed by this same vigilance was kept up. This child did not have to dress himself; he had servants who did that. Servants watched over him while he slept and while he was at play. He was not permitted to do anything that a servant could do for him. He had grown to the age of ten years. One day he was playing in the yard and noticed that the back gate had been left open. In all of his life he had never been outside of that gate alone, and naturally that was just the thing that he wished to do. During a moment when the servants were not looking he dashed out at the gate, and was run down and killed by an automobile before he reached the middle of the street.

He had used his servants' eyes until his own no longer served him as they might have done had he learned to rely upon them.

Twenty years ago the man whom I served as secretary sent his two sons away to school. One of them went to the University of Virginia and the other to a college in New York. Each month it was a part of my task to make out a check for $100.00 for each of these boys. This was their "pin money," to be spent as they wished. How profitably I remember the way I envied those boys as I made out those checks each month. I often wondered why the hand of fate bore me into the world in poverty. I could look ahead and see how these boys would rise to the high stations in life while I remained a humble clerk.

In due time the boys returned home with their "sheep-skins." Their father was a wealthy man who owned banks and railroads and coal mines and other property of great value. Good positions were waiting for the boys in their father's employ.

But, twenty years of time can play cruel tricks on those who have never had to struggle. Perhaps a better way to state this truth would be that time gives those who have never had to struggle a chance to play cruel tricks on themselves! At any rate, these two boys brought home from school other things besides their sheep-skins. They came back with well developed capacities for strong drink-capacities which 'they developed because the hundred dollars which each of them received each month made it unnecessary for them to struggle.

Theirs is a long and sad story, the details of which will not interest you, but you will be interested in their "finis" As this lesson is being written I have on my desk a copy of the newspaper published in the town where these boys lived. Their father has been bankrupted and his costly mansion, where the boys were born, has been placed on the block for sale. One of the boys died of delirium tremens and the other one is in an insane asylum.

Not all rich men's sons turn out so unfortunately, but the fact remains, nevertheless, that inaction leads to atrophy and this, in turn, leads to loss of ambition and self-confidence, and without these essential qualities a man will be carried through life on the wings of uncertainty, just as a dry leaf may be carried here and there on the bosom of the stray winds.

Far from being a disadvantage, struggle is a decided advantage, because it develops those qualities which would forever lie dormant without it. Many a man has found his place in the world because of having been forced to struggle for existence early in life. Lack of knowledge of the advantages accruing from struggle has prompted many a parent to say, "I had to work hard when I was young, but I shall see to it that my children have an easy time!" Poor foolish creatures. An "easy" time usually turns out to be a greater handicap than the average young man or woman can survive. There are worse things in this world than being forced to work in early life. Forced idleness is far worse than forced labor. Being forced to work, and forced to do your best, will breed in you temperance and self-control and strength of will and content and a hundred other virtues which the idle will never know.

Not only does lack of the necessity for struggle lead to weakness of ambition and will-power, but, what is more dangerous still, it sets up in a person's mind a state of lethargy that leads to the loss of Self-confidence. The person who has quit struggling because effort is no longer necessary is literally applying the principle of Auto-suggestion in undermining his own power of Self-confidence. Such a person will finally drift into a frame of mind in which he will actually look with more or less contempt upon the person who is forced to carry on.

The human mind, if you will pardon repetition, may be likened to an electric battery. It may be positive or it may be negative. Self-confidence is the quality with which the mind is re-charged and made positive.

Let us apply this line of reasoning to salesmanship and see what part Self-confidence plays in this great field of endeavor. One of the greatest salesmen this country has ever seen was once a clerk in a newspaper office.

It will be worth your while to analyze the method through which he gained his title as "the world's leading salesman."

He was a timid young man with a more or less retiring sort of nature. He was one of those who believe it best to slip in by the back door and take a seat at the rear of the stage of life. One evening he heard a lecture on the subject of this lesson, Self-confidence, and that lecture so impressed him that he left the lecture hall with a firm determination to pull himself out of the rut into which he had drifted.

He went to the Business Manager of the paper and asked for a position as solicitor of advertising and was put to work on a commission basis. Everyone in the office expected to see him fail, as this sort of salesmanship calls for the most positive type of sales ability. He went to his room and made out a list of a certain type of merchants on whom he intended to call. One would think that he would naturally have made up his list of the names of those whom he believed he could sell with the least effort, but he did nothing of the sort. He placed on his list only the names of the merchants on whom other advertising solicitors had called without making a sale. His list consisted of only twelve names. Before he made a single call he went out to the city park, took out his list of twelve names, read it over a hundred times, saying to himself as he did so, "You will purchase advertising space from me before the end of the month."

Then he began to make his calls. The first day he closed sales with three of the twelve "impossibilities." During the remainder of the week he made sales to two others. By the end of the month he had opened advertising accounts with all but one of the merchants that he had on the list. For the ensuing month he made no sales, for the reason that he made no calls except on this one obstinate merchant. Every morning when the store opened he was on hand to interview this merchant and every morning the merchant said "No." The merchant knew he was not going to buy advertising space, but this young man didn't know it. When the merchant said No the young man did not hear it, but kept right on coming. On the last day of the month, after having told this persistent young man No for thirty consecutive times, the merchant said:

"Look here, young man, you have wasted a whole month trying to sell me; now, what I would like to know is this - why have you wasted your time?"

"Wasted my time nothing," he retorted; "I have been going to school and you have been my teacher. Now I know all the arguments that a merchant can bring up for not buying, and besides that I have been drilling myself in Self-confidence."

Then the merchant said: "I will make a little confession of my own. I, too, have been going to school, and you have been my teacher. You have taught me a lesson in persistence that is worth money to me, and to show you my appreciation I am going to pay my tuition fee by giving you an order for advertising space."

And that was the way in which the Philadelphia North American's best advertising account was brought in. Likewise, it marked the beginning of a reputation that has made that same young man a millionaire.

He succeeded because he deliberately charged his own mind with sufficient Self-confidence to make that mind an irresistible force. When he sat down to make up that list of twelve names he did something that ninety-nine people out of a hundred would not have done-he selected the names of those whom he believed it would be hard to sell, because he understood that out of the resistance he would meet with in trying to sell them would come strength and Self-confidence. He was one of the very few people who understand that all rivers and some men are crooked because of following the line of least resistance.

I am going to digress and here break the line of thought for a moment while recording a word of advice to the wives of men. Remember, these lines are intended only for wives, and husbands are not expected to read that which is here set down.

From having analyzed more than 16,000 people, the majority of whom were married men, I have learned something that may be of value to wives. Let me state my thought in these words:

You have it within your power to send your husband away to his work or his business or his profession each day with a feeling of Self-confidence that will carry him successfully over the rough spots of the day and bring him home again, at night, smiling and happy. One of my acquaintances of former years married a woman who had a set of false teeth. One day his wife dropped her teeth and broke the plate. The husband picked up the pieces and began examining them. He showed such interest in them that his wife said:

"You could make a set of teeth like those if you made up your mind to do it."

This man was a farmer whose ambitions had never carried him beyond the bounds of his little farm until his wife made that remark. She walked over and laid her hand on his shoulder and encouraged him to try his hand at dentistry. She finally coaxed him to make the start, and today he is one of the most prominent and successful dentists in the state of Virginia. I know him well, for he is my father!

No one can foretell the possibilities of achievement available to the man whose wife stands at his back and urges him on to bigger and better endeavor, for it is a well known fact that a woman can arouse a man so that he will perform almost superhuman feats. It is your right and your duty to encourage your husband and urge him on in worthy undertakings until he shall have found his place in the world. You can induce him to put forth greater effort than can any other person in the world. Make him believe that nothing within reason is beyond his power of achievement and you will have rendered him a service that will go a long way toward helping him win in the battle of life.

One of the most successful men in his line in America gives entire credit for his success to his wife. When they were first married she wrote a creed which he signed and placed over his desk. This is a copy of the creed:

- I believe in myself.
- I believe in those who work with me.
- I believe in my employer.
- I believe in my friends.
- I believe in my family.
- I believe that God will lend me everything I need with which to succeed if I do my best to earn it through faithful and honest service.
- I believe in prayer and I will never close my eyes in sleep without praying for divine guidance to the end that I will be patient with other people and tolerant with those who do not believe as I do.
- I believe that success is the result of intelligent effort and does not depend upon luck or sharp practices or double-crossing friends, fellow men or my employer.
- I believe I will get out of life exactly what I put into it, therefore I will be careful to conduct myself toward others as I would want them to act toward me.
- I will not slander those whom I do not like.

- I will not slight my work no matter what I may see others doing.
- I will render the best service of which I am capable because I have pledged myself to succeed in life and I know that success is always the result of conscientious and efficient effort.
- Finally, I will forgive those who offend me because I realize that I shall sometimes offend others and I will need their forgiveness.

Signed ....

The woman who wrote this creed was a practical psychologist of the first order. With the influence and guidance of such a woman as a helpmate any man could achieve noteworthy success.

Analyze this creed and you will notice how freely the personal pronoun is used. It starts off with the affirmation of Self-confidence, which is perfectly proper. No man could make this creed his own without developing the positive attitude that would attract to him people who would aid him in his struggle for success.

This would be a splendid creed for every salesman to adopt. It might not hurt your chances for success if you adopted it. Mere adoption, however, is not enough. You must practice it! Read it over and over until you know it by heart. Then repeat it at least once a day until you have literally transformed it into your mental make-up. Keep a copy of it before you as a daily reminder of your pledge to practice it. By doing so you will be making efficient use of the principle of Auto-suggestion as a means of developing Self-confidence. Never mind what anyone may say about your procedure. Just remember that it is your business to succeed, and this creed, if mastered and applied, will go a long way toward helping you.

You learned in Lesson Two that any idea you firmly fix in your subconscious mind, by repeated affirmation, automatically becomes a plan or blueprint which an unseen power uses in directing your efforts toward the attainment of the objective named - in the plan.

You have also learned that the principle through which you may fix any idea you choose in your mind is called Auto-suggestion, which simply means a suggestion that you give to your own mind. It was this principle of Auto-suggestion that Emerson had in mind when he wrote:

"Nothing can bring you peace but yourself!"

You might well remember that Nothing can bring you success but yourself. Of course you will need the co-operation of others if you aim to attain success of a far-reaching nature, but you will never get that cooperation unless you vitalize your mind with the positive attitude of Self-confidence.

Perhaps you have wondered why a few men advance to highly paid positions while others all around them, who have as much training and who seemingly perform as much work, do not get ahead. Select any two people of these two types that you choose, and study them, and the reason why one advances and the other stands still will be quite obvious to you. You will find that the one who advances believes in himself. You will find that he backs this belief with such dynamic, aggressive action that he lets others know that he believes in himself. You will also notice that this Self-confidence is contagious; it is impelling; it is persuasive; it attracts others.

You will also find that the one who does not advance shows clearly, by the look on his face, by the posture of his body, by the lack of briskness in his step, by the uncertainty with which he speaks, that he lacks Self-confidence. No one is going to pay much attention to the person who has no confidence in himself.

He does not attract others because his mind is a negative force that repels rather than attracts.

In no other field of endeavor does Self-confidence or the lack of it play such an important part as in the field of salesmanship, and you do not need to be a character analyst to determine, the moment you meet him, whether a salesman possesses this quality of Self-confidence. If he has it the signs of its influence are written all over him. He inspires you with confidence in him and in the goods he is selling the moment he speaks.

We come, now, to the point at, which you are ready to take hold of the principle of Auto-suggestion and make direct use of it in developing yourself into a positive and dynamic and self-reliant person. You are instructed to copy the following formula, sign it and commit it to memory:

SELF-CONFIDENCE FORMULA

First: I know that I have the ability to achieve the object of my definite purpose, therefore I demand of myself persistent, aggressive and continuous action toward its attainment.

Second: I realize that the dominating thoughts of my mind eventually reproduce themselves in outward, bodily action, and gradually transform themselves into physical reality, therefore I will concentrate My mind for thirty minutes daily upon the task of thinking of the person I intend to be, by creating a mental picture of this person and then transforming that picture into reality through practical service.

Third: I know that through the principle of Auto-suggestion, any desire that I persistently hold in my mind will eventually seek expression through some practical means of realizing it, therefore I shall devote ten minutes daily to demanding of myself the development of the factors named in the sixteen lessons of this Reading Course on the Law of Success.

Fourth: I have clearly mapped out and written down a description of my definite purpose in life, for the coming five years. I have set a price on my services for each of these five years; a price that I intend to earn and receive, through strict application of the principle of efficient, satisfactory service which I will render in advance.

Fifth: I fully realize that no wealth or position can long endure unless built upon truth and justice, therefore I will engage in no transaction which does not benefit all whom it affects. 1 will succeed by attracting to me the forces I wish to use, and the co-operation of other people. I will induce others to serve me because I will first serve them. I will eliminate hatred, envy, jealousy, selfishness and cynicism by developing love for all humanity, because I know that a negative attitude toward others can never bring me success. I will cause others to believe in me because I will believe in them and in myself.

I will sign my name to this formula, commit it to memory and repeat it aloud once a day with full faith that it will gradually influence my entire life so that I will become a successful and happy worker in my chosen field of endeavor.

Signed...

Before you sign your name to this formula make sure that you intend to carry out its instructions. Back of this formula lies a law that no man can explain. The psychologists refer to this law as Auto-suggestion and let it go at that, but you should bear in mind one point about which there is no uncertainty, and that is the fact that whatever this law is it actually works!

Another point to be kept in mind is the fact that, just as electricity will turn the wheels of industry and serve mankind in a million other ways, or snuff out life if wrongly applied, so will this principle of Auto-suggestion lead you up the mountain-side of peace and prosperity, or down into the valley of misery and poverty, according to the application you make of it. If you fill your mind with doubt and unbelief in your ability to achieve, then the principle of Auto-suggestion takes this spirit of unbelief and sets it up in your subconscious mind as your dominating thought and slowly but surely draws you into the whirlpool of failure. But, if you fill your mind with radiant Self-confidence, the principle of Auto-suggestion takes this belief and sets it up as your dominating thought and helps you master the obstacles that fall in your way until you reach the mountain-top of success.

THE POWER OF HABIT

Having, myself, experienced all the difficulties that stand in the road of those who lack the understanding to make practical application of this great principle of Auto-suggestion, let me take you a short way into the principle of habit, through the aid of which you may easily apply the principle of Auto-suggestion in any direction and for any purpose whatsoever.

Habit grows out of environment; out of doing the same thing or thinking the same thoughts or repeating the same words over and over again. Habit may be likened to the groove on a phonograph record, while the human mind may be likened to the needle that fits into that groove. When any habit has been well formed, through repetition of thought or action, the mind has a tendency to attach itself to and follow the course of that habit as closely as the phonograph needle follows the groove in the wax record.

Habit is created by repeatedly directing one or more of the five senses of seeing, hearing, smelling, tasting and feeling, in a given direction. It is through this repetition principle that the injurious drug habit is formed. It is through this same principle that the desire for intoxicating drink is formed into a habit.

After habit has been well established it will automatically control and direct our bodily activity, wherein may be found a thought that can be transformed into a powerful factor in the development of Self-confidence. The thought is this: Voluntarily, and by force if necessary, direct your efforts and your thoughts along a desired line until you have formed the habit that will lay hold of you and continue,voluntarily, to direct your efforts along the same line.

The object in writing out and repeating the Self-confidence formula is to form the habit of making belief in yourself the dominating thought of your mind until that thought has been thoroughly embedded in your subconscious mind, through the principle of habit.

You learned to write by repeatedly directing the muscles of your arm and hand over certain outlines known as letters, until finally you formed the habit of tracing these outlines. Now you write with ease and rapidity, without tracing each letter slowly. Writing has become a habit with you.

The principle of habit will lay hold of the faculties of your mind just the same as it will influence the physical muscles of your body, as you can easily prove by mastering and applying this lesson on Self-confidence. Any statement that you repeatedly make to yourself, or any desire that you deeply plant in your mind through repeated statement, will eventually seek expression through your physical, outward bodily efforts. The principle of habit is the very foundation upon which this lesson on Self-confidence is built, and if you will understand and follow the directions laid down in this lesson you will soon know more about the law of habit, from first-hand knowledge, than could be taught you by a thousand such lessons as this.

You have but little conception of the possibilities which lie sleeping within you, awaiting but the awakening hand of vision to arouse you, and you will never have a better conception of those possibilities unless you develop sufficient Self-confidence to lift you above the commonplace influences of your present environment.

The human mind is a marvelous, mysterious piece of machinery, a fact of which I was reminded a few months ago when I picked up Emerson's Essays and re-read his essay on Spiritual Laws. A strange thing happened. I saw in that essay, which I had read scores of times previously, much that I had never noticed before. I saw more in this essay than I had seen during previous readings because the unfoldment of my mind since the last reading had prepared me to interpret more.

The human mind is constantly unfolding, like the petals of a flower, until it reaches the maximum of development. What this maximum is, where it ends, or whether it ends at all or not, are unanswerable questions, but the degree of unfoldment seems to vary according to the nature of the individual and the degree to which he keeps his mind at work. A mind that is forced or coaxed into analytical thought every day seems to keep on unfolding and developing greater powers of interpretation.

Down in Louisville, Kentucky, lives Mr. Lee Cook, a man who has practically no legs and has to wheel himself around on a cart. In spite of the fact that Mr. Cook has been without legs since birth, he is the owner of a great industry and a millionaire through his own efforts. He has proved that a man can get along very well without legs if he has a well developed Self-confidence.

In the city of New York one may see a strong able-bodied and able-headed young man, without legs, rolling himself down Fifth Avenue every afternoon,with cap in hand, begging for a living. His head is perhaps as sound and as able to think as the average.

This young man could duplicate anything that Mr. Cook, of Louisville, has done, if he thought of himself as Mr. Cook thinks of himself.

Henry Ford owns more millions of dollars than he will ever need or use. Not so many years ago, he was working as a laborer in a machine shop, with but little schooling and without capital. Scores of other men, some of them with better organized brains than his, worked near him. Ford threw off the poverty consciousness, developed confidence in himself, thought of success and attained it. Those who worked around him could have done as well had they thought as he did.

Milo C. Jones, of Wisconsin, was stricken down with paralysis a few years ago. So bad was the stroke that he could not turn himself in bed or move a muscle of his body. His physical body was useless, but there was nothing wrong with his brain, so it began to function in earnest, probably for the first time in its existence. Lying flat on his back in bed, Mr. Jones made that brain create a definite purpose. That purpose was prosaic and humble enough in nature, but it was definite and it was a purpose, something that he had never known before.

His definite purpose was to make pork sausage. Calling his family around him he told of his plans and began directing them in carrying the plans into action. With nothing to aid him except a sound mind and plenty of Self-confidence, Milo C. Jones spread the name and reputation of "Little Pig Sausage" all over the United States, and accumulated a fortune besides.

All this was accomplished after paralysis had made it impossible for him to work with his hands.

Where thought prevails power may be found!

Henry Ford has made millions of dollars and is still making millions of dollars each year because he believed in Henry Ford and transformed that belief into a definite purpose and backed that purpose with a definite plan. The other machinists who worked along with Ford, during the early days of his career, visioned nothing but a weekly pay envelope and that was all they ever got. They demanded nothing out of the ordinary of themselves. If you want to get more be sure to demand more of yourself. Notice that this demand is to be made on yourself!

There comes to mind a well known poem whose author expressed a great psychological truth:

> If you think you are beaten, you are;
> If you think you dare not, you don't;
> If you like to win, but you think you can't,
> It is almost certain you won't.
>
> If you think you'll lose you've lost,
> For out of the world we find
> Success begins with a fellow's will –
> It's all in the state of mind.

If you think you are outclassed, you are -
You've got to think high to rise.
You've got to be sure of yourself before
You can ever win a prize.

Life's battles don't always go
To the stronger or faster man;
But soon or late the man who wins
Is the man who thinks he can.

It can do no harm if you commit this poem to memory and use it as a part of your working equipment in the development of Self-confidence.

Somewhere in your make-up there is a "subtle something" which, if it were aroused by the proper outside influence, would carry you to heights of achievement such as you have never before anticipated. Just as a master player can take hold of a violin and cause that instrument to pour forth the most beautiful and entrancing strains of music, so is there some outside influence that can lay hold of your mind and cause you to go forth into the field of your chosen endeavor and play a glorious symphony of success. No man knows what hidden forces lie dormant within you. You, yourself, do not know your capacity for achievement, and you never will know until you come in contact with that particular stimulus which arouses you to greater action and extends your vision, develops your Self-confidence and moves you with a deeper desire to achieve.

It is not unreasonable to expect that some statement, some idea or some stimulating word of this Reading Course on the Law of Success will serve as the needed stimulus that will re-shape your destiny and re-direct your thoughts and energies along a pathway that will lead you, finally, to your coveted goal of life. It is strange, but true, that the most important turning-points of life often come at the most unexpected times and in the most unexpected ways. I have in mind a typical example of how some of the seemingly unimportant experiences of life often turn out to be the most important of all, and I am relating this ease because it shows, also, what a man can accomplish when he awakens to a full understanding of the value of Self-confidence. The incident to which I refer happened in the city of Chicago, while I was engaged in the work of character analysis. One day a tramp presented himself at my office and asked for an interview. As I looked up from my work and greeted him he said, "I have come to see the man who wrote this little book," as he removed from his pocket a copy of a book entitled Self-confidence, which I had written many years previously. "It must have been the hand of fate," he continued, "that slipped this book into my pocket yesterday afternoon, because I was about ready to go out there and punch a hole in Lake Michigan. I had about come to the conclusion that everything and everybody, including God, had it in for me until I read this book, and it gave me a new viewpoint and brought me the courage and the hope that sustained me through the night. I made up my mind that if I could see the man who wrote this book he could help me get on my feet again. Now, I am here and I would like to know what you can do for a man like me."

While he was speaking I had been studying him from head to foot, and I am frank to admit that down deep in my heart I did not believe there was anything I could do for him, but I did not wish to tell him so. The glassy stare in his eyes, the lines of discouragement in his face, the posture of his body, the ten days' growth of beard on his face, the nervous manner about this man all conveyed to me the impression that he was hopeless, but I did not have the heart to tell him so, therefore I asked him to sit down and tell me his whole story. I asked him to be perfectly frank and tell me, as nearly as possible, just what had brought him down to the ragged edge of life. I promised him that after I had heard his entire story I would then tell him whether or not I could be of service to him. He related his story, in lengthy detail, the sum and substance of which was this: He had invested his entire fortune in a small manufacturing business. When the world war began in 1914, it was impossible for him to get the raw materials necessary in the operation of his factory, and he therefore failed. The loss of his money broke his heart and so disturbed his mind that he left his wife and children and became a tramp. He had actually brooded over his loss until he had reached the point at which he was contemplating suicide.

After he had finished his story, I said to him: "I have listened to you with a great deal of interest, and I wish that there was something which I could do to help you, but there is absolutely nothing."

He became as pale as he will be when he is laid away in a coffin, and settled back in his chair and dropped his chin on his chest as much as to say, "That settles it." I waited for a few seconds, then said:

"While there is nothing that I can do for you, there is a man in this building to whom I will introduce you, if you wish, who can help you regain your lost fortune and put you back on your feet again." These words had barely fallen from my lips when he jumped up, grabbed me by the hands and said, "For God's sake lead me to this man."

It was encouraging to note that he had asked this "for God's sake." This indicated that there was still a spark of hope within his breast, so I took him by the arm and led him out into the laboratory where my psychological tests in character analysis were conducted, and stood with him in front of what looked to be a curtain over a door. I pulled the curtain aside and uncovered a tall looking-glass in which he saw himself from head to foot. Pointing my finger at the glass I said:

"There stands the man to whom I promised to introduce you. There is the only man in this world who can put you back on your feet again, and unless you sit down and become acquainted with that man, as you never became acquainted with him before, you might just as well go on over and `punch a hole' in Lake Michigan, because you will be of no value to yourself or to the world until you know this man better."

He stepped over to the glass, rubbed his hands over his bearded face, studied himself from head to foot for a few moments, then stepped back, dropped his head and began to weep. I knew that the lesson had been driven home, so I led him back to the elevator and sent him away. I never expected to see him again, and I doubted that the lesson would be sufficient to help him regain his place in the world, because he seemed to be too far gone for redemption. He seemed to be not only down, but almost out.

A few days later I met this man on the street. His transformation had been so complete that I hardly recognized him. He was walking briskly, with his head tilted back. That old, shifting, nervous posture of his body was gone. He was dressed in new clothes from head to foot. He looked prosperous and he felt prosperous. He stopped me and related what had happened to bring about his rapid transformation from a state of abject failure to one of hope and promise.

"I was just on my way to your office," he explained, "to bring you the good news. I went out the very day that I was in your office, a down-and-out tramp, and despite my appearance I sold myself at a salary of $3,000.00 a year. Think of it, man, three thousand dollars a year! And my employer advanced me money enough with which to buy some new clothes, as you can see for yourself. He also advanced me some money to send home to my family, and I am once more on the road to success. It seems like a dream when I think that only a few days ago I had lost hope and faith and courage, and was actually contemplating suicide.

"I was coming to tell you that one of these days, when you are least expecting me, I will pay you another visit, and when I do. I will be a successful man. I will bring with me a check, signed in blank and made payable to you, and you may fill in the amount because you have saved me from myself by introducing me to myself - that self which I never knew until you stood me in front of that looking-glass and pointed out the real me."

As that man turned and departed in the crowded streets of Chicago I saw, for the first time in my life, what strength and power and possibility lie hidden in the mind of the man who has never discovered the value of Self-reliance. Then and there I made up my mind that I, too, would stand in front of that same looking-glass and point an accusing finger at myself for not having discovered the lesson which I had helped another to learn. I did stand before that same looking-glass, and as I did so I then and there fixed in my mind, as my definite purpose in life, the determination to help men and women discover the forces that lie sleeping within them. The book you hold in your hands is evidence that my definite purpose is being carried out.

The man whose story I have related is now the president of one of the largest and most successful concerns of its kind in America, with a business that extends from coast to coast and from Canada to Mexico.

A short while after the incident just related, a woman came to my office for personal analysis. She was then a teacher in the Chicago public schools. I gave her an analysis chart and asked her to fill it out. She had been at work on the chart but a few minutes when she came back to my desk, handed back the chart and said, "I do not believe I will fill this out." I asked her why she had decided not to fill out the chart and she replied: "To be perfectly frank with you, one of the questions in this chart put me to thinking and I now know what is wrong with me, therefore I feel it unnecessary to pay you a fee to analyze me." With that the woman went away and I did not hear from her for two years. She went to New York City, became a writer of advertising copy for one of the largest agencies in the country and her income at the time she wrote me was $10,000.00 a year.

This woman sent me a check to cover the cost of my analysis fee, because she felt that the fee had been earned, even though I did not render her the service that I usually render my clients. It is impossible for anyone to foretell what seemingly insignificant incident may lead to an important turning-point in one's career, but there is no denying the fact that these "turning-points" may be more readily recognized by those who have well-rounded-out confidence in themselves.

One of the irreparable losses to the human race lies in the lack of knowledge that there is a definite method through which Self-confidence can be developed in any person of average intelligence. What an immeasurable loss to civilization that young men and women are not taught this known method of developing Self-confidence before they complete their schooling, for no one who lacks faith in himself is really educated in the proper sense of the term.

Oh, what glory and satisfaction would be the happy heritage of the man or woman who could pull aside the curtain of fear that hangs over the human race and shuts out the sunlight of understanding that Self-confidence brings, wherever it is in evidence.

Where fear controls, noteworthy achievement becomes an impossibility, a fact which brings to mind the definition of fear, as stated by a great philosopher:

"Fear is the dungeon of the mind into which it runs and hides and seeks seclusion. Fear brings on superstition and superstition is the dagger with which hypocrisy assassinates the soul."

In front of the typewriter on which I am writing the manuscripts for this Reading Course hangs a sign with the following wording, in big letters:

"Day by day in every way I am becoming more successful."

A skeptic who read that sign asked if I really believed "that stuff" and I replied, "Of course not. All it ever did for me was to help me get out of the coal mines, where I started as a laborer, and find a place in the world in which I am serving upwards of 100,000 people, in whose minds I am planting the same positive thought that this sign brings out; therefore, why should I believe in it?"

As this man started to leave he said: "Well, perhaps there is something to this sort of philosophy, after all, for I have always been afraid that I would be a failure, and so far my fears have been thoroughly realized."

You are condemning yourself to poverty, misery and failure, or you are driving yourself on toward the heights of great achievement, solely by the thoughts you think. If you demand success of yourself and back up this demand with intelligent action you are sure to win. Bear in mind, though, that there is a difference between demanding success and just merely wishing for it. You should find out what this difference is, and take advantage of it.

Do you remember what the Bible says (look it up, somewhere in the book of Matthew) about those who have faith as a grain of mustard seed? Go at the task of developing Self-confidence with at least that much faith if not more. Never mind "what they will say" because you might as well know that "they" will be of little aid to you in your climb up the mountain-side of life toward the object of your definite purpose. You have within you all the power you need with which to get whatever you want or need in this world, and about the best way to avail yourself of this power is to believe in yourself.

"Know thyself, man; know thyself."

This has been the advice of the philosophers all down the ages. When you really know yourself you will know that there is nothing foolish about hanging a sign in front of you that reads like this: "Day by day in every way I am becoming more successful," with due apologies to the Frenchman who made this motto popular. I am not afraid to place this sort of suggestion in front of my desk, and, what is more to the point, I am not afraid to believe that it will influence me so that I will become a more positive and aggressive human being.

More than twenty-five years ago I learned my first lesson in Self-confidence building. One night I was sitting before an open fire-place, listening to a conversation between some older men, on the subject of Capital and Labor. Without invitation I joined in the conversation and said something about employers and employees settling their differences on the Golden Rule basis. My remarks attracted the attention of one of the men, who turned to me, with a look of surprise on his face and said:

"Why, you are a bright boy, and if you would go out and get a schooling you would make your mark in the world."

Those remarks fell on "fertile" ears, even though that was the first time anyone had ever told me that I was bright, or that I might accomplish anything worthwhile in life. The remark put me to thinking, and the more I allowed my mind to dwell upon that thought the more certain I became that the remark had back of it a possibility.

It might be truthfully stated that whatever service I am rendering the world and whatever good I accomplish, should be credited to that off-hand remark.

Suggestions such as this are often powerful, and none the less so when they are deliberate and self-expressed. Go back, now, to the Self-confidence formula and master it, for it will lead you into the "power-house" of your own mind, where you will tap a force that can be made to carry you to the very top of the Ladder of Success.

Others will believe in you only when you believe in yourself. They will "tune in" on your thoughts and feel toward you just as you feel toward yourself. The law of mental telepathy takes care of this. You are continuously broadcasting what you think of yourself, and if you have no faith in yourself others will pick up the vibrations of your thoughts and mistake them for their own. Once understand the law of mental telepathy and you will know why Self-confidence is the second of the Fifteen Laws of Success.

You should be cautioned, however, to learn the difference between Self-confidence, which is based upon sound knowledge of what you know and what you can do, and egotism, which is only based upon what you wish you knew or could do. Learn the difference between these two terms or you will make yourself boresome, ridiculous and annoying to people of culture and understanding. Self-confidence is something which should never be proclaimed or announced except through intelligent performance of constructive deeds.

If you have Self-confidence those around you will discover this fact. Let them make the discovery. They will feel proud of their alertness in having made the discovery, and you will be free from the suspicion of egotism. Opportunity never stalks the person with a highly developed state of egotism, but brick-bats and ugly remarks do. Opportunity forms affinities much more easily and quickly with Self-confidence than it does with egotism. Self-praise is never a proper measure of self-reliance. Bear this in mind and let your Self-confidence speak only through the tongue of constructive service rendered without fuss or flurry.

Self-confidence is the product of knowledge. Know yourself, know how much you know (and how little), why you know it, and how you are going to use it. "Four-flushers" come to grief, therefore, do not pretend to know more than you actually do know. There's no use of pretense, because any educated person will measure you quite accurately after hearing you speak for three minutes. What you really are will speak so loudly that what you "claim" you are will not be heard.

If you heed this warning the last four pages of this one lesson may mark one of the most important turning-points of your life.

Believe in yourself, but do not tell the world what you can do-SHOW IT!

The complete text of the book behind this excerpt may be found in -

The Law of Success - In Sixteen Lessons

(Please see Bibliography for details.)

Julia Seton, M.D.

One of the first women to be admitted to the AMA, Julia Seton was also a New Thought pioneer, founding New Civilization Centers all over the world.

The excerpt here is from her "Science of Success", where she lays out several methods for you to create and achieve your own success with no more than your thoughts to start with.

And you will find her saying,

"The tools of conquest are in our hands! Our concentrated mind, our thought force carefully directed and intensified, at our own pleasure, make us the master of our fate and no matter what our place in life may be, we can show our greatness."

Science of Success

FOURTEENTH SUCCESS METHOD - CONCENTRATION

CENTURIES ago it was written, "Whatsoever thy hand findeth to do, do it with thy might." And that subtle law of doing everything we do with our might is the very heart of the law of success.

Upon concentration more than upon any other thing hangs our hope for ultimate self-perfection.

Concentration is the first step toward conscious direction and control, and without it we cannot hope to go far into the fulfillment of our own desires. The one who hopes to find something to do, who has an urging aspiration and then fails to do this thing with their might, is not fit to possess the thing for which they are longing.

It is possible to go through life idle and drifting, thinking the world owes us a living and we do get some things because the Universal life always floats an abundance of supply on its bosom, and anyone who wants to do so can eat the crumbs which fall from the idlers' table, but if we hope to come out into any definite form, use or value, we can only do it by bending nobly to life's oars.

In life's channel there are rocks everywhere and it is our own hand that must clear the channel and our own genius that must steer us past them. Some of the most wonderful successes have been born from the genius of concentration and they never surrendered one iota of their might until they accomplished their ends. The story is told of the late John W. Gates and his perfect manifestation of this success principle. He went to San Antonio, Texas and saw the great possibilities in Texas; he came to the state some years ago as the agent of a barbed wire company, and emphasized his belief to an old citizen now a resident of San Antonio.

This old citizen was complaining that he could only make a living here.

"Make a living!" said Gates. "Any man can get rich here in ten years."

"Well," said the old citizen, "I've been here more than ten years and I have not got rich."

"Perhaps not," remarked Gates, "wealth does not hunt one up and spring from some unseen angle. One has to keep constantly on the trail, and since there are so many trails leading in the right direction in Texas, if you will keep an eye on me I'll show you how the trick is turned."

Some years later when Gates became heavily interested in the lumber business in the eastern part of the state, someone said to him:

"You cannot make the lumber business go here, since there is no means of shipping it."

"Never mind," remarked Gates, "I'll make a place to ship it from and then I'll show you that there is enough lumber in Texas to weatherboard the universe."

Sometime after this he met the old man to whom he had talked about getting rich when he first came to Texas.

"I hear you are making it go," said the old man, "and that you are really getting rich, as you said you would."

"Making it go," remarked the man who saw possibilities. "Damn it! things are making me go. Things come so easily here that I am constantly on the dodge to keep from owning the whole state of Texas. It's the easiest game I ever played. No odds what kind of a hand one has, if he bets stiff enough he'll win."

There are thousands of failures simply because they did not have the genius to see an opportunity, but there are more failures because when opportunity was everywhere they lacked the thought force necessary to push it into form. This is not just the same as the law of "mind your own business."

There are many subtle breaks in this chain of doing and every break means failure. Living in one world and working there with our hands, while all our thoughts and wits are wandering in another, divides our forces. No one can serve two masters. Success demands that our mind shall be in all things we do, and all things in our mind, until we have established a long line of things which we can do automatically. When concentration is complete one can do a half dozen things at one time and direct as many more. The concentrated mind does not think in concepts, it thinks in ultimates, it does not think in pennies and dollars, it thinks in millions, it does not think in cities and states, it thinks in continents; nor does it think in minutes, hours, or days but in eternities.

Here are some of the well--known failure cases we meet, and who demand help and attention. One day I went to a restaurant and after seating myself said to the waitress, "Bring me a pot of tea."

Instead of bringing me a pot of tea, as I had ordered, she brought a cup of tea. She had not heard what I said. When she brought the cup of tea it was overflowing with tea which spilled over the saucer and the table. The waitress set the cup down and went away. I did not know where she had gone. She was not in sight nor finishing my order --- that was sure. It is written "Thou shalt have no other gods before me" and this waitress was not doing with her might what her hands found to do. She was thoroughly reckless, careless and regardless of the thing that she was in the restaurant to do.

I have watched the people in the work world. I went into a jewelry store and the girl at the counter was humming some ragtime song. Her mind was on the ragtime and she kept on singing and I hardly dared to interrupt her. When I asked for a bracelet she said, "Let me see." She proceeded to drag out some jewelry in a careless way from the shelves and continued to hum her interrupted song. Not seeing any article that appealed to my fancy, I asked, "Have you anything else?" I was simply forced to compel her to pay me some attention as a dentist forces a tooth. This girl did not know her stock, and did not care half as much about it as she did about the song. She was not there in the interest of jewelry, she was not doing what her hand found to do with all her might. She was not concentrated in her work. She was living in one world, while functioning in another.

Another incident of like character. I went to a coat store and asked the saleswoman to show me a coat. She stood like a statue and asked, "What kind of a coat do you want?" I replied, "I do not know, I want you to show me some coats." To this she replied, "Well, if you will tell me what sort you want, --- what color?" In desperation I said, "I don't care. I want to see if you have anything I want." She then walked around unconcerned and abstractedly and did not seem to know a thing about coats, yet she was selling coats, she should have known all about coats. I had had no choice, but just wanted to find something suitable for me in that store.

What would a concentrated saleswoman have done? A life that was in power, a saleswoman who was doing with her might what her hands found to do? She would have said, "Here are some coats." And then she would have piled up coats of all descriptions before me and she would have made suggestions in regard to them and mentioned their attractive prices and would have tempted me to try on half a dozen of them.

The girl in the coat store was only one of ten thousand of her kind who are walking the streets out of a job, and wondering why someone else has work and she has not. Finally I saw a coat on a rack and put it on myself and asked the saleswoman if the attached tag was the correct one, and being assured that it was I concluded to take this coat. Then I said to her, "I want to tell you something that you won't forget. You did not sell me this coat, I got it in spite of you. The man who employs you would have lost this sale as far as you are concerned, and if he had lost this sale to me he will lose twenty-five or thirty sales during the day because of you. And when on Saturday night he comes to you and says 'I have no use for you' you will shed bitter tears and ask what the matter is.

"You have not learned the first principles of keeping a position and nobody will then employ you. I am not a prophet, but I venture to say that you have been out of work half the time for the last five years, and you can't keep a place more than a few weeks." Afterward I found that I was right and that she was afraid that she would lose her place that very Saturday night.

The whole world of commerce and industry is looking for mascots, for people who can come in and help them to intensify their business, who will be a help to them, they are not looking for people like this sales girl, to stand around and let the customers buy their own goods, and sell it to themselves and almost make out their own checks. They are paying their help to be the link between their goods and the public that is seeking them, and until this is learned, people of this saleswoman type will wander and continue to wander over the face of the earth because they do not have that necessary concentration to hold them steadfast to their work. The fault is not in their employers, but in themselves. The saleswoman I have cited was one whom nobody liked. Why? Because she did not put anything into life, and consequently could take nothing out of it. I am taking this girl as a principle, because she is one of many of her kind who clog the world with failure and always asking themselves, "What is the matter with me?" Their methods are faulty.

Our first fundamental is that success is built upon one thing --- success methods, and failure is built upon one thing --- failure methods, and this saleswoman hoping for success was using failure methods and there is no relationship between them. One is the product of unconcentrated, unrelated, indifferent life, and the other is the product of a conscious, powerful, related and concentrated life.

"Do with your might what your hands find to do" and concentrate on that work until you are absolute master, no matter how much you dislike your work. If you had outgrown the thing you are doing, you would not have to do it, just as one lays down an old coat that is outgrown. The moment we are big enough to get rid of a thing, we are forced to leave that thing. We could not stay, for the larger law of our life displaces it, we cannot stay with it because the cosmic law will push it off.

Man's fitness is measured by his understanding and by his perfection in the place on his path; and so today if we are working in a place which we do not enjoy it is the measure of the state of consciousness we have intensified so highly that it cannot keep out of form.

A man once said to me, "What is the reason I always get such 'five cent' jobs? Why, I am a bigger man than that. I have a great deal of ability and I simply hate these 'five cent' jobs. I never get anything that is up to me; I can't do these little things with any degree of power or efficiency, because all the time it just grinds me to think I have these little positions. I want something that is as big as I am."

I said to him only the eternal truth when I replied: "You have a 'five cent' job because you have in you a 'five cent' man whom you have intensified so that he cannot keep out of form: No man ever had a 'five cent' job who had not the 'five cent' consciousness and that is the measure of your concentration." This man had concentrated only in the degree of power which represented the "five cent" man, and he will keep the five cent jobs until his mind and power are enough to get more than that. He will then be the biggest man in the "five cent" position and the "five cent" job will have to slip off. It is better to be a success in a five cent job than a failure in trying to do the work of a millionaire.

Again, women say to me: I want to attract a great big, God-man into my life. Now what is the reason I never meet the kind of a man I want to meet? What is the reason that all the men I meet are sort of 'five cent' men? They are not worthwhile." Don't you see that is the same story from the woman's side as the man with his work? These people picture an absolutely matchless sort of being and then wonder at their lack of success in obtaining him or her.

The reason of all this stands out clearly. It is because the God-man, strangely enough, by the law of God, must have a God-woman to mate with him. It is plain that there must be some state of consciousness in us that is intensified so that it cannot keep out of form, or we would not have attracted around us the "five cent" job, or the little man. Only as we pour out the whole strength of our selfhood and character can we displace these small things, and when the great bigness of our life is expressed, we then attract the position, person or object that fits that life.

When we know that no one gives to us but ourselves, and no one takes away from us but ourselves, and that we lose or gain through our own individual **law of attraction**, and that this attraction is based wholly on our power of concentration and ability to pass up the proofs of our fitness, then we have a new idea of success and failure. We begin to put the blame where it belongs --- upon ourselves --- and to really know that the perfect or imperfect expression of life is in our own hands.

There is only one world, and all things are in it! They do not wait around to fall into our laps without any visible lines of transference. The tools of conquest are in our hands! Our concentrated mind, our thought force carefully directed and intensified, at our own pleasure, make us the master of our fate and no matter what our place in life may be, we can show our greatness.

"All the world falls into line with the man who declares himself a master." And only one who knows how to be the divine thinker of their own thoughts can ever take a master's place and speak with authority.

Concentration first, then an unfaltering determination to do! Then, with eyes wide-open to life's gigantic opportunities, the Gates of Success swing wide, never to close again.

The complete text of the book behind this excerpt may be found in -

Law of Attraction: Science of Success

(Please see Bibliography for details.)

Summary

There could be many studies done which compare the various authors in this book. There probably have already been many, many studies.

I did one, it culminated in the "Go Thunk Yourself!" series of books – and a career in finding, editing, and publishing classic references for your use.

The bottom line with all these authors, regardless of their personal writing styles or beliefs, is that they all talk the same talk – and tell about a walk that you can walk. All of these authors bring an approach of how you can use this stuff in your own life, right now.

You could trace each of these authors back to earlier authors, until you get to Troward, who in turn studied all the major religions in their own languages. So we have a subject, under the New Thought tent, which has been extracted from the workable texts through history.

New Thought is probably the only school of thought which could pull this off. Organizationally, there is no central church or authority to clear how and what people say and research. New Thought itself has even evolved its approaches in dealing with God (or however you name that Source).

But I'd say, as Napoleon Hill does, to "keep your own counsel" in all these matters. Choose what you believe and base your beliefs on what works for you, personally, in your own current life.

I'm not one to tell you that you have to accept as gospel any of these books. Many could be offended by various phrases taken from these books in or out of context. And that's the great part about New Thought – you can find any of various versions that fit your particular beliefs. You can go from devout Christian to complete mystic to Eastern studies. Your choice.

And so the wide variety of authors included in this text.

Through this book, I've given you a glimpse into the wide variety of approaches just having to do with the Law of Attraction. You will note that they each don't redefine that law, but just tell you how you can apply it – and the consequences of doing so.

That is the key to any real study – that a widely disparate group of authors will come up with the same principles and find them workable. This means that there is a substantial chance you will find these principles to be useful in your own life.

There are really no limits to what you can achieve in your life. Wealth, Success, Health – anything you want, or could want.

For that's the thing – you can want anything and get anything.

Sure, there's responsibilities that go with this. Trine, Larson, Allen – all these tell that you really, really get exactly what you are on the inside. So you have to make darn sure that your inside is the exact best you can think and create it to be.

Now the great part about this book is that it isn't the end of your journey. Each of the books excerpted within are only that – excerpts. Haanel and Troward are the thick studies. Hill's "Law of Success" has 16 volumes of text to digest. Holmes' "Science of Mind" is over 500 pages in many editions.

But you will get the best education you can on this planet. For when you know the laws of how this universe is put together – and how it wants to serve you – then you can truly create the world you've always wanted, but were afraid to ask for.

Now's your chance: read and think and ask away!

I've included a list of additional resources for your studies. All of the above authors' books are now available for either hardcopy purchase or download. And I've been working on my own to get versions of these books back in print. You can buy my books, which I would appreciate, or search to get them as free downloads, in various formats. Some are only available as paid downloads, some are in very obscure locations for download.

But the point is to read and study for yourself, regardless of where you get the book or ebook you want and need. Read and study for yourself. That's your ticket to any quantity or quality of wealth, health, and success in your life.

And as the Irish blessing goes: "May the road rise up to meet you on your journey."

Bibliography

More Resources for Studying
The Law of Attraction

Here are the books that these excerpts came from.

I've spent considerable research and editing hours bringing these to you in readable formats – both as hardcopy and download versions. These listed books are available through Lulu.com

As well, you may be able to find most of these references in their various raw states through Gutenburg.org, the Internet Archive, and several other sources such as University of Pennsylvania's Online Books Page. Many have been published on Lulu and available through Amazon.

Why would I tell you to get others' versions of these books? Because having the data is more important than anything else. The point is that you have all the tools you can attract into your life – in order to create, change, improve that life into what you want it to be..

I support my own research through book sales – and I've spent several years getting to the point where I can offer this **Law of Attraction Classics Series** to you. My continuing research will be to offer ecourses and special reports concerning each of these authors and their works.

I can be reached through my blog, Go Thunk Yourself!

The Complete Thomas Troward Collection

by Judge Thomas Troward,
Dr. Robert C. Worstell, editor

Thomas Troward is perhaps the single most influential writer in self-help. Napoleon Hill (Think and Grow Rich), Charles F. Haanel (The Master Key System) and many other authors either quote Troward directly or have been influenced by those who studied Troward's lectures and books.

This is a collection of his complete works, with a combined table of contents and easy-to-read format. A reference no professional or casual student of self-help should be without.

This book contains the complete text of each of his published works:

- The Edinburgh Lectures
- The Dore Lectures
- The Creative Process in the Individual
- Bible Mystery and Bible Meaning
- The Law and The Word
- The Hidden Power

You will not find this complete collection in a single volume anywhere else at this time.

This is a key reference behind the successful Go Thunk Yourself! series.

The Complete Genevieve Behrend Collection

By Genevieve Behrend,
Dr. Robert C. Worstell, editor

ONLY ONCE EVERY CENTURY seems to come a chance to study and learn at the feet of a real master..

This is the scene which Genevieve Behrend created for herself. You see, she read and applied Thomas Troward's works in order to become his pupil - *and no one else did.*

In this book she not only clarifies Troward's works, but also:

- Gives precise instructions and details in using the Law of Attraction
- Outlines simple techniques to strengthen your will and eliminate fear from your life
- How to enable your body to begin Instantaneous Healing
- And many other simple actions you can take immediately to improve your life - with no more than reading this book.

This is a key book for anyone continuing their personal studies in self-help - or as a way to **quickly learn and apply basic techniques to improve your wealth, health, and success**.

Law of Attraction: Your Invisible Power

by Genevieve Behrend
Dr. Robert C. Worstell, editor,

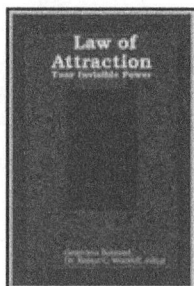

IMAGINE sitting at the feet of the most brilliant thinker of this century - as his only pupil.

This was the scene for this author, as she applied what she had learned from Thomas Troward:

"From the Edinburgh Lectures I had read something about the Law of Attraction, and from the Chapter of "Causes and Conditions" I had gleaned a vague idea of visualizing. So every night, before going to sleep, I made a mental picture of the desired $20,000... I wrote out my picture, saw myself buying my steamer ticket, walking up and down the ship's deck from New York to London, and, finally, saw myself accepted as Troward's pupil."

Now you can learn, as she did - with her unique and personal insight into Troward and his genius.

She writes in a modern, American style - translating his intense logical writing style into simple and readily applied basic data.

Part of the **Law of Attraction Classics** series - ready for your study.

Law of Attraction: Magic of Believing

by Claude M. Bristol
Dr. Robert C. Worstell, editor

DON'T READ this book and expect your life to be the same.

This one book contains the secret behind "Think and Grow Rich", and other bestsellers' successes:

- It can tell you why you are or aren't successful.
- It can tell you why you are rich or poor.
- It can give you the reason why something you really want to change - isn't and won't.

But you have to read it, first.

As recommended by Earl Nightingale, this book has been long out of print and is now recovered and published just so you could change your life. Edited and formatted for easy reading, in hardcopy or on-screen, this classic is a must for anyone who seriously wants to improve some chronic condition - FOREVER.

Not for the faint-at-heart, this book contains techniques a hard-nosed police reporter dug up from a lifetime of work and study into the workings of the mind.

Law of Attraction: Science of Mind

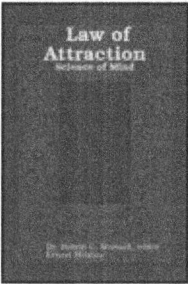

by Ernest Holmes,
Dr. Robert C. Worstell, editor

So you know how the Law of Attraction works?
How about the rest of the background theory which
ties it in to all Life?

Ernest Holmes wrote the textbook - second only to
Troward's work - on how the whole thing fits
together. There is such a thing as natural law, not just
gravity, but laws of the mind.

You can study these through Holmes' work and change your world into
the one you want to live.

This book has a unique approach to the **Law of Attraction** as it tells you
what goes on below the surface - and how to apply it in many, many new
ways in and around your new world.

Formatted for easy hardcopy and on-screen reading, this is a welcome
addition to any library on this subject.

Law of Attraction: Prosperity

by Charles Fillmore,
Dr. Robert C. Worstell, editor

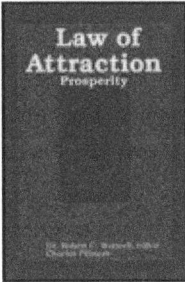

For those of us who would like to know more about the Law of Attraction and its many applications--

Charles Fillmore regained his health, started a publishing house and his own radio station - then went on to buy a 1400 acre estate where he built a church which has possibly the largest Christian congregation in the world. All from attending one lecture.

Yes, there was a lot of hard work, but wouldn't you like to know his secrets for prosperity and success?

In this one volume are included his famous "Prosperity" and as well the "Atom-Smashing Power of Mind" for your study and use.

Formatted for easy hardcopy and on-screen viewing, this is a vital book to have in any **Law of Attraction** library.

Law of Attraction: Dynamic Thought

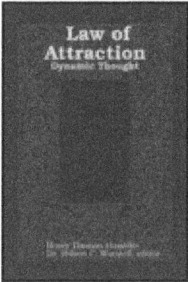

By Henry Thomas Hamblin,
Dr. Robert C. Worstell, editor

Are you interested in a very practical way to improve your Law of Attraction ability?

Hamblin wrote a very precise course back in 1923, one which takes you from where you are to beyond where you think is possible to achieve. It is written in very simple, direct steps which can be easily followed, even now - over 80 years later.

You can take these steps without having to have special coaches or mentors - something you can do in your own home. Right now, today.

Perfect for use in your own home or office, Hamblin's Dynamic Thought course has been formatted for easy hardcopy and on-screen reading. Also includes "Within You is the Power" - more examples of the personal abilities you can have.

Law of Attraction: Mental Chemistry

By Charles F. Haanel,
Dr. Robert C. Worstell, editor

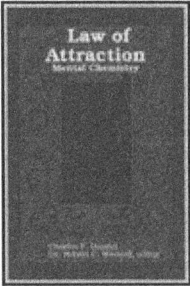

YOU MAY BE FAMILIAR with Haanel from his bestselling "Master Key System". 10 years after that publication, he authored this classic which explains the earlier book in simple terms.

Yet in this book, he gives more detail and application to the **Law of Attraction** than in his earlier work. In 19 short chapters, he covers about every applicable aspect of human existence - and this nearly a century ago.

You will find answers to questions which have been known - but remain a secret to all but a few. Your luck is in getting this and the other books in this Law of Attraction Classics Series to discover these secret answers for yourself - and create your world just the way you want it!

Law of Attraction: Ideal Made Real

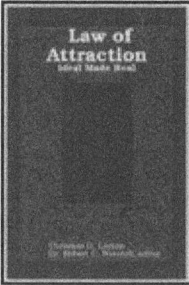

By Christian D. Larson,
Dr. Robert C. Worstell, editor

Ever wanted your dreams to become your reality?

Christian Larson made it possible for you and everyone else to make their ideal become real. As you grow, your dreams grow - so this book is one of the first steps you should take in your personal growth. Larson picked only the best ideas and methods for making your ideal real.

- 7 Prime essential steps
- How to get peace into your life
- How to forgive and gain both strength and wisdom
- How to tap into universal abundance around you
- Why gratitude works
- When harmony makes your dreams come true faster
- Talk Health, Happiness, and Prosperity - and become so
- Twelve Paths to Happiness
- And much more...

Also included in this volume: "Your Forces and How To Use Them" - where you learn the limits to personal progress lie only within...

Law of Attraction: In Tune With The Infinite

by <u>Ralph Waldo Trine,</u>
<u>Dr. Robert C. Worstell,</u> editor

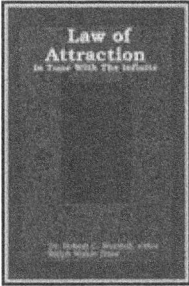

If you seek understanding of the Law of Attraction through the spiritual, this book is for you.

Ralph Waldo Trine predates Norman Vincent Peale in his alignment of metaphysical thoughts with those of the Carpenter from Galilee. Consider this statement:
"Each is building their own world. We both build from within and we attract from without. Thought is the force with which we build, for thoughts are forces. Like builds like and like attracts like."

Sound like something from <u>"The Secret"</u>? By reading these earlier works, you can find the underlying principals which all life operates from. Trine explains these in an easy manner, formatted for easy hardcopy and on-screen reading.

And so this book joins the Law of Attraction Classics series.

Also included: <u>"What All The World's A-Seeking"</u>.

Law of Attraction: Science of Success

By Julia Seton, M.D.,
Dr. Robert C. Worstell, editor

Seton outlines 20 success methods in this one book, writing as if she is across a table from you and telling you what she just discovered.

- Know Thyself
- Have a Plan
- Don't Hurry
- Clean Up Your Moods
- Mind Your Own Business
- The Use of Power
- Faith
- Selfness
- Yesterday, Today and Tomorrow
- Psychological Sins
- Business, But Not the Truth
- Personality and Individuality
- Enthusiasm
- Concentration
- Appreciation
- Hateful Comparisons
- Happiness
- Poise
- The Rules of the Game
- Compensation

Formatted for your easy reading either in hardcover or on-screen, this book also includes the full text of Freedom Talk Number II.

Law of Attraction: Thoughts Are Things

by Prentice Mulford,
Dr. Robert C. Worstell, editor

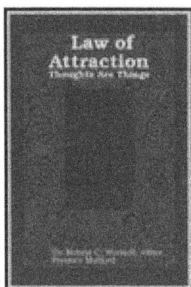

Just when you thought you had **Law of Attraction** mastered, you find someone who wrote before it was popular and "everybody knew".

Prentice Mulford was ages ahead of his time.

Factually, what he wrote in the 1800's is still being discovered today:

"When we dread a misfortune, or live in fear of any ill, or expect ill luck, we make also a construction of unseen element, thought,– which, by the same law of attraction, draws to it destructive, and to you damaging, forces or elements. Thus the law for success is also the law for misfortune..."

If you want the highly polished stuff that hypes your world, this author isn't for you. But if you want the pitch straight, with no curves - then Mumford is the way to get the straight bottom line.

Also contains the complete text of "The God In You".

Don't miss your chance to get a real classic.

Law of Attraction: Thought Vibration

by <u>William W. Atkinson,</u>
<u>Dr. Robert C. Worstell, editor</u>

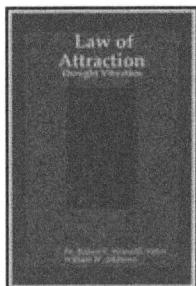

First in the **Law of Attraction Classics** series, this is the first in several books describing and detailing the Law of Attraction - the central point behind the underground hit "The Secret".

William Walker Atkinson was a key author and editor behind the popular New Thought Movement during the late 1800's well through the 1930's.

Three of his classics are included in this single volume,

- Thought Vibration
- Practical Mental Influence
- The Secret of Success

Each of these gives more detail to how the Law of Attraction is used. He says, *"We speak learnedly of the Law of Gravitation, but ignore that equally wonderful manifestation, THE LAW OF ATTRACTION IN THE THOUGHT WORLD."* And goes on to give in short chapters exactly how to apply this Law to your life.

Carefully edited to provide you readability in either hardcopy or on your computer, his original language and grammar have been preserved.

Law of Attraction: Power of Concentration

By Theron Q. Dumont,
Dr. Robert C. Worstell, editor

Get what you want in life by concentrating on it.
Now, you've probably been told variations of this by
teachers in public schools, supervisors at work, etc.
But Dumont gives you the reason it works - and can
help you achieve what you want in life.

As you study about the Law of Attraction, you have to
study Dumont. The problem has been that he is mostly unknown today.
And so this book.

This book ties the link between Hill (Think and Grow Rich), Coue
(Autosuggestion and Self-Mastery), and Haanel (Master Key System).
One can see how what you tell yourself and what you concentrate on is
exactly what you bring into your life.

It's a book you have to have in your library if you're serious about
personal change.

Also included: The Art and Science of Personal Magnetism.

Law of Attraction: Byways of Blessedness

by James Allen,
Dr. Robert C. Worstell, editor

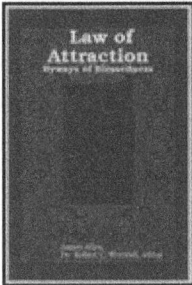

ANY STUDENT of the Law of Attraction is probably familiar with Allen's "As a Man Thinketh". Yet his later book, "Byways of Blessedness" addresses the Law.

In this continuing series, Allen's two works above are joined by his "The Path to Prosperity", in a format which is eminently readable both in hardcopy and on your computer monitor - while maintaining his original prose style and wordings.

This particular volume covers more than the average student of self-help wants - you will take the complete road of self-examination to find what you are attracting in your life through your very thoughts. And you'll find that you can tell what you've been thinking by what adverse as well as positive effects are happening to you.

Now for the faint of heart, however gently Allen tells you the inexorable effects of what you've been thinking about.

Truly a book everyone should have in their library.

Collect the whole **Law of Attraction Classics** series!

Haanel's Master Key System

by <u>Charles F. Haanel,</u>
<u>Dr. Robert C. Worstell, editor</u>

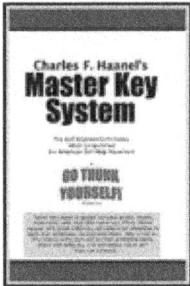

This is Haanel's classic self-help work published in 1912 which had sold over 200,000 copies by 1933. This book is based on a 1909 course which had 24 lessons, complete with review questions and answers.

This book has been formatted from the original text to ensure easy reading and study, both in hardcopy and on-screen.

Napoleon Hill (<u>Think and Grow Rich</u>) credits Haanel and this book with his early success. This is one of the principle sources for American Self-Help literature, describing and detailing many of the basics which later authors (Hill, Covey, Peale, among others) used to write their own best sellers.

Any serious student of self-help should have this volume for both study and continuing reference.

The <u>paperback edition</u> is also available.

THINK, THANK, THUNK!

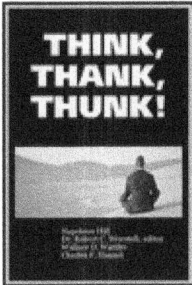

by Napoleon Hill,
Wallace D. Wattles,
Charles F. Haanel,
Dr. Robert C. Worstell, editor

THERE ARE THREE AUTHORS who have completely changed your world -

Charles F. Haanel - "The Master Key System"
Wallace D. Wattles - "The Science of Getting Rich"
Napoleon Hill - "Think and Grow Rich"

How they did it is point of study. But every major self-help author and every true success on this planet all use the same underlying system.

I cover this in "Go Thunk Yourself", but later research only confirms this system as actual and underlying all that exists in our world - which is as we create it.

In this volume are all these three authors' works.

Using them, you can work out the solution to any problem - if you apply what they teach to yourself and your dreams.

The Law of Success - In Sixteen Lessons

by Napoleon Hill,
Dr. Robert C. Worstell, editor

Before his Think and Grow Rich, Napoleon Hill had already created this 16-volume master work, exactly 20 years after Andrew Carnegie commissioned Hill to a **find the secrets of over 500 successful businessmen and millionaires**.

In 16 lessons, this book lays out the primary principles necessary to gaining success, wealth, and happiness.

This edition has been edited from the original to fit into a single hardcover volume. Nowhere else can you find a all these volumes condensed into a single text – perfect to fit in your library or on your desk.

Trade paperback edition also available.

Secrets Between Your Ears

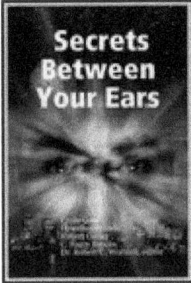

by Emile Coue,
Dorothea Brande,
Robert Collier,
C. Harry Brooks,
Dr. Robert C. Worstell, editor

While you may have heard that the only limits in your life are within you, **there is a way to re-program yourself to achieve the greatness you know is there**.

Contained in this volume are three masterworks:

"Wake Up and Live!" by Dorothea Brande,
"The Secret of the Ages" by Robert Collier, and
"Self-Mastery and the Practice of Autosuggestion"
by Emile Coue and C. Harry Brooks.

Each were bestsellers when originally published and are finding new popularity with "The Secret".

Within this text are the simple techniques (known and used by Napoleon Hill, author of "Think and Grow Rich") that will make it possible to acquire any amount of money, degree of happiness, and quality of health you desire.

Read, apply, and change your life forever!

Go Thunk Yourself!(TM) - Become Rich, Famous, A Success

by Robert C. Worstell

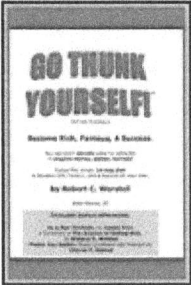

What do Napoleon Hill, Norman Vincent Peale, Dale Carnegie, and Stephen Covey have in common?

They all **THUNK** the same way. They each discovered the same basic secrets behind wealth, success, and fame - **and became wealthy, successful and famous.**

You can too.

This book's simple **14-day program** allows you to recreate your own life, just the way you want it to be!

All you have to do is invest some time each day to read these simple chapters and do the exercises. You can learn these secrets and start taking control over your own life, to start achieving the riches, fame and success you've always dreamed of.

Dreams CAN BECOME Reality!

About the Editor

Rev. Dr. Robert C. Worstell, M.Msc, MBA, PhD is an independent researcher and the author of several self-help and self-improvement books:

- "Thinking at Internet Speed" ,

- "How Self-Help Authors Write Bestsellers",

- "Go Thunk Yourself(TM)",

- "Go Thunk Yourself, Again!",

- "Go Thunk Yourself, S'more!", and

- "Go Thunk Yourself, Compleat!".

In addition to "The Complete Thomas Troward Collection", "Getting Rich, Being Healthy, Being Great ", and "Think, Thank, Thunk!", he has edited several publications. His most recent works include the recent Law of Attraction Series, containing works by over 15 major New Thought philosophers.

He has certificates in Computer Networking and Wireless Broadband, as well as degrees in Business Administration, Comparative Religions and Computer Science.

Worstell lives on a working farm in rural Missouri and is continually involved in research to improve the quality of life. He's spent over 35 years researching the human condition through personal studies of counseling, education, and self-improvement.